CAMBRIDGE
UNIVERSITY PRESS

Cambridge Lower Secondary
English

TEACHER'S RESOURCE 9

Patrick Creamer, Giles Clare & Helen Rees-Bidder

CAMBRIDGE
UNIVERSITY PRESS

Shaftesbury Road, Cambridge CB2 8EA, United Kingdom

One Liberty Plaza, 20th Floor, New York, NY 10006, USA

477 Williamstown Road, Port Melbourne, VIC 3207, Australia

314–321, 3rd Floor, Plot 3, Splendor Forum, Jasola District Centre, New Delhi – 110025, India

1103 Penang Road, #05–06/07, Visioncrest Commercial, Singapore 238467

Cambridge University Press is part of the University of Cambridge.

It furthers the University's mission by disseminating knowledge in the pursuit of
education, learning and research at the highest international levels of excellence.

www.cambridge.org
Information on this title: www.cambridge.org/9781108782166

© Cambridge University Press & Assessment 2021

First published 2014
Second edition 2021

20 19 18 17 16 15 14 13 12 11 10 9 8 7 6 5 4

Printed in Italy by Rotolito S.p.A

A catalogue record for this publication is available from the British Library

ISBN 978-1-108-78216-6 Paperback with Digital Access

Additional resources for this publication at www.cambridge.org/go

⟩ Contents

Digital resources

The following items are available on Cambridge GO. For more information on how to access and use your digital resource, please see inside front cover.

Active learning

Assessment for Learning

Developing learner language skills

Differentiation

Improving learning through questioning

Language awareness

Metacognition

Skills for Life

Letter for parents – Introducing the Cambridge Primary and Lower Secondary resources

Lesson plan template

Curriculum framework correlation

Scheme of work

Diagnostic check and answers

Mid-point test and answers

End-of-year test and answers

Answers to Learner's Book questions

Answers to Workbook questions

Glossary

You can download the following resources for each unit:

Differentiated worksheets and answers

Language worksheets and answers

Audio files

Extract sheets and audioscripts

End-of-unit tests and answers

> Introduction

Welcome to the new edition of our Cambridge Lower Secondary English series.

Since its launch, the series has been used by teachers and learners in over 100 countries for teaching the Cambridge Lower Secondary English curriculum framework.

This exciting new edition has been designed by talking to Lower Secondary English teachers all over the world. We have worked hard to understand your needs and challenges, and then carefully designed and tested the best ways of meeting them.

As a result of this research, we've made some important changes to the series. This Teacher's Resource has been carefully redesigned to make it easier for you to plan and teach the course.

The series now includes digital editions of the Learners' Books and Workbooks. This Teacher's Resource also offers additional materials available to download from Cambridge GO. (For more information on how to access and use your digital resource, please see inside front cover.)

The series uses the most successful teaching approaches like active learning and metacognition and this Teacher's Resource gives you full guidance on how to integrate them into your classroom.

Formative assessment opportunities help you to get to know your learners better, with clear learning intentions and success criteria as well as an array of assessment techniques, including advice on self and peer assessment.

Clear, consistent differentiation ensures that all learners are able to progress in the course with tiered activities, differentiated worksheets and advice about supporting learners' different needs.

All our resources include extra language support to enable learning and teaching in English. They help learners build core English skills with vocabulary and grammar support, as well as additional language worksheets.

We hope you enjoy using this course.

Eddie Rippeth

Head of Primary and Lower Secondary Publishing, Cambridge University Press

> How to use this series

All of the components in the series are designed to work together.

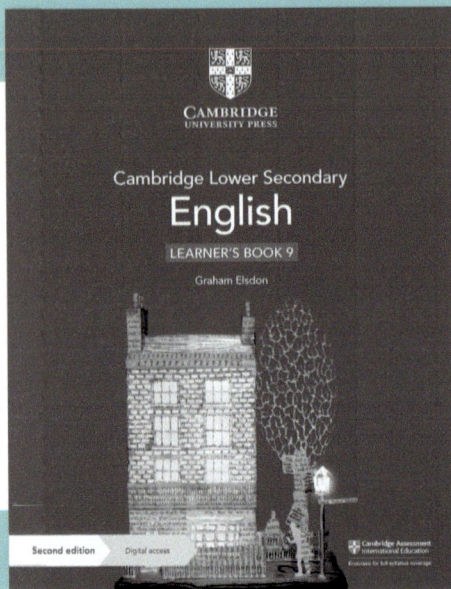

The Learner's Book is designed for learners to use in class with guidance from the teacher. It offers complete coverage of the curriculum framework. A variety of activities, texts and images motivate learners and help them to develop the necessary skills. Each unit contains opportunities for formative assessment, differentiation and reflection so you can support your learners' needs and help them progress.

A digital version of the Learner's Book is included with the print version and available separately. It includes simple tools for learners to use in class or for self-study.

The skills-focused write-in Workbook provides further practice of all the reading and writing skills presented in the Learner's Book and is ideal for use in class or as homework. A three-tier, scaffolded approach to skills development promotes visible progress and enables independent learning, ensuring that every learner is supported. Teachers can assign learners activities from one or more tiers for each session, or learners can progress through each of the tiers in the session.

A digital version of the Workbook is included with the print version.

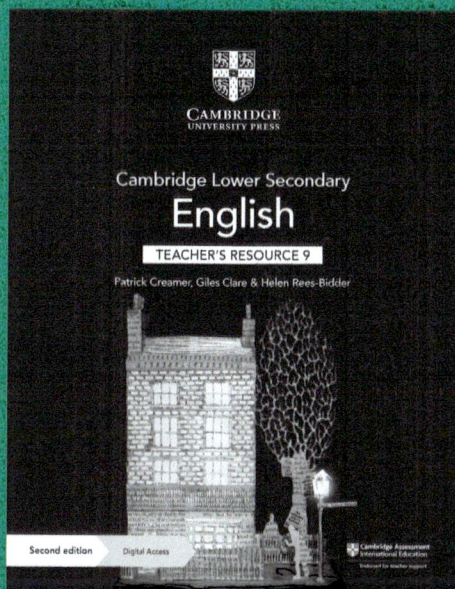

The Teacher's Resource is the foundation of this series and you'll find everything you need to deliver the course in here, including suggestions for differentiation, formative assessment and language support, teaching ideas, audio, audioscripts, answers, tests and extra materials. Each Teacher's Resource includes:

- **a print book** with detailed teaching notes for each session
- **digital access** with all the material from the book in digital form plus editable planning documents, downloadable answers, audio, audioscripts, worksheets and more.

A letter to parents, explaining the course, is available to download from Cambridge GO (as part of this Teacher's Resource).

> How to use this Teacher's Resource

This Teacher's Resource contains both general guidance and teaching notes that help you to deliver the content in our Cambridge Lower Secondary English resources. Some of the material is provided as downloadable files, available on **Cambridge GO**. (For more information about how to access and use your digital resource, please see inside front cover.) See the Contents page for details of all the material available to you, both in this book and through Cambridge GO.

Teaching notes

This book provides **Teaching notes** for each unit of the Learner's Book and Workbook. Each set of teaching notes contains the following features to help you deliver the unit.

The **Unit plan** summarises the sessions covered in the unit, including the number of learning hours recommended for each session, an outline of the learning content and the Cambridge resources that can be used to deliver the session.

Session	Approximate number of learning hours	Outline of learning content	Resources
1.1 Relic	2 hours, 30 minutes	Learners read, explore, discuss and summarise their impressions of a story opening, and consider genre and story structure.	Learner's Book Session 1.1 Workbook Session 1.1

The **Background knowledge** feature explains prior knowledge required to access the unit and gives suggestions for addressing any gaps in your learners' prior knowledge.

Learners' prior knowledge can be informally assessed through the **Getting started** feature in the Learner's Book.

BACKGROUND KNOWLEDGE

This unit examines three main forms of writing: prose, drama and travel writing. It is useful to consider the structure and language features common to these forms. For example, if you are not already familiar with the layout conventions of scripts it is worth exploring these in play scripts or film scripts (many of which are available online).

The **Teaching skills focus** feature covers a teaching skill and suggests how to implement it in the unit.

> ### TEACHING SKILLS FOCUS
>
> Assessment for Learning is a method for building regular assessment into the learning cycle. Assessment may be by learners themselves, their peers or teacher.
>
> Three key techniques can be used to obtain information about learners' progress: asking, observing and analysing.

Reflecting the Learner's Book, each unit consists of multiple sessions.

At the start of each session, the **Learning plan** table includes the learning objectives, learning intentions and success criteria that are covered in the session.

It can be helpful to share learning intentions and success criteria with your learners at the start of a lesson so that they can begin to take responsibility for their own learning.

LEARNING PLAN

Learning objectives	Learning intentions	Success criteria
9Rs.01, 9Ri.01, 9Ri.03, 9Ra.02, 9Wc.06, 9SLm.03, 9SLg.02, 9SLg.03	Learners will: • read a story opening and discuss genre	Learners can: • identify a fiction genre based on a story's key features

The **Language support** feature contains suggestions for how to support learners who may need extra language support.

> ### LANGUAGE SUPPORT
>
> This session asks learners to analyse explicit information, so it may be useful to recap the difference between explicit and implicit information with learners. Remind them that explicit information is information that is stated clearly and in detail, leaving no room for misunderstanding, doubt or confusion. Implicit information suggests or *implies* something, without expressing it directly.

There are often **Common misconceptions** associated with particular learning areas. These are listed, along with suggestions for identifying evidence of the misconceptions in your class and suggestions for how to overcome them.

Misconception	How to identify	How to overcome
State verbs cannot express a dynamic meaning.	Write the following examples on the board and ask learners if they describe states or events: • *You're being difficult.* • *We're having a celebration.* Discuss learners' responses.	Point out that the verbs *be*, *being* and *have* are often categorised as state verbs, but in these examples they have a dynamic meaning – that is, they describe: • someone acting in a 'difficult' way • the event of a party/celebration.

For each session, there is a selection of **Starter ideas**, **Main teaching ideas** and **Plenary ideas**. You can pick out individual ideas and mix and match them depending on the needs of your class. The activities include suggestions for how they can be differentiated or used for assessment. **Homework ideas** are also provided.

Starter idea

Interesting places (10 minutes)

Resources: Learner's Book, Session 1.5, Getting started activity

Description: Ask learners to recall an interesting place they have visited. If they feel they have not travelled anywhere very interesting, they could think of a place they would like to visit (perhaps a place they have read about or seen on television). Then organise learners into pairs and ask them to discuss the Getting started activity. Remind them to focus on what made the place memorable, or what makes them want to visit.

Main teaching ideas

1 The meaning of implicit and explicit information (40 minutes)

Learning intention: Explore the implications of explicit information

Resources: Learner's Book, Session 1.5, 'Coober Pedy: Getting below the surface' Extract 1, Activities 1 and 2

Description: Recap the meanings of explicit and implicit information, and the terms 'imply' and 'infer' (see the Language support in Session 1.1 of this Teacher's Resource). Emphasise that explicit information will be clear and detailed, and will allow readers to understand the main points in a text. Implied meaning is when a writer *suggests* something rather than stating it directly.

The **Cross-curricular links** feature provides suggestions for linking to other subject areas.

CROSS-CURRICULAR LINK

Science (wind energy): Learners could find out more about how William Kamkwamba generated electricity using wind. They could find out about wind farms, how they work, where they are situated and the role they play in providing cleaner, cheaper electricity and aiding decarbonisation.

Note: some texts used in the Learner's Book and Workbook have been abridged, so please be aware that learners may not be presented with the full version of the text.

Digital resources to download

This Teacher's Resource includes a range of digital materials that you can download from Cambridge GO. (For more information about how to access and use your digital resource, please see inside front cover.) This icon ⬇ indicates material that is available from Cambridge GO.

Helpful documents for planning include:

- **Letter for parents – Introducing the Cambridge Primary and Lower Secondary resources:** a template letter for parents, introducing the Cambridge Lower Secondary English resources.

- **Lesson plan template:** a Word document that you can use for planning your lessons.

- **Curriculum framework correlation:** a table showing how the Cambridge Lower Secondary English resources map to the Cambridge Lower Secondary English curriculum framework.

- **Scheme of work:** a suggested scheme of work that you can use to plan teaching throughout the year.

Each unit includes:

- **Differentiated worksheets:** these worksheets are provided in variations that cater for different abilities. Worksheets labelled 'A' are intended to support less confident learners, while worksheets labelled 'C' are designed to challenge more confident learners. Answer sheets are provided.

- **Language worksheets:** these worksheets provide extra language support. Answer sheets are provided.

- **Extract sheets:** these are copies of all the texts in the Learner's Book which can be shared and annotated by learners.

- **Audioscripts:** these are transcripts of all the listening activities in the Learner's Book.

- **End-of-unit tests:** these provide quick checks of the learners' understanding of the concepts covered in the unit. Answers are provided. Advice on using these tests formatively is given in the Assessment for Learning section of this Teacher's Resource.

Additionally, the Teacher's Resource includes:

- **Diagnostic check and answers:** a test to use at the beginning of the year to discover the level that learners are working at. The results of this test can inform your planning.

- **Mid-point test and answers:** a test to use after learners have studied half the units in the Learner's Book. You can use this test to check whether there are areas that you need to go over again.

- **End-of-year test and answers:** a test to use after learners have studied all units in the Learner's Book. You can use this test to check whether there are areas that you need to go over again, and to help inform your planning for the next year.

- **Answers to Learner's Book activities**

- **Answers to Workbook activities**

- **Glossary**

In addition, you can download more detailed information about teaching approaches.

🎧 **Audio** is available for download from Cambridge GO (as part of this Teacher's Resource and as part of the digital resources for the Learner's Book).

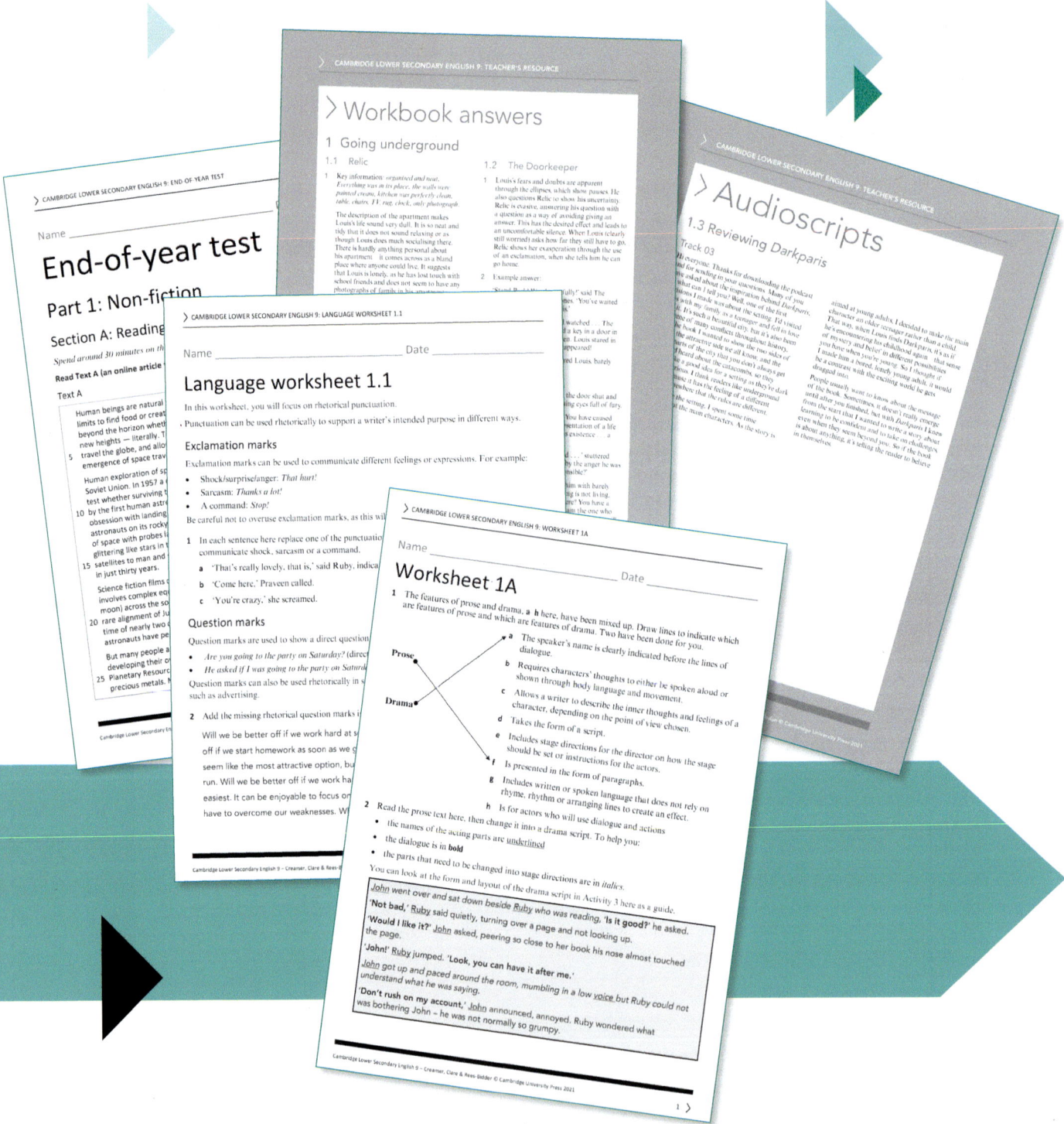

> Workbook answers

1 Going underground

1.1 Relic

1 Key information: *organised and neat. Everything was in its place, the walls were painted cream, kitchen was perfectly clean, table, chairs, TV, rug, clock, only photograph.*

The description of the apartment makes Louis's life sound very dull. It is so neat and tidy that it does not sound relaxing or as though Louis does much socialising there. There is hardly anything personal about his apartment. It comes across as a bland place where anyone could live. It suggests that Louis is lonely, as he has lost touch with school friends and does not seem to have any photographs of family in his apartment.

2 Example answer:

1.2 The Doorkeeper

1 Louis's fears and doubts are apparent through the ellipses, which show pauses. He also questions Relic to show his uncertainty. Relic is evasive, answering his question with a question as a way of avoiding giving an answer. This has the desired effect and leads to an uncomfortable silence. When Louis tellearly still worried asks how far they still have to go, Relic shows her exasperation through the use of an exclamation, when she tells him he can go home.

> Audioscripts

1.3 Reviewing *Darkparis*

Track 03

Hi everyone. Thanks for downloading the podcast and for sending in your questions. Many of you asked about the inspiration behind *Darkparis*...

Name _____

End-of-year test

Part 1: Non-fiction

Section A: Reading

Spend around 30 minutes on th...

Read Text A (an online article on th...

Text A

Human beings are natural... limits to find food or creat... beyond the horizon wheth... new heights — literally. T... travel the globe, and allo... emergence of space trav...

Human exploration of sp... Soviet Union. In 1957 a... test whether surviving, t... by the first human astr... obsession with landing, astronauts on its rocky... of space with probes i... glittering like stars in... satellites to man and... in just thirty years.

Science fiction films... involves complex eq... moon) across the so... rare alignment of Ju... time of nearly two... astronauts have pe...

But many people a... developing their o... Planetary Resourc... precious metals. M...

Name _____   Date _____

Language worksheet 1.1

In this worksheet, you will focus on rhetorical punctuation.

Exclamation marks

Exclamation marks can be used to communicate different feelings or expressions. For example:

- Shock/surprise/anger: *That hurt!*
- Sarcasm: *Thanks a lot!*
- A command: *Stop!*

Be careful not to overuse exclamation marks, as this wil...

1 In each sentence here replace one of the punctuation... communicate shock, sarcasm or a command.
  a 'That's really lovely, that is,' said Ruby, indica...
  b 'Come here,' Praveen called.
  c 'You're crazy,' she screamed.

Question marks

Question marks are used to show a direct question...

- *Are you going to the party on Saturday?* (direct...
- *He asked if I was going to the party on Saturd...*

Question marks can also be used rhetorically in s... such as advertising.

2 Add the missing rhetorical question marks i...

Will we be better off if we work hard at s... off if we start homework as soon as we g... seem like the most attractive option, bu... run. Will we be better off if we work ha... easiest. It can be enjoyable to focus on... have to overcome our weaknesses. W...

Name _____   Date _____

Worksheet 1A

1 The features of prose and drama, **a**–**h** here, have been mixed up. Draw lines to indicate which are features of prose and which are features of drama. Two have been done for you.

Prose

Drama

  a The speaker's name is clearly indicated before the lines of dialogue.
  b Requires characters' thoughts to either be spoken aloud or shown through body language and movement.
  c Allows a writer to describe the inner thoughts and feelings of a character, depending on the point of view chosen.
  d Takes the form of a script.
  e Includes stage directions for the director on how the stage should be set or instructions for the actors.
  f Is presented in the form of paragraphs.
  g Includes written or spoken language that does not rely on rhyme, rhythm or arranging lines to create an effect.
  h Is for actors who will use dialogue and actions.

2 Read the prose text here, then change it into a drama script. To help you:

- the names of the acting parts are underlined
- the dialogue is in **bold**
- the parts that need to be changed into stage directions are in *italics*.

You can look at the form and layout of the drama script in Activity 3 here as a guide.

John went over and sat down beside Ruby *who was reading,* 'Is it good?' *he asked.*

'Not bad,' Ruby *said quietly, turning over a page and not looking up.*

'Would I like it?' John *asked, peering so close to her book his nose almost touched the page.*

'John!' Ruby *jumped.* 'Look, you can have it after me.'

John *got up and paced around the room, mumbling in a low* voice *but Ruby could not understand what he was saying.*

'Don't rush on my account,' John *announced, annoyed. Ruby wondered what was bothering John – he was not normally so grumpy.*

> About the authors

Giles Clare

Giles Clare is an experienced teacher and educational author. He has written multiple titles for major educational publishers for the UK and international markets. He has written books and resources for a wide age range of learners, from Reception to GCSE, including revision and test materials, home learning resources and teacher guides, as well as fiction and non-fiction titles. He believes in engendering a love of language in learners. He has helped provide local authority teacher training and has presented at a national languages conference.

Patrick Creamer

Patrick is an English Language and Literature teacher, and an author of learning resources for children, adolescents and adults, specialising in writing guidance and supporting materials for teachers. His main areas of interest are metacognition, teachers' use of questioning strategies, active learning and linguistics.

Graham Elsdon

Graham has been an English leader in a successful school in the north of England and he is an experienced examiner. He is a visiting lecturer at Newcastle University, and presents staff and student training on English courses for a variety of organisations and training providers. In addition, Graham has authored several GCSE and A level study guides and textbooks.

Helen Rees-Bidder

Helen taught in the UK for 27 years. She is now a freelance educational consultant and her current roles include working as an examiner. Helen has delivered face-to-face and online training courses and enrichment workshops in a number of countries. She is passionate about developing oracy skills across the curriculum.

> About the curriculum framework

The information in this section is based on the Cambridge Lower Secondary English curriculum framework (0861) from 2020. You should always refer to the appropriate curriculum framework document for the year of your learners' assessment to confirm the details and for more information. Visit www.cambridgeinternational.org/lowersecondary to find out more.

The Cambridge Lower Secondary English curriculum framework has been designed to help learners to become confident communicators. They will learn to apply reading, writing, speaking and listening skills in everyday situations, as well as developing a broad vocabulary and an understanding of grammar and language. Through this curriculum, learners will develop evaluation skills, learn to appreciate texts from different cultures and learn to write for different audiences and purposes.

The Cambridge Lower Secondary English curriculum framework is split into three strands: reading, writing, and speaking and listening. For more information, visit the Cambridge Assessment International Education website.

A curriculum framework correlation document (mapping the Cambridge Lower Secondary English resources to the learning objectives) and scheme of work are available to download from Cambridge GO (as part of this Teacher's Resource).

> About the assessment

Information concerning the assessment of the Cambridge Lower Secondary English curriculum framework is available on the Cambridge Assessment International Education website: **www.cambridgeinternational.org/lowersecondary**

> Approaches to learning and teaching

The following are the teaching approaches underpinning our course content and how we understand and define them.

Active learning

Active learning is a teaching approach that places learner learning at its centre. It focuses on how learners learn, not just on what they learn. We, as teachers, need to encourage learners to 'think hard', rather than passively receive information. Active learning encourages learners to take responsibility for their learning and supports them in becoming independent and confident learners in school and beyond.

Assessment for Learning

Assessment for Learning (AfL) is a teaching approach that generates feedback that can be used to improve learners' performance. Learners become more involved in the learning process and, from this, gain confidence in what they are expected to learn and to what standard. We, as teachers, gain insights into a learner's level of understanding of a particular concept or topic, which helps to inform how we support their progression.

Differentiation

Differentiation is usually presented as a teaching approach where teachers think of learners as individuals and learning as a personalised process. Whilst precise definitions can vary, typically the core aim of differentiation is viewed as ensuring that all learners, no matter their ability, interest or context, make progress towards their learning intentions. It is about using different approaches and appreciating the differences in learners to help them make progress. Teachers therefore need to be responsive and willing and able to adapt their teaching to meet the needs of their learners.

Language awareness

For all learners, regardless of whether they are learning through their first language or an additional language, language is a vehicle for learning. It is through language that learners access the learning intentions of the lesson and communicate their ideas. It is our responsibility, as teachers, to ensure that language doesn't present a barrier to learning.

Metacognition

Metacognition describes the processes involved when learners plan, monitor, evaluate and make changes to their own learning behaviours. These processes help learners to think about their own learning more explicitly and ensure that they are able to meet a learning goal that they have identified themselves or that we, as teachers, have set.

Skills for Life

How do we prepare learners to succeed in a fast-changing world? To collaborate with people from around the globe? To create innovation as technology increasingly takes over routine work? To use advanced thinking skills in the face of more complex challenges? To show resilience in the face of constant change? At Cambridge, we are responding to educators who have asked for a way to understand how all these different approaches to life skills and competencies relate to their teaching. We have grouped these skills into six main Areas of Competency that can be incorporated into teaching, and have examined the different stages of the learning journey and how these competencies vary across each stage.

These six key areas are:

- Creativity – finding new ways of doing things, and solutions to problems
- Collaboration – the ability to work well with others
- Communication – speaking and presenting confidently and participating effectively in groups
- Critical thinking – evaluating what is heard or read, and linking ideas constructively
- Learning to learn – developing the skills to learn more effectively
- Social responsibilities – contributing to social groups, and being able to talk to and work with people from other cultures.

More information about these approaches to learning and teaching is available to download from Cambridge GO (as part of this Teacher's Resource).

Cambridge learner and teacher attributes

This course helps develop the following Cambridge learner and teacher attributes.

Cambridge learners	Cambridge teachers
Confident in working with information and ideas – their own and those of others.	**Confident** in teaching their subject and engaging each learner in learning.
Responsible for themselves, responsive to and respectful of others.	**Responsible** for themselves, responsive to and respectful of others.
Reflective as learners, developing their ability to learn.	**Reflective** as learners themselves, developing their practice.
Innovative and equipped for new and future challenges.	**Innovative** and equipped for new and future challenges.
Engaged intellectually and socially, ready to make a difference.	**Engaged** intellectually, professionally and socially, ready to make a difference.

Reproduced from Developing the Cambridge learner attributes *with permission from Cambridge Assessment International Education.*

> Approaches to learning and teaching English

Structure of the course

The Learner's Book contains nine units, each based on exciting themes like 'Law and order' and 'That's entertainment'. Most units contain a range of international fiction, non-fiction, poetry and drama text extracts, reflecting the interests and diverse cultural backgrounds of your learners. There are two units which are different (Unit 3: 'The Red-Headed League' and Unit 7: 'The Journey Within'). Each of these two units focuses on one full short story, promoting reading for pleasure and allowing students to delve deeper into language and meaning.

Every unit contains six sessions, each designed to take around 2.5 hours of teaching time including the Workbook and Worksheets. If your timing is different, we hope the materials are flexible enough for you to be able to fit them to your requirements.

The Workbook accompanies the Learner's Book, providing supplementary and extension material. The content mirrors the content of the Learner's Book to support:

- reinforcement of concepts introduced in the Learner's Book
- the 'Language focus' parts of some sessions
- differentiated activities
- independent work or homework.

Skills development

Cambridge Lower Secondary English offers an integrated approach to the four language skills (speaking, listening, reading and writing) allowing you to cover learning objectives from each strand of the curriculum framework in your English lessons.

Speaking and listening

Speaking and listening underpin this course. Each session offers opportunities to consolidate and develop the speaking and listening sub-strands (making yourself understood, showing understanding, group work and discussion, performance, and reflection and evaluation). Listening activities are included in the Learner's Book with accompanying recordings available in this Teacher's Resource. (If you are unable to play the recordings, audioscripts in this Teacher's Resource allow you to read the text out to your class instead.) Audio tracks actively promote good pronunciation of English and you will find recordings of all the texts from the Learner's Book in this Teacher's Resource as well as in the Digital Learner's Book.

Reading and writing

We ensure rich coverage of each reading and writing sub-strand as follows:

- **Word structure (spelling):** students are encouraged to explore the etymology of words and improve their spelling through checking their own and others' work.

- **Vocabulary and language:** we provide multiple opportunities for securing vocabulary, exploring context, grammatical features and word families. We also explore texts with learners to reflect on writers' choices of vocabulary and language. You will find further vocabulary practice in the Workbook and Language worksheets (available to download from this Teacher's Resource).

- **Grammar and punctuation:** while mindful of reading for pleasure and text coherence, we focus on the grammar and punctuation arising from a text so that learners experience new structures and grammar rules in context. Wherever you find a Language focus box in the Learner's Book, there is further practice in the corresponding Workbook session. We have respected both teachers' and learners' capacity for understanding and using correct metalanguage in the classroom, especially in writing activities.

- **Structure of texts:** an exciting range of authentic texts is provided for discussion, performance, reflection and as models for learners' own writing. This is especially true in the final sessions of each unit when learners aim to write within the support of frameworks or scaffolds.

- **Interpretation of and creation of texts:** while the units provide a rich and broad selection of texts, it is also expected that learners enjoy texts outside of the course, especially aligned in some way to the topic or theme. Differentiation within each activity ensures that all learners can explore authentic texts and experiment with creative ideas and writing.

- **Appreciation and reflection of reading:** we support the ethos of reading for pleasure and encourage learners to reflect and evaluate their wider reading. In particular, the two short story units allow students the satisfaction of reading a story from beginning to end.

- **Presentation and reflection of writing:** we encourage learners to adopt a write, reflect/evaluate and improve cycle of working. We encourage them to present their own work and listen for feedback as well as to talk about and reflect on their own and others' ideas.

〉 Setting up for success

Our aim is to support better learning in the classroom with resources that allow for increased learner autonomy while supporting teachers to facilitate student learning. Through an active learning approach of enquiry-led tasks, open-ended questions and opportunities to externalise thinking in a variety of ways, learners will develop analysis, evaluation and problem-solving skills.

Some ideas to consider to encourage an active learning environment are as follows:

- set up seating to make group work easy
- create classroom routines to help learners to transition between different types of activity efficiently (e.g. move from pair work to listening to the teacher to independent work)
- source mini-whiteboards, which allow you to get feedback from all learners rapidly
- start a portfolio for each learner, keeping key pieces of work to show progress at parent–teacher days
- have a display area with learner work and vocab flashcards.

Planning for active learning

We recommend the following approach to planning.

1 **Plan learning intentions and success criteria:** these are the most important feature of the lesson. Teachers and learners need to know where they are going in order to plan a route to get there.

2 **Plan language support:** think about strategies to help learners overcome the language demands of the lesson so that language does not present a barrier to learning.

3 **Plan starter activities:** include a 'hook' or starter to engage learners using imaginative strategies. This should be an activity where all learners are active from the start of the lesson.

4 **Plan main activities:** during the lesson, try to: give clear instructions, with modelling and written support; coordinate logical and orderly transitions between activities; make sure that learning is active and all learners are engaged; create opportunities for discussion around key concepts.

5 **Plan Assessment for Learning and differentiation:** use a wide range of Assessment for Learning techniques and adapt activities to a wide range of abilities. Address misconceptions at appropriate points and give meaningful oral and written feedback which learners can act on.

6 **Plan reflection and plenary:** at the end of each activity and at the end of each lesson, try to: ask learners to reflect on what they have learnt compared to the beginning of the lesson; build on and extend this learning.

7 **Plan homework:** if setting homework, it can be used to consolidate learning from the previous lesson or to prepare for the next lesson.

To help planning using this approach, a blank lesson plan template is available to download from Cambridge GO (as part of this Teacher's Resource).

For more guidance on setting up for success and planning, please explore the Professional Development pages of our website: **www.cambridge.org/education/PD**

❯ 1 Going underground

Unit plan

Session	Approximate number of learning hours	Outline of learning content	Resources
1.1 Relic	2 hours, 30 minutes	Learners read, explore, discuss and summarise their impressions of a story opening, and consider genre and story structure.	Learner's Book Session 1.1 Workbook Session 1.1
1.2 The Doorkeeper	2 hours, 30 minutes	Learners explore a writer's structural and language choices, examine rhetorical punctuation and continue a story in the style of an author.	Learner's Book Session 1.2 Workbook Session 1.2 ⬇ Language worksheet 1.1
1.3 Reviewing *Darkparis*	2 hours, 30 minutes	Learners discuss book recommendations with their peers, explore how personal context affects reading and writing, and write a review.	Learner's Book Session 1.3 Workbook Session 1.3
1.4 The second test	2 hours, 30 minutes	Learners act out a dramatic scene and practise using voice and gesture in drama. They also write their own dramatic scene.	Learner's Book Session 1.4 Workbook Session 1.4 ⬇ Differentiated worksheets 1A, 1B and 1C
1.5 Visiting Coober Pedy	2 hours, 30 minutes	Learners explore the impact of explicit information on the meaning of a text and analyse extended metaphors and other language choices.	Learner's Book Session 1.5 Workbook Session 1.5 ⬇ Language worksheet 1.2
1.6 Living under the ground	2 hours, 30 minutes	Learners explore the structure, language and themes of travel writing, and produce their own piece of travel writing.	Learner's Book Session 1.6 Workbook Session 1.6

BACKGROUND KNOWLEDGE

For the teacher

This unit examines three main forms of writing: prose, drama and travel writing. It is useful to consider the structure and language features common to these forms. For example, if you are not already familiar with the layout conventions of scripts it is worth exploring these in play scripts or film scripts (many of which are available online). Travel writing can be particularly enjoyable to read, and it may be useful to find examples that you think would appeal to your learners, and mention these in class in addition to studying the examples in the Learner's Book.

CONTINUED

For the learner

Learners would benefit from reading sections of plays or film scripts and then comparing these with the same stories in novel form. As general preparation for this unit, you could ask learners to consider a favourite scene in a novel, film or play, then compare how this scene is presented differently in the form of a novel, or a play or film script.

This unit also gives special focus to rhetorical punctuation, specifically:

- exclamation marks for indicating shock, surprise, sarcasm or commands
- question marks for rhetorical questions
- ellipses to show a pause, an unfinished thought or a time lapse.

So, it will benefit learners if they are confident with the correct use of punctuation in general (full stops, commas, question marks, semi-colons and colons) before considering how punctuation can be used for rhetorical purposes, such as in persuasive speaking and writing.

TEACHING SKILLS FOCUS

Assessment for Learning

Assessment for Learning is a method for building regular assessment into the learning cycle. Assessment may be by learners themselves, their peers or teacher.

Three key techniques can be used to obtain information about learners' progress: asking, observing and analysing.

- Asking is when teachers ask learners about their thoughts, feelings, opinions, ideas, interests, likes, dislikes, etc. To be an effective teacher is to frequently ask learners what they think about the topic and learning activities.

- Observing is when teachers listen, watch, feel or use any other sense to assess what is happening for their learners in the classroom and during learning activities. Observation may take place during pair or group discussion, performance in drama, talks or presentations, reading aloud or in any other interaction. This provides valuable information for assessing learners' progress.

- Analysing is when teachers examine and analyse learners' speech or writing to discover errors in their language use or thinking.

Suggestions for self-, peer and teacher assessment follow each of the teaching ideas in this resource.

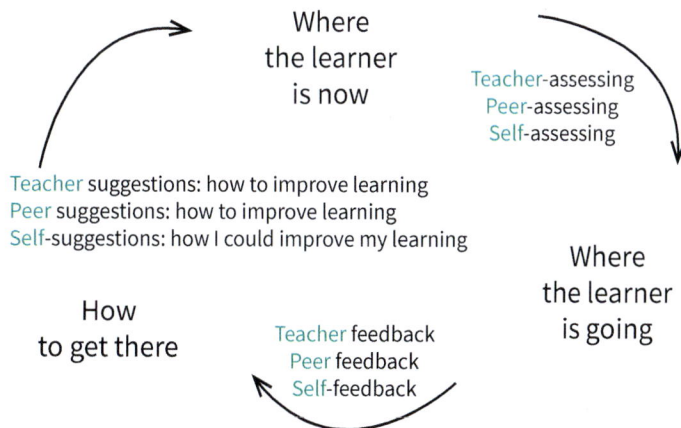

Where the learner is now

Teacher-assessing
Peer-assessing
Self-assessing

Teacher suggestions: how to improve learning
Peer suggestions: how to improve learning
Self-suggestions: how I could improve my learning

How to get there

Teacher feedback
Peer feedback
Self-feedback

Where the learner is going

1.1 Relic

LEARNING PLAN

Learning objectives	Learning intentions	Success criteria
9Rs.01, 9Ri.01, 9Ri.03, 9Ra.02, 9Wc.06, 9SLm.03, 9SLg.02, 9SLg.03	Learners will: • read a story opening and discuss genre • explore how key information helps readers understand a character's actions • consider the effect of story structure • discuss and summarise their impressions of a story opening.	Learners can: • identify a fiction genre based on a story's key features • understand how explicit information helps a reader understand a character's actions • comment on the effect of story structure • express their opinion of a story opening and summarise their own and others' ideas.

LANGUAGE SUPPORT

This session asks learners to analyse explicit information, so it may be useful to recap the difference between explicit and implicit information with learners. Remind them that explicit information is information that is stated clearly and in detail, leaving no room for misunderstanding, doubt or confusion. Implicit information suggests or *implies* something, without expressing it directly. Some learners may confuse 'imply' and 'infer'. Remind them that to infer something is to reach a conclusion based on implicit information. You can clarify this by explaining that a writer or speaker *implies* something, while a reader or listener *infers* something.

Starter idea

Beginnings . . . (10 minutes)

Resources: Learner's Book, Session 1.1, Getting started activity

Description: Read the following two summaries of story openings to learners:

- The main character wakes up, has a shower, brushes their teeth, eats breakfast and then decides to go on an adventure.

- The main character is in great danger in the middle of an adventure; the first chapter ends on a cliffhanger and later chapters explain how the adventure started.

Ask learners which opening they find most interesting. Explain that writers can start their story at any point in the plot, but writers usually try to make the opening engaging, to grab the reader's attention. Learners should then complete the Getting started activity in pairs.

Main teaching ideas

1 Discussing genre (20 minutes)

Learning intention: Read a story opening and discuss genre.

Resources: Learner's Book, Session 1.1, *Darkparis* Extract 1, Activity 1

Description: Remind learners that a genre is a style or category of literature, art, film or music.

To categorise a text we usually compare its features with other texts and look for similarities in features such as setting, events, characters and themes. For example:

- historical fiction features characters and events in a historical setting

- fairy tales are usually written for children and may feature magical creatures

- science fiction is typically set in the future or on other planets with actual, imagined or potential science

- young adult fiction often emphasises real-life experiences such as friendship, romance, family life, or commentary on social issues.

Explain that there are many different genres, and that stories will often be categorised as a sub-genre within a genre (e.g. science fiction or fantasy within young adult fiction, such as *The Hunger Games*).

Learners should then read the extract from *Darkparis* and complete Activity 1 in pairs.

> Differentiation ideas:

- Support: Explain the concept of genre with examples other than fiction, which may be easier for learners to understand. Ask learners to sort the following items into groups: cheese, apples, butter, carrots, oranges, milk, onions, potatoes, bananas. How did they categorise the items?

- Challenge: Ask learners to compare the extract from *Darkparis* with any other stories or films they have seen, then write a short list of features common to that genre.

> Assessment ideas: Listen to learners' discussions and assess how clearly they consider the underground setting as a possible indicator that this might be a thriller or adventure story. Assess also whether they discuss the theme of making friends or meeting people for the first time and link this to young adult fiction.

2 Analysing explicit information (30 minutes)

Learning intention: Explore how key information helps readers understand a character's actions.

Resources: Learner's Book, Session 1.1, *Darkparis* Extract 1, Activity 2

Description: Write this quotation on the board: *Jinn and Phyllis were spending a wonderful holiday, in space, as far away as possible from the inhabited stars.* Explain that it is the first sentence of a novel called *Planet of the Apes.* Point out that that it contains explicit information that has important implications for the rest of the story – that other planets are inhabited and that space travel is possible. Ask learners: *What implications could this explicit information have for the story?* Get several responses from different learners.

Next, read Extract 1 from *Darkparis* again to the class and ask learners what explicit information it contains. If they give examples of information that they have inferred rather than being explicit information, point out the difference between explicit (directly stated) and implicit (indirectly stated) meaning. Write any correct examples of explicit information on the board. Then, ask learners to complete Activity 2 on their own.

> Differentiation ideas:

- Support: To clarify the difference between explicit and implicit information use this example: *That early morning class may not be best for him.* (Implied meaning: he has trouble getting up early in the morning or does not like getting up early.) An explicit statement would be: *He has trouble getting up early.*

- Challenge: Ask learners to write two paragraphs. The first should analyse the explicit information and the second the implicit information in the extract.

> Assessment ideas: Read learners' paragraphs. Assess how clearly they have explained how the explicit information in the extract has helped them understand what might happen later in the story.

3 Analysing story structure (30 minutes)

Learning intention: Consider the effect of story structure.

Resources: Learner's Book, Session 1.1, Activity 3

Description: Remind learners that 'structure' is how a writer organises a story or text, including the order of events (perhaps using devices such as flashbacks) and when to introduce certain characters. A plot has a beginning, a middle and an end, but writers may reorder plot events for effect.

Give the following example:

> **Plot outline:** Ruby and Praveen are brother and sister. Praveen says Ruby is not a good athlete, so she challenges him to a race. At first, she thinks she might lose and regrets suggesting the race (beginning). However, she trains very hard. Praveen sees Ruby training and decides he should also put the effort in (middle). The race happens, Ruby wins and Praveen learns to respect her more (end).
>
> **Possible structural choices for the writer:**
>
> a Start with Ruby and Praveen arguing and then Ruby worrying about the race and training hard, followed by Praveen training and him respecting her more after she wins.
>
> b Start with the race and Praveen learning to respect Ruby more, then show a flashback to Ruby and Praveen arguing and then Ruby's worrying about and training for the race, followed by Praveen's training.
>
> c Start with Praveen training for the race; during his training show a flashback to the argument with Ruby where she challenges him to the race, then return to Praveen's training, then the race, and then show Praveen respecting Ruby more.

Ask learners to read Activity 3 in pairs and then to write brief notes in answer to the question: *For each of the bullet points in Activity 3, what effects does this structural choice have on the reader?* Learners should then use these notes in their discussion for Activity 3.

> **Differentiation ideas:**

*   Support: Tell learners that the early part of a story (the *exposition*) normally includes background information about characters or previous plot events that helps the reader understand the rest of the story. Then ask them to make brief notes on what they learn about the characters' backstories and previous events in the extract from *Darkparis* to use in their discussion.

*   Challenge: Ask learners to write a second set of answers that includes at least one new idea from their discussions.

> **Assessment ideas:** Before beginning their discussions, ask learners to give each other feedback on the notes they prepared. How useful are they? How could they be improved?

4 Reactions to a story opening (50 minutes)

Learning intention: Discuss and summarise impressions of a story opening.

Resources: Learner's Book, Session 1.1, Activities 4 and 5

Description: Read Activity 4 to the class, then ask for a show of hands based on each of the bullet points (do not go into reasons for their response at this point). Ask:

*   Did you find the extract interesting?
*   Is the extract well-structured?
*   Are you interested in the two main characters?

Put learners into mixed groups of those who expressed different opinions for the Activity 4 discussion. Before they start, read the Speaking tip and emphasise that learners should explore why they agree or disagree about each of the bullet points. Tell learners they will be writing a summary of the discussion afterwards, so they should try to remember the key points.

After the discussion, learners should work independently to write their paragraphs for Activity 5.

> **Differentiation ideas:**

*   Support: For Activity 5, give learners the following writing frame:

    *   Paragraph 1: Interest in the story – explain why people found the story interesting; include any points from peers who were not interested in the story.

    *   Paragraph 2: Structure of the story – write about whether and how the story structure grabs the reader's attention.

    *   Paragraph 3: The two main characters – write about how the two characters come across to readers – what are their personalities?

*   Challenge: For Activity 5, ask learners to write one paragraph on each of the bullet points, including points of agreement and disagreement in each paragraph.

> **Assessment ideas:** Observe and listen closely to learners' group discussions. Assess how clearly they express their ideas or opinions, and how well they listen to, comment on and reflect ideas that differ from their own.

Plenary idea

Choosing an opening (10 minutes)

Description: Read learners the following plot outline:

> Arif is angry at her father Madesh because he suggests that women are no good at making money. So, she makes lemonade and sells it on a stand outside her house and makes lots of money. At first, Madesh is embarrassed to be proved wrong and tries to make excuses, but when Arif wins a Young Businesswoman of the Year award, Madesh is extremely proud of his daughter and respects what she has achieved, so they become closer.

Ask learners to decide where they would start this story and explain why to a partner.

Homework idea

Learners should complete Workbook Session 1.1.

1.2 The Doorkeeper

LEARNING PLAN		
Learning objectives	**Learning intentions**	**Success criteria**
9Rv.02, 9Rg.01, 9Rs.01, 9Rs.02, 9Ri.01, 9Ri.09, 9Wv.01, 9Wv.02, 9Wg.01, 9Wg.03, 9Wc.01, 9Wc.02, 9Wp.01	Learners will: • explore the effect of structural and language choices • consider how punctuation choices can be used to present a character • write the continuation of a story in the style of an author.	Learners can: • analyse the effect of a writer's structural and language choices • comment on how punctuation choices help to create a distinctive character • use specific language, structural and grammatical techniques to write in the style of another author.

LANGUAGE SUPPORT

The extract in this session contains dialogue as direct speech. It may help learners to review the format of direct speech and consider what alternatives are available.

Direct speech reports the actual words spoken, which are enclosed in speech marks. Direct speech also uses a **reporting verb** (for example 'said', 'shouted'), which may be followed by an <u>adverb or prepositional phrase</u>:

- 'I'm here,' she **said**.
- 'I'm here,' she **said** <u>excitedly</u>.

Indirect speech is when the narrator reports what was said, rather than quoting the actual words spoken: *She said she had arrived.*

Free direct speech is a variation on direct speech, such as using speech marks without reporting verbs:

- 'I'm here,' she said. (direct speech)
- 'I'm here.' (free direct speech)

Free indirect speech usually represents a character's thoughts, rather than their actual words:

- 'Time to go?' he asked. (direct speech)
- He asked if it was time to go. (indirect speech)
- Time to go? He wondered if he had stayed too long. (free indirect speech).

Starter idea

Mysterious characters (15 minutes)

Resources: Learner's Book, Session 1.2, Getting started activity

Description: Write some synonyms for the word 'mysterious' on the board (e.g. *strange, secretive, puzzling, unknown*). Explain that these adjectives can be used to modify the word 'character' (*strange character*, etc.). Put learners into pairs and ask them to think of characters from books and films that they find are mysterious, secretive, etc. and to discuss what makes them seem like this.

Main teaching ideas

1 Writer's choices: structure and language (30 minutes)

Learning intention: Explore the effect of structural and language choices.

Resources: Learner's Book, Session 1.2, *Darkparis* Extract 2, Activity 1

Description: Tell learners that for Activity 1, they will need to comment on the different effects created by the writer's structural choices. Recap what we mean by 'effects' by reading these two examples (or writing them on the board):

a   With the heavy curtains still drawn, Ruby awoke in darkness. A sound and a feeling that she was not alone made her alert very quickly. She felt a hand cover her mouth.

b   Ruby awoke quickly when she felt a hand cover her mouth. The room was still dark as the heavy curtains were still drawn.

Ask learners what effect each example has on them as a reader. Elicit that example a builds suspense and tension by establishing **a** dark, unsettling setting, and ends with a dramatic event, making us want to read on. Example **b** does not establish or build tension through description and ends in a dull way, less likely to engage the reader.

Learners should then read the extract and complete Activity 1 on their own.

> **Differentiation ideas:**

- Support: Draw the table in Activity 1 on the board and read the first three paragraphs of the extract with learners. Ask: *What effect does the description of the setting here have on you?* Write answers on the board. They can then read the rest of the extract and complete the table on their own. If learners need further support, suggest some effects to get them started, such as feeling tense, frightened or excited.

- Challenge: After completing the table, ask learners to write a paragraph combining the notes they have made in the 'Effects' column into an analysis of the extract as a whole.

> **Assessment ideas:** Review learners' tables and assess whether they have described clearly their emotional response and any ideas they had. For example, have they identified:

- the description of the setting as frightening, atmospheric, mysterious, etc.

- the choice about the tunnels as exciting

- the cliffhanger as creating suspense or tension and making them want to know what happens next?

2 The effects of language features (55 minutes)

Learning intentions: Explore the effect of structural and language choices. Consider how punctuation choices can be used to present a character.

Resources: Learner's Book, Session 1.2, Activities 2 and 3; Language worksheet 1.1

Description: Activities 2 and 3 are both discussion activities, so they can be run consecutively in the following way.

Write on the board an outline of the language features that learners will be discussing in both activities, with some examples:

- figurative/metaphorical language: *the car's brakes screeched* (aural imagery); *the scent of the flowers was delightful* (olfactory imagery); *the light blinded her for a moment* (visual imagery); *his sports vest proudly displayed the five overlapping rings of the Olympics* (symbol)

- rhetorical devices: *That's one small step for a man, one giant leap for mankind* (antithesis/contrast)

- punctuation used for rhetorical purposes: *And now . . . here it is* (three-dot ellipsis); *I insist you leave now!* (exclamation mark); *How did that actor win an Oscar?* (rhetorical question).

Put learners into pairs and ask them to take their time to read Activities 2 and 3, the Language focus information and all the Key word definitions. They should then spend 10–15 minutes discussing how metaphorical language and rhetorical devices help to create mystery (Activity 2) and a further 10–15 minutes analysing how punctuation is used for rhetorical purposes to characterise The Doorkeeper (Activity 3).

In the remaining 20–25 minutes, ask learners to complete Language worksheet 1.1 to consolidate understanding of rhetorical punctuation.

> **Differentiation ideas:**

- Support: List the three language features on the board and ask learners for examples of each. Write correct examples on the board and clarify issues with any incorrect examples. Ensure that learners understand all the terms and examples.

- Challenge: Not all learners will need the outline of language features and examples on the board. So, at the beginning of the lesson ask learners to complete Activities 2 and 3 in 20–25 minutes. In the remaining 15–20 minutes they should write two paragraphs analysing all the language features, with a focus on their effects (they can use and expand on the points from their pair discussions).

> **Assessment ideas:** Assess learners' responses to each activity as follows:

- Creating mystery: This 'how' question asks learners to analyse, so assess how well they use the language examples in Activity 2 to reach conclusions about the effects on the reader (for example, the imagery creating a sense of darkness and confusion, disorientation or fear).

- Punctuation: This 'what is suggested' question also asks for analysis, so assess if learners reach conclusions about the effects of punctuation in characterising The Doorkeeper (such as the question mark/rhetorical question and exclamation mark making him seem strong, confident and in charge).

3 Continuing the story (40 minutes)

Learning intention: Write the continuation of a story in the style of an author.

Resources: Learner's Book, Session 1.2, Activity 4

Description: Review what has happened in the first two extracts of *Darkparis,* and recap the writer's structural choices and language techniques and their effects:

- What has happened: Louis meets Relic in the catacombs; he follows her underground and meets The Doorkeeper, who presents him with a test.

- Structural choices: Some parts of the story follow the plot chronologically, others use flashback. Some parts of the story use a cliffhanger.

- Language techniques: Figurative/metaphorical language; rhetorical devices; punctuation.
- Effects: It creates a mysterious and disorientating atmosphere; characterises The Doorkeeper as strong, confident and in charge.

Read Activity 4 as a class. Point out that the next part of the plot has been outlined for them, so they can focus closely on using the three language techniques and writing in the same style. Read the Writing tip and then ask learners to complete the activity independently.

> **Differentiation ideas:**

- Support: Give learners a rough plan for how they could write the next 200 words of the story: 50 words describing Louis travelling through a dark, winding tunnel and catching up with The Doorkeeper; 50 words of description and dialogue between The Doorkeeper and Louis, where he advises him to turn back and follow his own path; 50–100 words describing Louis arriving back at The Fork and then finding his way to a huge maze.

- Challenge: Ask learners to either invent an alternative plot for the next part of the story and write that in the same style as the original, or to write 200 words for Activity 4 as instructed, then invent an alternative plot for the next part of the story and write that in the same style as the original.

> **Assessment ideas:** Learners should complete the Peer assessment, reading their stories aloud and giving each other feedback.

Plenary idea

Exploring effects (10 minutes)

Description: Put learners into pairs and ask them to list the structural choices and language techniques they have studied in this session. Next, ask them to think of a story or film they have read or seen recently that used interesting structural choices or language techniques – for example, a film that told its story non-chronologically or a novel with metaphorical descriptions of settings or characters. In small groups, learners should discuss why these choices and techniques were interesting.

Homework idea

Learners should complete Workbook Session 1.2.

1.3 Reviewing *Darkparis*

LEARNING PLAN

Learning objectives	Learning intentions	Success criteria
9Ri.05, 9Ri.06, 9Ri.10, 9Ra.01, 9Ra.02, 9Ra.03, 9Ra.04, 9Ra.05, 9Wv.03, 9Wg.04, 9Wg.05, 9Ws.02, 9Wp.02, 9SLs.01	Learners will: • make some book recommendations • explore how personal context affects the reading and writing of texts • synthesise information from different sources • write a formal review.	Learners can: • listen to the type of books people are interested in and make some recommendations • understand how personal context influences writers' choices and readers' reactions to a text • use different strategies to synthesise information from a range of sources • write a formal review using standard English.

LANGUAGE SUPPORT

In Activity 4 in this session, learners are reminded to write using standard English. The Common misconception below explains the important distinction between standard English and Received Pronunciation (RP). Other points to emphasise are:

- standard English is the form of English that has the most prestige or status compared to other forms of English

- standard English is not attached to any particular region or location

- standard English is not widely used in speech; it is mostly found in writing

- depending on the context, non-standard English is usually acceptable in speech (such as when speaking with or writing to friends), but is usually not acceptable in formal writing.

A good grasp of standard English is an important skill for life, as the ability to use the grammar, vocabulary, spelling and punctuation of standard English in writing will allow learners to progress confidently through school and university.

Common misconception

Misconception	How to identify	How to overcome
Standard English is about pronouncing words correctly.	Write this sentence on the board and ask different learners to say it aloud: *Did you see the sign at the end of the garden path?* Ask learners if they can distinguish different ways people pronounce the word *path*. For example, some learners may pronounce it with a *v* sound ('parve'). Other learners may pronounce it with a longer *ar* sound and with a *th* sound at the end ('par-th').	Point out that the sentence is written in standard English. This term describes grammar, vocabulary, spelling and punctuation – *not* pronunciation. Standard English can be spoken in a wide variety of accents. The accent that some people might confuse with standard English is called Received Pronunciation (RP). RP is sometimes called 'Queen's English', 'BBC English' or 'Oxford English'. RP is not widely used even in the UK (only 3 percent use it), but it is the accent on which phonemic transcriptions in dictionaries are based.

Starter idea

Favourite books (10 minutes)

Resources: Learner's Book, Session 1.3, Getting started activity

Description: Write a list of some popular young adult fiction on the board, such as *The Boy in the Striped Pyjamas*, *The Hunger Games*, *Noughts and Crosses*, *Stormbreaker*, *The Fellowship of the Ring*, *The Ruby in the Smoke*. Put learners into pairs and ask them to discuss the Getting started activity, using the examples you have listed if they need to. Ask learners to write a list of the books they would recommend to their friends and peers.

Main teaching ideas

1 Discussing book recommendations (30 minutes)

Learning intention: Make some book recommendations.

Resources: Learner's Book, Session 1.3, Activity 1

Description: Point out that in bookshops and online stores, books are organised according to genre:

science fiction and fantasy, literature and fiction, mysteries and thrillers, romance, historical fiction, biographies, and so on.

Put learners into groups and ask them to complete Activity 1 using their notes from the Getting started activity. They should: mention the titles of the books on their list, decide which genres those books belong to, ask their peers which genres they prefer and explain why they would recommend the books in their list which fit that genre.

> **Differentiation ideas:**

- Support: Tell groups that every learner has 3–4 minutes to talk about the books on the list, explaining which they would recommend and why. This provides a more formal turn-taking structure and will encourage all learners to speak and listen, rather than some learners dominating the discussion.

- Challenge: As well as discussing genres, ask learners to draw a table of the top five books that were recommended, noting the genre of these books and how many times they were recommended by different learners.

> **Assessment ideas:** This is likely to be an informal discussion so it is a good opportunity to observe learners' turn-taking skills, as some might be enthusiastic about the books they have read and forget to listen to their peers' views. Assess whether learners routinely compromise in turn-taking. If they do, give some positive feedback after the discussions. If they do not, remind learners that listening is an important skill to develop alongside speaking, because we learn a lot through listening, as well as communicating respect to other speakers.

2 What influences readers' responses? (30 minutes)

Learning intention: Explore how personal context affects the reading and writing of texts.

Resources: Learner's Book, Session 1.3, Activity 2

Description: Remind learners that context refers to the personal and social background of a reader or writer, which might include someone's age, the type of community they have grown up in or prefer (for example, a large city or a small village), their views on social issues (for example, the role of women in society), their general or personal preferences (for example, liking or disliking science fiction) and their life experiences (for example, travel, hardship).

As a class, read the three reactions to *Darkparis* in Activity 2. Suggest that some of these contextual factors will have influenced Ayesha, Vanessa and Alexei's responses, but emphasise that learners can consider other factors, such as how a reader might feel about the story's setting, characters or plot, or what effect language and symbolism might have on them. Learners should then write answers to Activity 2 on their own.

> **Differentiation ideas:**

- Support: After reading the activity, point out the following: the age of each reader has been given; two of the readers are very close in age whereas the other is older, so their age may have influenced their views; the views and living situation of some readers appear to have influenced their responses to *Darkparis*.

- Challenge: After learners have completed Activity 2, ask them to write a paragraph explaining their own response to the *Darkparis* extracts. They should reflect on their own personal and social context and include these reflections in their paragraph.

> **Assessment ideas:** Ask learners to swap their answers with a partner and give each other feedback, considering the following:

- Has their partner clearly explained their answers?

- Do their answers make sense?

- How could their answers be improved?

3 Discussing and synthesising different views (65 minutes)

Learning intention: Synthesise information from different sources.

Resources: Learner's Book, Session 1.3, Activities 3 and 4; Workbook Session 1.3

> ⬇ **Download the audioscript for Activity 3 from Cambridge GO (Track 03).**

Description: Remind learners of all the points they considered about personal and social context in Activity 2, then explain that these are relevant for writers as well as readers. Read Activity 3 and make sure that learners understand that they need to choose a clear way to make their notes. Read the Listening tip as a class, then play the recording while learners make notes on each of the bullet points.

To prepare learners for the synthesis task in Activity 4, ask learners to complete the three activities in Workbook Session 1.3. Allow 15–20 minutes for this, then read Activity 4, the Reading tip and the Key word definitions to the class. Check that learners understand the definitions and clarify any confusion (e.g. explain the difference between skimming and scanning as 'getting the overall idea' contrasted with 'finding specific details'). Then put learners into groups to complete Activity 4 using their notes from Activity 2.

> **Differentiation ideas:**

- Support: Before the listening activity, remind learners to listen out for key words and their synonyms:

  - why she chose the setting – key words: setting, location, place names (i.e., Paris); chose, choice, pick, select, decision(s)

  - why she chose Louis as a central character – key words: character, character names (i.e. Louis); chose, choice, pick, select, decision(s)

  - what she says about the message of her book – key words: message, moral, theme, communicate, 'what it's about'.

- Challenge: After Activity 4, give learners 5–10 minutes to write a one-paragraph summary of the views expressed in their small group discussion.

> **Assessment ideas:** Ask learners to use the Reflection questions to assess their ability to understand and synthesise information from multiple sources.

Plenary idea

Synthesising information (15 minutes)

Description: Remind learners that synthesising information means combining details from different sources, usually to find links and make an overall point. Once they have synthesised information, they can communicate it in writing or visually, make predictions, or solve problems.

Write the following table on the board, which shows the results of a survey of favourite books in a school.

Book title	Genre	Votes
The Boy in the Striped Pyjamas	literary fiction	33
The Hunger Games	science fiction	51
Noughts and Crosses	literary fiction	29
Stormbreaker	thriller	31

Ask learners to analyse this information in pairs. Which is the most popular book? Which is the most popular genre? Then ask learners to predict which book would be the most popular out of the following in the same school, and to give reasons for their answers:

- a story about young environmental campaigners

- a time-travel adventure story

- a mystery story with a teenage detective.

CROSS-CURRICULAR LINK

Maths (percentages and graphs): This session could lead to some independent research investigating the popularity of books by genre, after which learners could present their findings using percentages and graphs. For example, ask learners to do a survey of the favourite books and genres of their peers in class or across the whole school, then to work out and present the following:

- percentages of learners who like the top five books

- percentage of learners who like the top five genres

- a pie chart showing the percentage of learners who like the top five books

- a pie chart showing the percentage of learners who like the top five genres.

Homework idea

Learners should complete Activity 5, the book review, for homework. Remind them to reread Extracts 1 and 2 of the story from the previous sessions, and make notes on the characters and settings, the appeal of the storyline and whether the novel is likely to be popular with 12–18-year-old readers. Reiterate that the review should consider what appeal the text has for readers, not simply summarise the story. If necessary, give learners the following structure for their writing:

1   A short paragraph explaining the book's main themes and the author's intentions.

2   A short paragraph summarising the extracts.

3   A paragraph on the book's positive points.

4   A paragraph on the book's negative points.

5   A final paragraph evaluating the balance between the book's positive and negative points.

1.4 The second test

LEARNING PLAN

Learning objectives	Learning intentions	Success criteria
9Rs.01, 9Ri.01, 9Ri.05, 9Ri.07, 9Ri.08, 9Ws.01, 9Wc.01, 9Wc.03, 9Wc.04, 9Wc.07, 9SLm.02, 9SLm.03, 9SLm.04, 9SLp.01, 9SLp.03, 9SLr.01	Learners will: • use voice and gesture to convey character and theme in drama • explore a theme across several texts • explore the effect of structural choices in a script • write a dramatic scene.	Learners can: • use voice and gesture to convey character and emotion in a dramatic performance • analyse how a theme is presented and developed in different texts • comment on the effect of different structural choices in a script • write a dramatic scene, maintaining the voice and personality of the characters.

LANGUAGE SUPPORT

The dramatic scene in this session contains several examples of rhetorical devices. These are common in drama and speeches, and learners will benefit from being able to identify and comment on them. They include the following (examples are from the scene in this session):

• Questioning and answering self: *What's this about? I want to leave!* (This is different from a rhetorical question, where the writer does not provide an answer.)

• Balanced phrases: *Bad choices – but they weren't your choices to make; I have. I refuse.*

• Repetition: *You chose the third tunnel, Louis. You chose your own route. You chose.*

• Three-part list: *This is why you're here, Louis. To prove yourself through the choices you make. To choose your new life.*

Starter idea

Delivering lines effectively in drama (10 minutes)

Resources: Learner's Book, Session 1.4, Getting started activity

Description: Ask nine learners to each read one of the lines below. Explain that *(pause)* indicates a half-a-second pause and that underlined words should be emphasised.

To be (*pause*) or <u>not</u> to be. That is the question.

To be <u>or</u> not to be. That is the question.

To be or <u>not</u> to be. That is the question.

To be or not to <u>be</u>. That is the question.

To be or not to be. <u>That</u> is the question.

To be or not to be. That <u>is</u> the question.

To be or not to be. That is <u>the</u> question.

To be or not <u>to</u> be. That is the question.

To be (*pause*) or not to be. That is the <u>question</u>.

Point out that the lines seem to mean something different depending on where the pauses and emphases come. Then, put learners into small groups or pairs and ask them to practise different ways of delivering the line in the Getting started activity.

Main teaching ideas

1 Using gesture and voice in drama (40 minutes)

Learning intentions: Use voice and gesture to convey character and theme in drama. Explore a theme across several texts.

Resources: Learner's Book, Session 1.4, *Darkparis* – the play, Activities 1 and 2

Description: Read the Speaking tip, pointing out how it is possible to vary the volume, tone and pace of voice when reading a play. Explain that in performance, learners can also use body language to express feelings and show character – for example by:

- moving around the stage or space they are in

- changing height (lying down, kneeling, sitting, standing, etc.)

- using hand gestures (pointing, making a fist, rubbing hands together, etc.)

- lowering their head or posture to seem obedient or raising their head and chest to seem confident.

Emphasise that in this scene from the play version of *Darkparis*, they will be exploring the theme of power, so they should experiment with voice and gestures that show how weak or powerful different characters are.

Organise learners into groups of four and give them 15 minutes to read the scene aloud for Activity 1. They should then move straight on to Activity 2 and begin acting out the play, experimenting with speaking the lines and adding movements and gestures to express the theme of power.

> **Differentiation ideas:**

- Support: Visit groups as they rehearse and give them directions as if you were the director in the theatre. For example, advise how they could dramatise Relic suspended above a fast-moving river (could a learner stand on a chair?) or the Old Man gazing into a glass ball (would hand gestures be useful here?).

- Challenge: Reduce the read-through for Activity 1 to 5–10 minutes, then in the remaining time ask learners to experiment with playing the different roles, so each learner tries two or more parts. Afterwards, ask learners to include feedback on the different roles they played during the Peer assessment.

> **Assessment ideas:** Learners should complete the Peer assessment feature.

2 Exploring themes in prose and drama (45 minutes)

Learning intention: Explore a theme across several texts.

Resources: Learner's Book, Session 1.4, Activity 3; Differentiated worksheets 1A, 1B and 1C

Description: Use Differentiated worksheets 1A, 1B or 1C to prepare learners for Activity 3. Allow 25–30 minutes for learners to complete the worksheets.

Organise learners into pairs and ask them to reread the extracts from *Darkparis* in Sessions 1.1 and 1.2, then to complete Activity 3 together. Remind learners to focus on:

- *finding examples* to support their ideas and so sustain an in-depth discussion

- *exploring* how Louis develops from a powerless character to one who has power

- *discussing* how the theme of power is communicated in both prose and drama texts.

> **Differentiation ideas:**

- Support: Before learners start, explain the theme of power in more detail. Point out that it can mean: one person having power over another; a character having power and at first using it for good deeds but then later using it for bad deeds (i.e. becoming corrupted); a character's quest to achieve power through gaining money, strength, skills or intelligence. Note that the following stories that they may have heard of all explore the theme of power: *Harry Potter*, *The Lord of the Rings*, *Star Wars*, *Animal Farm*, *Macbeth*.

- Challenge: In the final five minutes, ask learners to write a summary of points from their discussion. This could also include learners' thoughts on the self-assessment questions opposite.

> **Assessment ideas:** Ask learners to self-assess their contribution to the paired discussion, focusing on the following questions.

- How well were they able to express their ideas and opinions in detail, for example, on reflection, could they have communicated their ideas more clearly? How?

- Did they vary how they communicated, for example did they sometimes listen and sometimes speak? Did they sometimes use plain language and at other times use similes or metaphors?

3 Exploring and writing drama (45 minutes)

Learning intentions: Explore the effect of structural choices in a script. Write a dramatic scene.

Resources: Learner's Book, Session 1.4, Activities 4 and 5

Description: Draw an outline of the structure of this scene on the board (see the following diagram). Point out that the writer could have made different choices. For example: the scene could have started with all three characters on stage and ended with a cliffhanger; Louis and The Doorkeeper could have continued their dialogue and/or Louis could have challenged The Doorkeeper's authority; new characters could have been introduced. Ask learners what effect these different choices might have had on an audience and collect several responses. Then ask learners to write their answers for Activity 4.

Read the Writing tip as a class. Emphasise the importance of planning the events and how the scene will end. Suggest to learners that they can draw a diagram similar to the one on the board when planning drama scenes. Learners then write their scenes for Activity 5.

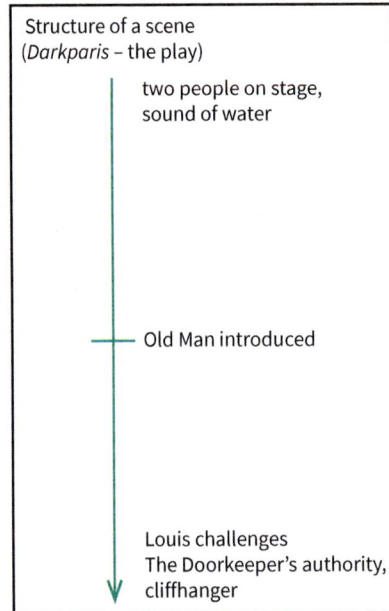

> Structure of a scene
> (*Darkparis* – the play)
>
> two people on stage, sound of water
>
> Old Man introduced
>
> Louis challenges The Doorkeeper's authority, cliffhanger

> **Differentiation ideas:**

- Support: Give learners an outline of a new scene and ask them to write the dialogue and stage directions for it:

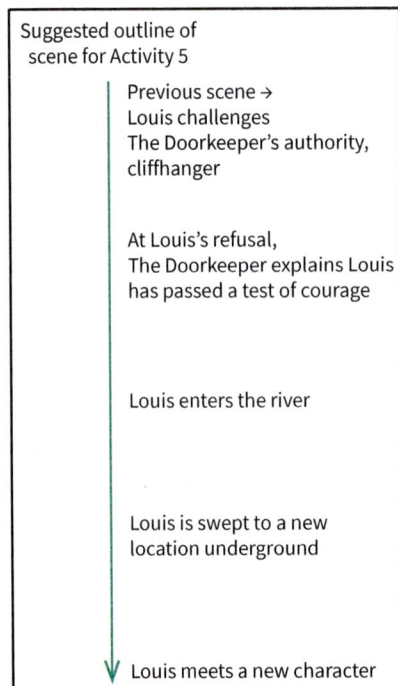

> Suggested outline of scene for Activity 5
>
> Previous scene →
> Louis challenges The Doorkeeper's authority, cliffhanger
>
> At Louis's refusal, The Doorkeeper explains Louis has passed a test of courage
>
> Louis enters the river
>
> Louis is swept to a new location underground
>
> Louis meets a new character

- Challenge: After Activity 5, ask learners to draw an outline of how they would continue the play version of *Darkparis*, imagining as many events as possible, including the climax and the end of the play.

> **Assessment ideas:** Read learners' dramatic scenes and look at any diagrams they have produced. Have they maintained the voice and personality of the characters? Have they retained Louis's challenge to The Doorkeeper? If not, have they made believable any changes in Louis's character? Have learners written a satisfying ending to their scenes, for example, has the story moved forward? Does their ending make the audience want to know what happens next? If not, give some feedback on other choices learners could have made.

Plenary idea

Responding to prose and drama (10 minutes)

Description: Get three learners to read aloud the drama script from Differentiated worksheets Activity 3. One learner should read the stage directions, and two others the parts of mother and daughter. Read learners the example script given in the answers, then put learners into pairs and ask them to discuss which they preferred, the drama or prose text, and why.

Homework idea

Learners should complete Workbook Session 1.4.

1.5 Visiting Coober Pedy

LEARNING PLAN

Learning objectives	Learning intentions	Success criteria
9Rv.02, 9Rv.03, 9Ri.02, 9Ri.03, 9Ri.04, 9Ri.07, 9SLm.03	Learners will: • explore the implications of explicit information • consider how extended metaphors contribute to the purpose and effect of a text • analyse a writer's language choices.	Learners can: • identify and comment on the implications of explicit information in a piece of travel writing • explain how imagery, including extended metaphors, can be used for purpose and effect • analyse the effect of a writer's language choices precisely and perceptively.

LANGUAGE SUPPORT

Travel writing, like much descriptive writing, makes frequent use of adjectives. These are a common language feature used to add detail and depth to description so it may help learners to recap how adjectives are used within sentences. Remind them that adjectives add details and qualities to *nouns*. In travel writing, this may be detail about rural landscapes, towns, cities, etc. Adjectives are typically found in three positions in sentences:

- immediately before a noun: *the <u>hungry</u> children*
- after a noun phrase: *the children, <u>hungry</u> for lunch, began to fight*
- after verbs and referring to the subject: *the children became <u>hungry</u>.*

Note that adjectives can also take the present participle, for example: *a fascinat<u>ing</u> person, a stimulat<u>ing</u> book, the amaz<u>ing</u> stunt.*

Common misconception

Misconception	How to identify	How to overcome
Adjectives are only *describing* words.	Ask learners to imagine they are sitting with friends at a table with lots of different plates. Someone says: 'the plate'. Ask learners: *Would it be clear which plate they were talking about?* Write these examples on the board and ask learners to say which words are adjectives: • *the blue plate* • *my plate* • *your plate* • *that plate.*	Explain that *blue, my, your* and *that* are all adjectives; 'my', 'your', 'his', 'her', 'its', 'our', 'their', and 'whose' are *possessive adjectives*, and 'that' functions as an adjective when it is used to modify a noun. The only word that describes a particular quality or detail in the example given here is *blue*. All the other adjectives specify something extra about the noun *plate*, so it can be identified correctly.

Starter idea

Interesting places (10 minutes)

Resources: Learner's Book, Session 1.5, Getting started activity

Description: Ask learners to recall an interesting place they have visited. If they feel they have not travelled anywhere very interesting, they could think of a place they would like to visit (perhaps a place they have read about or seen on television). Then organise learners into pairs and ask them to discuss the Getting started activity. Remind them to focus on what made the place memorable, or what makes them want to visit.

Main teaching ideas

1 The meaning of implicit and explicit information (40 minutes)

Learning intention: Explore the implications of explicit information

Resources: Learner's Book, Session 1.5, 'Coober Pedy: Getting below the surface' Extract 1, Activities 1 and 2

Description: Recap the meanings of explicit and implicit information, and the terms 'imply' and 'infer' (see the Language support in Session 1.1 of this Teacher's Resource). Emphasise that explicit information will be clear and detailed, and will allow readers to understand the main points in a text. Implied meaning is when a writer *suggests* something rather than stating it directly.

Ask a volunteer to read the article extract aloud, then (without giving specific examples) point out that the writer implies several things about Coober Pedy, and expresses their attitude to the place. Read Activity 1 as a class, and suggest to learners that for part (b) they will need to closely analyse the language in paragraphs 1 and 4. Learners then complete the activity in pairs.

Read Activity 2. Point out that the extract contains explicit information about the history of Coober Pedy and its distance from Canberra (do not identify where this information is in the text). Join learner pairs into groups of four or six to discuss the effect of explicit information in response to Activity 2.

> **Differentiation ideas:**

- Support: Before their discussion, give learners specific examples of implied meaning, voice and attitude, as well as explicit information, for example: *no wi-fi, effectively a hole in the ground, I was the unwilling heroine, three days travelling, precious opals.*

- Challenge: As part of Activity 2, ask learners to discuss and write one or two sentences in answer to this question: *What meaning do you infer from the writer using the phrase 'in a desperate attempt to get rich quick'?*

> **Assessment ideas:** Listen to the pair discussions for Activity 1. Assess whether learners understand that the writer implies Coober Pedy is a difficult place to live by listening for comments about there being

no wi-fi, that it is very far from towns and cities and that it does not offer a lot of comfort.

2 Analysing language choices (60 minutes)

Learning intentions: Consider how extended metaphors contribute to the purpose and effect of a text. Analyse a writer's language choices.

Resources: Learner's Book, Session 1.5, Activity 3; Language worksheet 1.2

Description: Use the information in Language support at the start of the session and in the answers for Language worksheet 1.2 to explain adjectives and their positions within sentences. Then give learners 20–30 minutes to complete Language worksheet 1.2 on their own.

Read through the Language focus feature and Key word definitions in the Learner's Book. Point out that writers make a variety of language choices, including:

- a balance of pre- and post-modification in sentences
- the type and number of adjectives and adverbs used
- when to use different sentence types (simple, compound, complex and compound-complex)
- words with particular connotations
- different kinds of figurative language (simile, metaphor, extended metaphor, personification, symbols, imagery).

All these language choices have effects on a reader that learners can comment on in their analyses.

Learners should write their article for Activity 3 on their own. Remind them to analyse specifically the comparisons the writer makes between Coober Pedy and Mars, as well as any other choices they think are relevant or interesting.

> **Differentiation ideas:**

- Support: Focus learners' attention on the specific comparisons the writer makes between Coober Pedy and Mars by writing some examples from the text on the board. Tell learners to base their analysis of the language choices on these examples.
- Challenge: Ask learners to write a longer analysis, perhaps 200–300 words, in which they comment on the effects of the writer's use of

figurative language, adjectives and words with particular connotations.

> **Assessment ideas:** Read learners' written work. Have they used specific, appropriate and short quotations as examples to comment on and analyse? Do they use accurate terms to describe the writer's language choices (for example simile, extended metaphor)? Do learners explain the effects of these choices on the reader?

3 Analysing a whole text (30 minutes)

Learning intention: Analyse a writer's language choices.

Resources: Learner's Book, Session 1.5, Activity 4

Description: Ask a learner to read the Reading tip aloud. Write on the board some of the key terms used in it, such as *perceptive analysis, implications/bigger issues in the text as a whole*, and discuss these using the following explanations:

- Perceptive analysis: This is an analysis in which the reader shows sensitivity to a writer's language choices and fully understands both their explicit and implied meanings.
- Implications/bigger issues in the text as a whole: An extended metaphor might cover one or two sentences or a paragraph, but a theme or main idea could extend across a whole article, story or book. To look at a text as a whole is to consider what the main ideas or themes are. Sometimes these themes are evident in patterns in the writer's language choices – these are the implications raised by the whole text.

Learners should then complete Activity 4 in pairs.

> **Differentiation ideas:**

- Support: Give learners some synonyms for 'alien' and ask whether they think these synonyms describe ideas the writer implies about Coober Pedy ('Coober Pedy seems alien – as if it is not normal').
- Challenge: Ask learners to write a 200-word analysis of the article. They should analyse the writer's language choices across the text and comment specifically on how the writer communicates the indirect meaning of Coober Pedy seeming alien or like another planet.

> **Assessment ideas:** Learners should complete the Self-assessment feature in the Learner's Book.

Plenary idea

Implied meanings and effects (10 minutes)

Description: Write this sentence on the board: *The teacher put eye-drops on his pupils during the lesson.* Put learners into pairs and ask them to identify the specific word with a double meaning and what effects this creates.

CROSS-CURRICULAR LINK

Maths (conversions): The Coober Pedy article contains distances stated in miles (*The nearest town is 400 miles away . . . It's 1,800 miles from Canberra*). Learners could research the formula for converting between miles and kilometres (if they do not already know it) and then perform this calculation on the figures in the article.

Homework idea

Learners should complete Workbook Session 1.5.

1.6 Living under the ground

LEARNING PLAN

Learning objectives	Learning intentions	Success criteria
9Rs.01, 9Ri.02, 9Ri.04, 9Ri.10, 9Ra.02, 9Wv.01, 9Wv.02, 9Ws.01, 9Wc.01, 9Wc.05, 9Wc.07, 9Wp.04, 9SLm.02, 9SLm.03, 9SLg.03	Learners will: • explore the effect of structural choices in travel writing • discuss and give a personal response to themes and ideas • produce and edit a piece of travel writing.	Learners can: • analyse the effect of structural choices in travel writing • discuss and give a personal response to themes and ideas • write, evaluate and edit a piece of travel writing.

LANGUAGE SUPPORT

In this session, the extract is structured through mixed paragraphing. Some paragraphs focus on direct speech while others focus on the writer's reflections about Coober Pedy. Learners may find it useful to review different approaches to paragraphing across different text types.

One contrast to highlight is the use or not of paragraphs with topic sentences. These tell the reader what the main focus of the paragraph will be. For example, paragraph 4 of Extract 2 in this session begins with the topic sentence: *The town feels like it is living on its past rather than looking to its future.* The rest of the paragraph develops this topic and focus, exploring ideas about Coober Pedy's past and possible future. Topic sentences are an important feature of academic writing such as essays.

Topic sentences are not as common in many other text types, including newspaper articles and fiction writing. Here, paragraph length, style and structure will vary widely. For example, they may include paragraphs that are only a single sentence, used for dramatic effect (you could give the concluding sentence of Extract 1 from Session 1.5 as an example of this: *But it did make for some nice photos*). In contrast, many older fiction texts use very long sentences.

Starter idea

Impressions of Coober Pedy (15 minutes)

Resources: Learner's Book, Session 1.6, Getting started activity

Description: Ask learners to describe the content of Extract 1 from Session 1.5. If necessary, give learners a few minutes to reread the extracts. Then organise learners into pairs and ask them to discuss the questions in the Getting started activity. Emphasise that they should focus on:

- impressions, ideas and feelings they gained from reading the travel writing extracts
- would they like to visit Coober Pedy – why or why not
- would they like to live in Coober Pedy – why or why not?

Main teaching ideas

1 Discussing and exploring the language of a travel article (30 minutes)

Learning intention: Explore the effect of structural choices in travel writing.

Resources: Learner's Book, Session 1.6, 'Coober Pedy: Getting below the surface' Extract 2, Activities 1 and 2

Description: Ask a volunteer to read Extract 2 to the class. Then go through the instructions for Activities 1 and 2. Before you organise learners into pairs, prompt their thinking on key points with the questions below. Make sure that learners understand you do not want answers to these questions now, but that they should reflect on them during their discussions for these activities.

- How would you describe Alinta's feelings towards Coober Pedy?
- The writer describes Alinta's response as 'comic' but 'tired'. What is meant by this?
- In the final paragraph, the writer reflects on the differences between life in Canberra and life in Coober Pedy. What seem to be the big differences from the writer's point of view?
- How does noticing these differences alter the writer's opinion of Coober Pedy?

Learners then complete Activities 1 and 2 in pairs.

> **Differentiation ideas:**

- Support: After asking each of the questions above, give some hints for learners to think

about: Alinta's feelings (hint: she defends Coober Pedy – ask learners how they feel when they want to defend something); the contrast between Canberra and Coober Pedy (hint: when in Canberra the writer mentions some specific things that make it seem busier and less peaceful than Coober Pedy).

- Challenge: Ask learners to write a paragraph that explains the key points of their discussions from Activities 1 and 2.

> **Assessment ideas:** Listen to learners' discussions and note whether they comment on Alinta's defence of Coober Pedy (i.e. that she feels positively towards it and defends it against the idea that it is behind the times), as well as whether they comment on the contrast the writer makes between life in Canberra (hectic and busy with traffic and the pinging of the mobile phone) and life in Coober Pedy (simpler and quieter without traffic and wi-fi).

2 In the fishbowl (40 minutes)

Learning intention: Discuss and give a personal response to themes and ideas.

Resources: Learner's Book, Session 1.6, Activity 3

Description: Read (or write on the board) the following statement by Henry Miller about travelling: *One's destination is never a place, but rather a new way of looking at things.* Ask learners to reflect on this quotation before, during and after the discussion in this session.

Tell learners that for the discussion they will use a 'fishbowl' format as follows. Some learners are seated inside the 'fishbowl' and discuss a topic, while others stand in a circle around them, listening carefully to the ideas presented. Learners can take turns in these roles, so that they practise being both contributors and listeners in a group discussion (15 minutes each).

Put chairs in a circle to create the fishbowl. Leave enough room for learners to stand around the chairs. You could have half your learners in the fishbowl and half outside listening.

Before they start, give all learners five minutes to reread both extracts from the Coober Pedy article, and Activity 3. Remind the learners in the fishbowl to focus their comments on the bullet points in the activity.

When the first 15 minutes is up, swap over the groups so the speakers become listeners and vice versa.

> 2 Law and order

Unit plan

Session	Approximate number of learning hours	Outline of learning content	Resources
2.1 Right and wrong	2 hours, 15 minutes	Learners discuss the implications of key information in a text, explore the effects of different sentence types and compare features of two texts on the same theme.	Learner's Book Session 2.1 Workbook Session 2.1
2.2 Join the police	2 hours, 30 minutes	Learners consider the features of an informative text, explore views on a complex topic and practise using colons and semi-colons.	Learner's Book Session 2.2 Workbook Session 2.2 ⬇ Language worksheet 2.1
2.3 The art detective	2 hours, 30 minutes	Learners discuss their own and others' views on an article, summarise a discussion and write a descriptive account.	Learner's Book Session 2.3 Workbook Session 2.3
2.4 Young detectives	2 hours, 30 minutes	Learners perform a dramatic scene and explore the characters, events, tone and structure of a mystery story.	Learner's Book Session 2.4 Workbook Session 2.4
2.5 Making deductions	2 hours, 30 minutes	Learners continue to explore the implications of key information in texts, compare characters in two texts and write their own character study.	Learner's Book Session 2.5 Workbook Session 2.5
2.6 Detective fiction	2 hours, 30 minutes	Learners identify the conventions on detective fiction and explore and express views about the genre. They also consider bias, figurative language and grammar in a text.	Learner's Book Session 2.6 Workbook Session 2.6 ⬇ Language worksheet 2.2 ⬇ Differentiated worksheets 2A, 2B and 2C

BACKGROUND KNOWLEDGE

For the teacher

Much of this unit is based on detective fiction, so if you are not already familiar with some of the main features and conventions of this genre, it may be useful to prepare for this. It may also be useful to think about the following concepts as preparation:

- purposes of texts – to entertain, persuade, inform, instruct, etc.

- intended audiences for texts – young adults, children, etc.
- how writers shape their language to appeal to an audience and achieve a purpose.

Session 2.2 takes a close look at the uses and effects of colons and semi-colons, and Session 2.6 examines the impact of pronoun use, so these are also good areas to prepare in a little more detail before teaching.

CONTINUED

For the learner

As this unit discusses detective fiction across several sessions, it may be useful for learners to familiarise themselves with the genre in advance. You could recommend that learners try reading some detective fiction or, if they watch any detective TV shows, to pay particular attention to the plots, characters, tone and themes. Learners could also prepare for this unit by thinking about their role as a reader or viewer of these stories.

For example, they could consider these questions:

- What are the effects of this text on me? Am I entertained, amused, frightened, etc.?
- Is this text aimed at me? Or is it aimed at someone younger, older or with different interests?
- How has the writer of this text used language to affect me? How have the plot and characters been shaped? What themes does this story deal with?

TEACHING SKILLS FOCUS

Metacognition

Metacognition can be defined as having three parts:

- self-awareness of your beliefs and ideas
- self-awareness of how you know something
- awareness of techniques for learning and the ability to use them to deepen knowledge.

These three parts exist on a scale and can be continually developed. Activities can be set up in the classroom to help learners develop three aspects of metacognition. For example, a reading strategy might be for learners to write a summary of a text. It is useful to see summary writing as developing metacognition rather than simply as a writing and editing task. To write a summary,

learners must use metacognition in their reading, so they can focus on the information needed for the summary and decide what information can be left out. This involves reviewing all the information in a text. It also means the learner has to develop techniques to evaluate the information – that is, learners must decide what information is important and what is not. Having to organise their thinking in writing in this way will develop the metacognitive abilities listed above.

This unit contains several summary-writing activities. It will be useful to consider how these activities help learners' metacognitive development, as well as improve their writing ability.

2.1 Right and wrong

LEARNING PLAN

Learning objectives	Learning intentions	Success criteria
9Rg.02, 9Rg.03, 9Rs.02, 9Ri.02, 9Ri.03, 9Ri.06, 9Ri.08, 9Ra.05	Learners will: • consider the implications of key information in an explanatory text • explore the effects of different sentence types • compare language, purpose and context in related texts.	Learners can: • use reading strategies to identify key information in a non-fiction text and discuss its implications • understand how the placement of different sentence types supports the purpose of a text • analyse language and purpose in related texts, and explain how context affects reader reaction.

LANGUAGE SUPPORT

This session contains examples of, and an activity that includes consideration of, minor sentences. Minor sentences can take several different forms, so it may help to remind learners of some of these. Examples of minor sentences (in addition to those covered in the Learner's Book) include:

• Headlines: *Hundreds of arrests.*
• Advertisements: *Smith's Sweets.*
• Notices: *No parking.*
• Abbreviated forms: *Wish you were here.*
• Interjections: *Hey!, Ouch!*

• Formula expressions: *Thank you!, How do you do?*
• Proverbs or sayings: *Like father, like son.*
• Commands: *How about a drink?, You should be so lucky!, Let's go!*
• Some questions.
• Exclamations.

Minor sentences do not conform to the main rules of grammar – for example, they may lack a subject or a verb, or if they contain a verb its use may not be typical.

Starter idea

Feeling sorry: guilt, remorse and regret (10 minutes)

Resources: Learner's Book, Session 2.1, Getting started activity

Description: Read the Getting started activity to learners. Explain that, in this context, *guilt* means feeling sorry for something that you have done or failed to do in the past. Point out that synonyms for *guilt* could be *remorse* or *regret*. Emphasise that *guilt*, *remorse* and *regret* are similar because they all involve recognising when we have acted badly in the past and feeling sorry or sad about that. Then, organise learners into pairs and ask them to discuss the Getting started activity together.

Main teaching ideas

1 Exploring an article (55 minutes)

Learning intentions: Consider the implications of key information in an explanatory text. Explore the effects of different sentence types.

Resources: Learner's Book, Session 2.2, 'The importance of conscience', Activities 1 and 2

Description: Ask three volunteers to read one section of the article each. Afterwards, write two single-sentence explanations of the article on the board:

- *Humans have evolved to feel bad when they are not sensitive to the needs of other people.*

- *Humans have evolved to have negative feelings when they have done something they think is wrong.*

Ask learners which of these is the clearest explanation of the overall meaning of the article. When a learner responds, ask them to give reasons. Get two or three responses from different learners, then give learners 10–15 minutes to write their notes for Activity 1.

Ask a volunteer to read the Key word definitions of the different sentence types to the class and clarify any questions they have about these. Then ask another learner to read the Language focus information aloud. Ensure that learners understand the main point: that they need to vary sentence types depending on purpose and effect. This is most clear when switching between compound and complex sentences or complex and simple sentences.

Give the following example:

a *Before Sunday dinner with my family, <u>I had a tough football match</u>. The other team defended really well.* (complex sentence followed by simple sentence)

b *After playing football, <u>I had Sunday dinner with my family</u>. My father had some big news and we were all very surprised.* (complex sentence followed by compound sentence)

The main clause in the complex sentences is underlined – each one focuses on a different thing because the purpose is different. In **a** the purpose is to tell a story about the football match and in **b** it is to tell a story about what happened at dinner. The conjunctions (*before* / *after*) structure the ideas. Emphasise that there are many other subordinate

conjunctions. Note that the complex sentences in these examples are followed by a different sentence type for variety and effect.

Once learners are secure in this understanding, ask them to reread the article and then complete Activity 2 independently.

> **Differentiation ideas:**

- Support: Explain that subordinate clauses show different kinds of connections between ideas: contrast (*Although I like school . . .*); reason (*He can't come because he has work to do*); possibility (*If I had a lot of money . . .*); and time (*When the teacher arrives . . .*). Then ask learners to continue with Activity 2 by looking for two clauses similar to these in the article and consider the writer's reason for using them.

- Challenge: As an addition to Activity 2, give learners this scenario: 'On Saturday morning you did homework, in the afternoon you met up with a friend'. Ask learners to write two different combinations of sentence types, with one version focusing on the homework and the other focusing on the meeting. The structures they use should fit these purposes.

> **Assessment ideas:** Read learners' paragraphs in answer to Activity 2. Assess if they have chosen a combination of sentence types from the article and if they have given an appropriate explanation of the purpose for why the writer used these sentence types.

2 Exploring the features of blogs (40 minutes)

Learning intention: Explore the effects of different sentence types.

Resources: Learner's Book, Session 2.1, 'To do – or not to do . . .', Activities 3 and 4

Description: Organise learners into small groups and ask them to read the blog text 'To do – or not to do . . .' several times. Next, read Activity 3 to learners. Point out that they are being asked to analyse the text's intended audience, purpose and structure, and then to use this information to explain how and why the writer's language choices will appeal to the audience. Give learners 15–20 minutes to discuss Activity 3. Each group should then report back to the class on the key points from their discussion.

Outline the information on minor sentences in Language support at the start of the session. Check understanding and clarify any questions learners have about this sentence form. Then ask them to write their answers to Activity 4 on their own.

> Differentiation ideas:

- Support: After outlining the information on minor sentences, point out some of the main effects they can have: creating a dramatic tone; communicating surprise; creating emphasis; and creating an informal, casual or conversational tone. Learners should write their answers to Activity 4 considering how relevant each of these effects are.

- Challenge: Ask learners to write two paragraphs for Activity 4: one in which they explain the effects of minor sentences and a second in which they explain the effects of rhetorical questions in the blog post.

> Assessment ideas: Read learners' answers to Activity 4. Have learners explained the effect of minor sentences in the blog post? Look specifically to see if learners mention that minor sentences have the effects listed above.

3   Comparing two texts (35 minutes)

Learning intention: Compare language, purpose and context in related texts.

Resources: Learner's Book, Session 2.1, Activity 5

Description: Ask for three volunteers to read aloud to the class. One should reread the article, another the blog post and the third should read the instructions for Activity 5 and the Reading tip.

Organise learners into small groups and ask them to discuss Activity 5 together. Each group should elect a timekeeper and a note taker. Explain that they should spend five minutes discussing each bullet point and make notes to share with the class. After 15–20 minutes, come back together as a class to share notes. Discuss the similarities between each groups' notes and the main points about both texts.

> Differentiation ideas:

- Support: Write the following questions on the board to prompt learners' comparisons of the article and the blog:

  - What differences of language and punctuation can you find? How would you explain the different effects of these?

  - How would you describe the different attitudes of the two writers?

  - Can you explain the different ways readers might respond to each text?

- Challenge: In the final five minutes of the lesson, ask learners to write a short paragraph that collates and summarises the notes and main points reported back from all groups.

> Assessment ideas: Learners should complete the Reflection feature to assess their understanding of texts and their contexts, as well as how they can use this skill in the future.

Plenary idea

Language and context (10 minutes)

Description: Explain that articles are a longer format than blogs, and they usually appear in printed newspapers or magazines (even if they are also read online), whereas blog posts are shorter and usually read only online. Then put learners into pairs and ask them to work out the average number of words per sentence in the article compared to the blog post (there are six sentences in the article's first paragraph and 103 words, so learners can divide these for an average and do the same for the blog post). Then ask learners to discuss whether the context, audience and purpose of each text has influenced the writer in using shorter or longer sentences.

Homework idea

Learners should complete Workbook Session 2.1.

2.2 Join the police

LEARNING PLAN

Learning objectives	Learning intentions	Success criteria
9Rg.01, 9Rs.01, 9Ri.02, 9Ri.06, 9Ri.07, 9Wg.01, 9Wg.04, 9SLm.02, 9SLm.03, 9SLg.02, 9SLg.04, 9SLr.01	Learners will: • identify the purpose, audience and structural features of a text • explore the views of others on a complex topic • use colons and semi-colons for effect.	Learners can: • identify and comment on the purpose, audience and structural features of a text • contribute to an effective discussion on different views of a complex topic • use colons and semi-colons to organise my writing and create different effects.

LANGUAGE SUPPORT

It may be useful to remind learners about colons and semi-colons before they start work on this session.

Semi-colons connect two statements that are closely linked. Consider these two sentences: *Ruby does well in science. Praveen is better at maths.* They could be joined using a comma and a conjunction:

• Ruby does well in science, but Praveen is better at maths.
• Although Ruby does well in science, Praveen is better at maths.

Alternatively, they can be joined using a semi-colon: *Ruby does well in science; Praveen is better at maths.*

Colons can introduce a list or be used before details or explanations:

• The days of the week are: Monday, Tuesday, Wednesday, Thursday and Friday.
• He was really late: he came running in, breathing hard and saying sorry over and over again.
• He was really late: his car would not start and then the bus he took was very behind schedule.

Semi-colons should be used to separate longer items in a list, for clarity: *My top five films are: Avengers Endgame; The Fault in Our Stars; X-Men Apocalypse; The Maze Runner; and Spider-Man: Homecoming.*

Starter idea

Authority and authority figures (15 minutes)

Resources: Learner's Book, Session 2.2, Getting started activity

Description: Write these two definitions on the board:

• *authority = the power or right to give orders, make decisions, and enforce obedience*
• *authority figure = a person with authority over others and who can inspire or demand obedience, e.g. parents, teachers and police officers.*

Put learners into pairs and ask them to discuss the Getting started activity using the terms and definitions on the board to guide their discussion. Point out that there is a two-part focus here: first, the positive, helpful experiences with authority figures; second, the challenges, difficulties and rewards of being an authority figure.

Main teaching ideas

1 Identifying the purpose, audience and structure of a text (40 minutes)

Learning intention: Identify the purpose, audience and structural features of a text.

Resources: Learner's Book, Session 2.2, 'Why should you become a police officer?', Activities 1 and 2

Description: Read the article 'Why should you become a police officer?' to learners once yourself, then ask for four volunteers to read the article a second time aloud, taking one section each. Afterwards, read through Activities 1 and 2 and the Reading tip.

List the bullet points in Activity 1 on the board in the form of questions (for example *What is the overall purpose of the text?*, etc.), and do the same for Activity 2: *What positive examples of being a police officer are presented?*

Then, organise learners into pairs to complete Activities 1 and 2. Remind them they should make notes of their answers. Afterwards, pairs should report back to the class.

> **Differentiation ideas:**

- Support: As you are listing the questions on the board, offer hints, clues and suggestions to prompt learners' thinking. For example, for the first bullet you could point out the text describes policing as an attractive career and this is related to the purpose of the text; for the second and third bullets you could ask learners to imagine why they would read or be interested in this text.

- Challenge: Add an extra task to Activity 1, getting learners to make notes on how the writer uses pronouns, rhetorical questions and punctuation to persuade readers that policing is an attractive career.

> **Assessment ideas:** As learner pairs are reporting back key points, check they have notes and answers on all five questions. In particular, assess if learners make the connection between the text's structure and the purpose and audience (that is, it is structured to answer questions someone might have about a police career, but also to present as many attractive benefits of policing as possible).

2 Using colons and semi-colons in a summary (85 minutes)

Learning intentions: Explore the views of others on a complex topic. Use colons and semi-colons for effect.

Resources: Learner's Book, Session 2.2, Activities 3 and 4

Description: Read the Language focus information to learners, then use the Language support feature at the start of the session to remind them of the additional information about colons and semi-colons. Write the examples from both sections on the board to help with your explanations and to focus learners' attention on the different uses of colons and semi-colons. To consolidate understanding, hand out Language worksheet 2.1 for learners to complete.

Afterwards, organise learners into pairs and give them 15–20 minutes to discuss Activity 3 together. Remind learners to give reasons *why* they agree or disagree with each view.

After the discussions, learners should write their summaries for Activity 4 on their own. Before they start, tell learners to reread the article and the three views in Activity 3 and then decide which view they will write about. Remind them to use colons and semi-colons in their summary.

> **Differentiation ideas:**

- Support: Remind learners of the summary-writing techniques they studied in Stage 8:
  - read the text several times to ensure they understand it
  - understand the instructions for the summary
  - make notes using bullet points, focusing on the main ideas in the text and combining repeated ideas into one bullet point
  - write the summary in standard English, using linking expressions and referring to the subject of the summary in the first sentence
  - edit the draft and check they are within the correct word count.

- Challenge: Ask learners to choose two of the views from Activity 3 and write two separate summaries of 150 words each.

> **Assessment ideas:** Read learners' summaries and assess their use of colons and semi-colons.

Specifically, assess whether learners have correctly used semi-colons to connect two statements that are closely linked and colons to add detail and explanation.

Plenary idea

Punctuation and clarity of meaning (10 minutes)

Description: Write these two sentences on the board:

- *I hate lazy learners who don't do their homework; like you, I think it shows they take their education for granted.*

- *I hate lazy learners who don't do their homework like you; I think it shows they take their education for granted.*

Put learners into pairs and ask them to discuss the different meanings created by the positioning of the semi-colon.

Homework idea

Learners should complete Workbook Session 2.2.

2.3 The art detective

LEARNING PLAN		
Learning objectives	**Learning intentions**	**Success criteria**
9Ri.02, 9Ri.03, 9Ri.04, 9Ri.07, 9Ra.02, 9Ww.01, 9Wv.01, 9Wc.07, 9Wp.02, 9SLs.01, 9SLg.02, 9SLp.01, 9SLp.02	Learners will: • read aloud with confidence and expression • discuss their own and others' views about an article • summarise points of agreement and disagreement from a discussion • write a descriptive account.	Learners can: • read a non-fiction text aloud with confidence and expression • contribute effectively to a group discussion, exploring their own and other people's views • summarise points from a discussion and explain areas of disagreement • write an imaginative descriptive account in a particular voice.

LANGUAGE SUPPORT

This session contains a text that includes the Arabic word *sheikh*. There are many words and phrases used in English that originally came from other languages. These words are known as loanwords. It may be useful to familiarise learners with this concept and to explore some of the most frequently used loanwords and phrases in English. Note that the three most common original languages for loanwords in English are Latin, German and French.

Some frequently used loanwords in English:

carpe diem (Latin) = make the most of the present time ('seize the day!')

mea culpa (Latin) = an acknowledgement that something is your own fault ('by my fault')

per se (Latin) = by itself/in themselves

ad infinitum (Latin) = forever ('to infinity')

per capita (Latin) = for each person ('by heads')

doppelgänger (German) = a double of someone who looks exactly like them ('double-goer')

blitzkrieg (German) = a violent and fast military campaign ('lightning war')

zeitgeist (German) = the characteristic spirit of a particular historical period ('time spirit')

schadenfreude (German) = a feeling of satisfaction when something bad happens to someone else ('harm joy')

laissez-faire (French) = a non-interference approach to something ('allow to do')

tête-à-tête (French) = a private conversation ('head-to-head')

raison d'être (French) = the most important reason for someone/thing's existence ('reason for being')

déjà vu (French) = the sense of having experienced the present situation before ('already seen')

Starter idea

Fictional detectives (10 minutes)

Resources: Learner's Book, Session 2.3, Getting started activity

Description: Write the names of some famous fictional detectives on the board, such as Sherlock Holmes, Inspector Goole and Hercule Poirot. Then, put learners into pairs and ask them to think of other fictional detectives they know from film, TV or literature as they discuss the Getting started questions. Remind learners to consider how the work of a real detective might be different from that of a fictional detective.

Main teaching ideas

1 Reading and exploring an article (45 minutes)

Learning intentions: Read aloud with confidence and style. Discuss their own and others' views on the content of an article.

Resources: Learner's Book, Session 2.3, 'Confessions of an art detective', Activities 1 and 2

Description: Tell learners they will be reading an article and then discussing it in groups. They will need to take accurate notes during the discussion because they will later use these to write a summary of where their peers agreed and disagreed.

Organise learners into pairs and give them 10–15 minutes to read the 'Confessions of an art detective' article for Activity 1.

Afterwards, combine pairs into small groups and read them the Listening tip. They should draft a table as described to keep track of the views expressed in their discussion. They should then complete Activity 2, using the bullet-point statements and paying close attention to where group members agree and disagree.

> **Differentiation ideas:**

- Support: Tell learners to focus only on the points of agreement and disagreement rather than linking all comments back to the specific person who made them. This will allow learners to focus more on *what* was said rather than worrying about *who* said it. This will also allow learners to focus more on taking part in the discussion themselves.

- Challenge: Tell learners that in their summary they should link all comments to the specific person who made them (these are called 'attributed' comments). This makes for a more demanding note-taking task.

> **Assessment ideas:** Listen to learners' group discussions. Assess how well they explore points of agreement and disagreement. Specifically, assess if learners: recognise and comment on when they agree and then explore why; recognise and comment on when they disagree and then explore why; and use agreement *and especially disagreement* to identify detailed points where further understanding would be useful.

2 Writing a well-structured summary (40 minutes)

Learning intention: Summarise points of agreement and disagreement from a discussion.

Resources: Learner's Book, Session 2.3, Activity 3

Description: Read Activity 3 to the class. Tell learners that they should aim to write 250–300 words in this summary. Before they start, write the following outline with headings and sub-headings on the board to help learners organise their writing if necessary:

- points of agreement:
  - points of strongest agreement (50 words)
  - points of weaker agreement (50 words)
- points of disagreement:
  - points of weakest disagreement (50 words)
  - points of strongest disagreement (50 words)
- explanation of points of disagreement (50–100 words).

Learners can use their own structure if they prefer. Remind them to closely consult their notes from Activity 2 when writing their summaries.

When they have finished, ask learners to respond to the Reflection feature in the Learner's Book.

> **Differentiation ideas:**

- Support: Suggest a simpler outline and shorter word count of 150 words for learners' summaries: points of agreement (50 words), points of disagreement (50 words) and explanation of points of disagreement (50 words).

- Challenge: Ask learners to write no more than 250 words and to use an integrated structure for their summaries, in which each significant point of the discussion has its own paragraph. Within each paragraph, learners should summarise where people agreed and explain why they disagreed.

> **Assessment ideas:** Read learners' summaries and assess how well their writing summarises the points on which people agreed and disagreed, how much and why.

3 Writing descriptively (45 minutes)

Learning intention: Write a descriptive account.

Resources: Learner's Book, Session 2.3, Activity 4

Description: Tell learners that they are now going to write a descriptive account. Explain that descriptive writing involves using details and sensory imagery (sights, sounds, smells, etc.) and that this kind of writing describes a person, a setting (a place) or an object in such a way that a strong sense of it comes across to the reader. Read the following short extract as an example:

> My father turns and marches towards the kitchen. He slips slightly, and I notice the soles of his shoes are completely clean, as if new. As he flicks the kitchen light on there's a harsh glare from the naked bulb. He is rummaging in the fridge. To the left of the kitchen door is my father's desk, cluttered with books and papers. There's a pin-board above the desk with dozens of leaflets, notes and takeaway menus, plus a simple calendar – the kind with no pictures but just the dates in a grid, which is blank.

Ask learners: *Do you get a sense of the father or the place in this extract?* If they answer 'Yes', ask the follow-up: *How? Which words, phrases or techniques create this sense?* If learners answer 'No', ask the follow-up: *How could the writer have improved this description?* Discuss these questions for 5–10 minutes.

Next, read Activity 4 and the Writing tip as a class. Emphasise again the point about sensory description. Learners then complete the activity on their own.

> **Differentiation ideas:**

- Support: Give learners additional examples of sensory imagery, as below, and check that they understand which words (underlined) appeal to a specific sense.
  - *The glow from the candle was warm.* *(sight)*
  - *The wolf snarled and growled.* *(sound)*

- *As she walked by, the <u>sweetness</u> of her <u>perfume</u> caught his attention. (smell)*

- *The tool felt <u>cold</u> and <u>heavy</u>. (touch)*

- Challenge: Ask learners to write two versions in the following way. First, they should write their descriptive account in 10–15 minutes. They should then read though this first version and spend a few minutes considering how they could improve their descriptions. They then take another 15 minutes to write a second version. Finally, learners should compare their two versions and decide which is better and why.

> **Assessment ideas:** Assess whether learners have used sensory imagery and figurative language such as similes, metaphors, extended metaphors and personification in their writing. How well does the imagery work? Does the description create a strong sense of Arthur Brand's feelings as he looks at the painting? Is there a vivid description of the painting itself?

Plenary idea

Exploring details (10 minutes)

Description: Point out to learners that the details have been important in both the factual (non-fiction) and the fictional texts in this session. For example, factual details were important in writing a summary – for example, specific details about where people agreed or disagreed – and fictional details were important in writing a descriptive account – for example, specific details about sights, sounds, smells, etc. In pairs, ask learners to discuss why details are important in both types of writing.

> ### CROSS-CURRICULAR LINK

> **Art (art history):** One of Arthur Brand's most famous cases involved finding a famous painting by Pablo Picasso, which had been missing for 20 years. Ask learners to search online for 'Picasso's *Bust de Femme*' to see images of the painting and find out about its history. They could then research more details about how the painting went missing and how it was found again. Finally, learners could be asked to write a paragraph summarising the history of the painting and then compare their summaries with their peers to see if they focused on the same details.

Homework idea

Learners should complete Workbook Session 2.3.

2.4 Young detectives

LEARNING PLAN		
Learning objectives	**Learning intentions**	**Success criteria**
9Rs.01, 9Ri.01, 9Ri.03, 9Ri.04, 9SLm.04, 9SLp.01, 9SLp.03, 9SLr.01	Learners will: • give a dramatic performance of a scene from a detective story • explore the characters, events and tone of a detective story • consider the effect of story structure.	Learners can: • give a dramatic performance of a scene from a detective story, using voice, gesture and movement to express character • comment on characters and events in a story and identify its tone • analyse the effect of structural choices in a detective story.

In this session, learners explore a fiction extract with frequent use of direct speech. It may be useful to recap the use of direct speech with learners, as well as the use of reporting verbs and adverbs.

Sometimes a writer will present direct speech followed by a **reporting verb**, perhaps with an <u>adverb</u>:

- 'Well, there it is,' **said** Liz.
- 'What do we do now?' **whispered** Jeff.
- 'You heard him,' **said** Dan <u>cheerfully</u>.
- 'Well, no,' **confessed** Sir Jasper.

- 'The big one hit me on the head,' **said** Sir Jasper <u>sadly</u>.

Writers avoid repeating the same reporting verbs and adverbs by first describing a character's **action** (or thought) and then presenting their direct speech:

- *Jeff nodded. 'Well, don't just stand there, Sherlock. Detect something!'*
- *Sir Jasper jumped up enthusiastically, and immediately took charge. 'You all go outside and pretend to be stealing the painting . . .'*
- *Dan nodded. 'What happened then?'*

Starter idea

Book covers and their stories (10 minutes)

Resources: Learner's Book, Session 2.4, Getting started activity

Description: Tell learners that the author Margaret Atwood once said that if she sees spaceships on a book cover she expects spaceships inside. She was saying that she did not want to be misled about the content of a story by the cover. Ask learners to discuss briefly in pairs what they expect to find out about a book from its cover. Then ask pairs to read the Getting started activity and make some predictions about this story based on the bullet points. What would they expect to see on the cover of this book?

Main teaching ideas

1 Giving a dramatic performance (60 minutes)

Learning intention: Give a dramatic performance of a scene from a detective story.

Resources: Learner's Book, Session 2.4, *The Case of the Missing Masterpiece* Extract 1, Activity 1

Description: Read Extract 1 of the story to learners and answer any questions about the scene described. Then read the instructions to Activity 1 so learners understand that they are going to rehearse and then perform the extract as a dramatic scene. Use the information in Language support above to help learners understand how to speak some of the character dialogue (sadly, cheerfully, etc.).

Organise learners into groups of three, and write the instructions below on the board. Learners can begin working their way through the steps as you are writing.

First 25 minutes:

1. Reread Extract 1, Activity 1 and the Speaking tip.
2. Decide which role each of you will take.
3. Write out the lines of dialogue.
4. Learn the dialogue and cues (when you need to say your lines – which character speaks just before you and what they say).

Second 25 minutes:

5. Reread the prompts for each character in Activity 1 and the Speaking tip.
6. Rehearse the scene several times, experimenting with voice and movement.
7. Decide as a group how you will approach your final performance.
8. Perform a final version of the scene.

Emphasise that learners should use movements, gestures, actions and their voices to convey their character.

When learners have finished their final performance, ask them to complete the Self-assessment exercise in the Learner's Book.

> **Differentiation ideas:**

- Support: Work with learners to write out the lines of dialogue and spend 5–10 minutes teaching them about cue lines – for example, half way through the scene Dan has the line: *You heard him. Steal the painting. You and Mickey can be the robbers.* His cue for this is Jeff's whispered line: *What do we do now?* Point out that in this example Dan can say his lines as a response to Jeff's question.

- Challenge: Between steps 2 and 6, ask learners to experiment with playing different characters in the scene. At step 7, learners should decide which role they will play in the final version of their scene.

> **Assessment ideas:** Watch learners rehearse and perform their dramatic scenes. Use the following questions to assess their speaking and listening skills:

- Do learners begin well by dividing and choosing their roles decisively or with enthusiasm?

- Do they experiment with different movements, gestures, actions and their voices to express their character and perform the scene?

- Do they explore how to create drama or humour as they rehearse and perform?

2 Identifying humour (25 minutes)

Learning intention: Explore the characters, events and tone of a detective story.

Resources: Learner's Book, Session 2.4, *The Case of the Missing Masterpiece* Extract 1, Activity 2

Description: Tell learners that you are going to reread Extract 1 to them and that you want them to remember any parts they find particularly amusing or serious (or parts where they think that was the writer's intention). They should also think about who the intended audience is for this story, and how the writer has used language to appeal to these readers.

After reading the extract, explain that humour is *subjective* and *personal* – that is, the same joke or event will make some people laugh while others will not find it funny. However, in writing we can usually tell when a writer intended something to be funny by analysing how events or characters are described and by the writer's language choices. Emphasise that we can understand *objectively* if something is intended to be funny, even if we do not find it

funny ourselves (you could point out *objective* is the opposite of *subjective*).

Then organise learners into pairs and ask them to complete Activity 2 together. Remind each learner to make their own notes during the pair discussion.

> **Differentiation ideas:**

- Support: Prompt learners to identify humour (or intended humour) by analysing closely the character of Sir Jasper. If they need further support, ask them to look at the parts of the text where Sir Jasper shouts *Aha, caught in the act!* and the lines that follow, and to consider if these might be intended to be funny and how we can tell that from the language.

- Challenge: Ask learners to write two or three sentences explaining how the writer has made parts of the scene funny through his use of language. They should identify one or two examples and then describe the specific language choices the writer has used to create humour.

> **Assessment ideas:** Ask learners to swap the notes they made and peer-assess them by giving feedback and suggestions based on the following questions:

- Did their partner identify specific parts of the text that are amusing or were intended to be amusing?

- Did their partner make note of the kind of audience the story was written for?

- Did their partner make any notes on specific language choices made by the writer?

3 Analysing story structure (45 minutes)

Learning intention: Consider the effect of story structure.

Resources: Learner's Book, Session 2.4, *The Case of the Missing Masterpiece* Extract 1, Activities 3 and 4

Description: Remind learners about the terms *protagonist* (main/central character) and *antagonist* (enemy/rival character). Point out that in a detective story the protagonist is often the detective and the antagonist is a character who does something wrong or who is at the heart of the mystery. However, this could be reversed, and there may also be other antagonists, such as rival detectives. The mystery or problem is a key part of detective stories. There may be several suspects, or no obvious suspects at all, to keep the reader guessing.

Ask learners who the protagonist is in this extract (Dan). Who is the victim (Sir Jasper)? They should then complete Activity 3 on their own, analysing the development of Dan's character and what Sir Jasper adds to the story at this point.

Read Activity 4 as a class and recap what deductions are in the context of a detective story. Ask learners to read the end of the extract again, then complete Activity 4.

> **Differentiation ideas:**

- Support: Before Activity 3, read the extract to learners once, then read it a second time pausing at key points and asking learners questions to prompt their thinking. For example, pause after *Or would he?* and ask learners how Liz, Jeff and Dan have been characterised by the writer so far. Or, pause after *just as I was on the actual night* and ask learners how Sir Jasper has been characterised by the writer.

- Challenge: When they have finished Activity 4, ask learners to write a humorous description of losing something trivial (e.g. a sock) in their bedroom and searching for it like they are a master detective following clues.

> **Assessment ideas:** Assess learners' answers to both activities together. Have learners explored how the writer uses language and story structure to show Dan's and Sir Jasper's characters? Have they explained the type of mystery created and what the description reveals about the characters?

Plenary idea

The structure of detective stories (10 minutes)

Description: Remind learners about the idea of an 'inciting incident' in a plot: an event or action that sets the story in motion and creates a problem for characters to resolve. Suggest that a mystery or crime provides writers with a strong inciting incident and problems to solve: How will the detective solve the mystery? Will the villains escape or get caught? What happens to the victims? Addressing these questions in a story provides dramatic action and leads to a climax and resolution.

In pairs, learners should think of an example detective story (in a book, film or on TV) they are both familiar with. They should discuss and decide if the structural points you have outlined are features in their example.

CROSS-CURRICULAR LINK

Science (forensics): Learners could be encouraged to think about how science is used in detective work. For example, they could research one of the following areas and its role in solving crimes or mysteries, then prepare a short talk (3–5 minutes) where they present the findings of their research to the rest of the class:

- forensic science
- DNA collection and identification
- toxicology.

Homework idea

Learners should complete Workbook Session 2.4.

2.5 Making deductions

LEARNING PLAN

Learning objectives	Learning intentions	Success criteria
9Rs.01, 9Ri.01, 9Ri.03, 9Ri.04, 9Ri.07, 9Ri.08, 9Ra.02, 9Ww.01, 9Ww.03, 9Wp.01, 9SLm.02, 9SLg.04	Learners will: • explore the implications of information in a story • consider the process of deduction as a structural feature • write a character study • compare characters and ideas in two texts.	Learners can: • analyse the meaning and implications of information in a story • understand the effect of structural choices such as the steps of deduction in detective fiction • write a character study, exploring actions and motivation • interpret and compare characters and ideas in two texts.

LANGUAGE SUPPORT

Previously, learners examined the use of minor sentences. Some minor sentences are referred to as 'fragments' or 'sentence fragments'. In the extract from *The Case of the Missing Masterpiece* in this session, the writer makes deliberate use of sentence fragments. For example:

- *Anything else? His voice? His hands?*
- *Being sold. Torn down for flats and offices.*
- *Oh yes, and one more thing.*

Remind learners that sentence fragments like these can be used for different effects:

- to create surprise or drama (*Hey! Stop!*)
- to express a sudden emotional or physical reaction (*Ouch! Yuk! Ugh!*)
- to make direct speech sound more realistic (*Agreed? I suppose. Sure? Enough!*).

Explore the effects of the sentence fragments in the extract here as part of the session.

Starter idea

What makes a good detective? (10 minutes)

Resources: Learner's Book, Session 1.5, Getting started activity

Description: Ask learners to imagine they are watching a comedy about a detective who is terrible at solving crimes. You can tell the detective is bad because they are:

- silly and immature
- forgetful, inattentive and unobservant
- clumsy and loud

- useless and impractical
- inexperienced and unprofessional.

Organise learners into pairs and ask them to list the skills and qualities of a *good* detective as they complete the Getting started activity.

Main teaching ideas

1 Deductions: Real life versus fiction (25 minutes)

Learning intention: Explore the implications of information in a story.

Resources: Learner's Book, Session 2.5, *The Case of the Missing Masterpiece* Extracts 1 and 2, Activity 1

Description: Remind learners about deduction. Define it as 'a process of thinking where your conclusions follow from general principles, theories or premises'. Give this example of deductive thinking:

- Premise 1 – All learners in this class speak English.
- Premise 2 – Ruby is a learner in this class.
- Conclusion – Ruby speaks English.

In this example, the conclusion is *deduced* from the premises – and the conclusion will be correct if the premises are correct. Deduction can be contrasted with induction. Explain induction as 'a process of thinking where you make specific observations, look for patterns and then come to a conclusion'. Give this example of inductive thinking:

- the teacher always brings a bottle of water to class
- therefore, the teacher will bring a bottle of water to class today.

Emphasise that these definitions are for real life, but fictional detectives are often described as using deduction to solve clues and catch criminals. Readers of detective stories will be using their thinking skills when they try to solve the clues in the story.

Finally, organise learners into pairs and ask them to carefully reread both extracts before they discuss Activity 1 together.

> **Differentiation ideas:**

- Support: Give learners a specific example of a clue and deduction in the extracts, such as: Clue: They wore masks. *Oh yes and the one who helped me was* <u>worried</u> *about his hat. He was wearing one of those woollen caps sailors sometimes wear. He kept* <u>fiddling</u> *with it, pulling it down to meet his mask.* Dan's deduction: One of the criminals has a very nervous manner (disposition).

- Challenge: Ask learners to write a list of all the clues and evidence given in both extracts, then write the conclusion that Dan reaches based directly on the evidence from the clues.

> **Assessment ideas:** Ask learners to peer-assess their paired discussion. They should give specific feedback on how well they took turns to speak and listen and, if necessary, how they could improve their turn taking in future.

2 Character and construction (45 minutes)

Learning intention: Consider the implications of information in a story.

Resources: Learner's Book, Session 2.5, *The Case of the Missing Masterpiece* Extracts 1 and 2, Activities 2 and 3

Description: Remind learners of the story arc by drawing the structure of a detective story on the board:

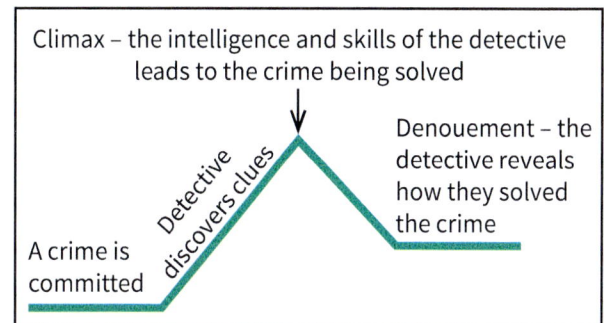

Read through Activities 2 and 3 with learners. Emphasise that the detective's intelligence and deductive skills are key features of mystery and detective stories, which help move the plot towards its climax and denouement, as indicated in the diagram. Explain 'denouement' as the final part of a story where the plot is resolved (in a detective story this is where the detective explains how they solved the crime).

Learners should then reread Extracts 1 and 2 and write their answers to Activities 2 and 3 independently. Remind learners to use short, relevant quotations to support their answers to Activity 3.

> **Differentiation ideas:**

- Support: Read through both extracts with learners. Whenever a clue is given, ask learners to make a note of it, then ask: *What could this clue indicate?* Learners should note down their thoughts and use these notes when they write their answers to Activities 2 and 3.

- Challenge: When they have finished Activity 3, remind learners of the definitions you gave for Activity 1. Ask learners to write out two examples each of deductive thinking and inductive thinking.

> **Assessment ideas:** Read learners' answers to Activity 3. Assess if learners have:

- stated clearly their agreement or disagreement with the comment by using phrases such as 'I agree with the comment because' or 'I disagree with the comment because'

- explained their reasons for agreeing or disagreeing with the comment with phrases such as '. . . for these reasons, first, . . . Second . . .' followed by a list of the learner's reasons

- supported their reasons with short, relevant quotations from the extracts.

3 Motivations for crime (60 minutes)

Learning intentions: Compare characters and ideas in two texts. Write a character study.

Resources: Learner's Book, Session 2.5, Activities 4 and 5

Description: Point out that some people enjoy stories about real detectives as well as fictional ones – this genre is known as 'true crime'.

Read the first bullet point Activity 4 and ask learners to name some synonyms for *motivates* in this sentence. Get several responses and write them on the board. Good responses may include *drives*, *inspires*, *influences* or *pushes*.

Read the Writing tip and suggest that the ideas about how a character develops could also be applied to real people such as Arthur Brand, the art detective.

Learners should complete Activities 4 and 5 using the following instructions and timings:

1 Reread the 'Confessions of an art detective' article. (3 minutes)

2 Reread Extracts 1 and 2 of *The Case of the Missing Masterpiece*. (6 minutes)

3 Respond to Activity 4. (15 minutes)

4 Respond to Activity 5. (15 minutes)

5 Check spelling, punctuation and grammar in their answers to Activity 5. (5 minutes)

> **Differentiation ideas:**

- Support: Before learners work on the activities, ask them to imagine these two scenarios:

  a A personal possession they love has been stolen from their home.

  b A friend of theirs has been attacked and robbed of a favourite possession.

- How would they think and feel in each of these scenarios? Point out that these thoughts and feelings would be their own motivations and values. Note that **a** is similar to 'Confessions of an art detective' and **b** is similar to *The Case of the Missing Masterpiece* so they can more easily imagine how Arthur Brand and Dan Robinson might think or feel.

- Challenge: Ask learners to write an additional paragraph where they explain which text they prefer and why.

> **Assessment ideas:** For Activity 5, assess learners' summaries. Have they summarised Dan's actions and motivations in 200 words or fewer? Have learners correctly identified the intended audience (young adults)? Have they given an explanation for why the character of Dan might appeal to this audience (because he is a similar age)?

Plenary idea

Motive, means and opportunity (10 minutes)

Description: Tell learners that detectives sometimes emphasise three key factors in solving crimes: motive (the reason for committing the crime), means (the tools or methods used to do so) and opportunity (the situation that allows the crime to take place). Organise learners into pairs and ask them to discuss whether motive, means and opportunity help them further understand the crimes and characters in 'Confessions of an art detective' and *The Case of the Missing Masterpiece*.

Homework idea

Learners should complete Workbook Session 2.5.

2.6 Detective fiction

Learning objectives	Learning intentions	Success criteria
9Rv.02, 9Rv.03, 9Rg.03, 9Ri.02, 9Ri.03, 9Ri.04, 9Ra.01, 9Ra.03, 9Ra.05, 9SLs.01	Learners will: • identify the conventions of detective fiction • consider the purpose of a text and whether it is biased • explore a writer's language and grammar choices • listen to and summarise opinions on detective fiction and express their own.	Learners can: • recognise and comment on the conventions of detective fiction • analyse the purpose of a text and assess whether it shows bias • analyse the meaning and effect of a writer's language and grammar choices • understand and summarise a variety of attitudes towards detective fiction.

LANGUAGE SUPPORT

Use the following table to review the different categories and functions of pronouns to help with Activity 4 in this session.

Personal pronouns	
First person: refer to the speaker(s) or writer(s)	I, me, mine, myself, we, us, our, ours, ourselves
Second person: refer to the audience	you, your, yours, yourself, yourselves
Third person: refer to anyone/anything else	she, her, hers, herself, he, him, his, himself, it, its, itself, they, them, their, theirs, themselves
Other types of pronoun	
Possessive pronouns: communicate ownership/ possession	my, your, his, her, its, our, their
Reflexive pronouns: connect to a noun or pronoun in the clause	myself, herself, himself, yourself, itself, ourselves, themselves
Interrogative pronouns: used to ask questions about nouns	who, whom, which, what, whose
Demonstrative pronouns: communicate distance or nearness	this, that, these, those
Indefinite pronouns: communicate an unspecific meaning	some, any, many, each, much, few, none, one, someone, somebody, something, anyone, anybody, anything
Relative pronouns: link relative clauses to head nouns in a phrase	who, whom, which, that, whose

Starter idea

Why do people like detective stories? (10 minutes)

Resources: Learner's Book, Session 2.6, Getting started activity

Description: Point out that detective stories are very popular in film, TV and literature. Suggest some possible reasons for this, such as: the world of crime and detective work are unfamiliar so they seem interesting; villains and detectives are naturally in conflict, which creates good drama; and detective stories allow writers and readers to explore their values. Then organise learners into pairs and ask them to discuss these reasons alongside the question in the Getting started activity.

Main teaching ideas

1 The ingredients of a detective story (35 minutes)

Learning intention: Identify the conventions of detective fiction.

Resources: Learner's Book, Session 2.6, 'The thrill of the dark', Activity 1; Differentiated worksheets 2A, 2B and 2C

Description: Hand out the appropriate Differentiated worksheet (2A, 2B or 2C) to learners and allow 15 minutes for the class to complete them. Then read the introduction to the extract in the Learner's Book. Ask for a volunteer to read the whole advertisement. Learners then complete Activity 1 on their own.

> **Differentiation ideas:**

- Support: After hearing the extract, point out one or two examples of conventions that are mentioned in the article – such as the villain being caught at the end or seeing a mystery solved. Then ask learners to carefully reread the article and the extracts in 2.4 and 2.5 and make notes of every possible example of a convention they find.

- Challenge: After Activity 1, ask learners to think of another story genre (for example science fiction, fantasy, adventure, romance) and write a list of the conventions of that genre. They could share their lists in small groups and add to each others' lists of conventions, or identify if any are reader assumptions.

> **Assessment ideas:** Ask learners to swap their Worksheets and their answers to Activity 1 with a partner to compare and discuss their work. In particular, ask learners to identify any disagreements they have about what is or is not a convention of detective stories. Learners should decide whether their disagreement is about textual conventions or assumptions.

2 Bias, extended metaphors and pronouns (50 minutes)

Learning intentions: Consider the purpose of a text and whether it is biased. Explore a writer's language and grammar choices.

Resources: Learner's Book, Session 2.6, Activities 2–4; Language worksheet 2.2

Description: Organise learners into pairs and ask them to read the Reading tip before rereading 'The thrill of the dark'. Give learners 10–15 minutes to discuss Activity 2 together, then ask learners to continue working in pairs to write a paragraph analysing the extended metaphor in the article for Activity 3.

Come together as a class to read Activity 4, then hand out Language worksheet 2.2 and ask learners to complete it to prepare for the work on pronouns. When learners have finished the worksheet, they should complete Activity 4 on their own then join up with a partner to compare analyses.

> **Differentiation ideas:**

- Support: For Activity 3, remind learners of the definition of an extended metaphor with an example, such as 'a comparison between two things that continues over a series of sentences, a paragraph or longer text (for example *His heart was frozen, his blood frosty, the warm, red liquid that used to flow was now full of sharp icicles; and his words chilled me to the bone*).' Ask learners for one or two examples of their own extended metaphors.

- Challenge: For Activity 4, ask learners to write two paragraphs examining how the writer has used the following language features and what effects these have on the reader: pronouns, figurative language, rhetorical questions and other punctuation.

> **Assessment ideas:** Read learners' written analyses for Activity 4. Have they quoted examples of pronoun use from the article? Do they use any

quoted examples of pronoun use to support their ideas? Do they give an explanation of how and why the writer has used pronouns? Have learners linked the writer's use of pronouns to the purpose of the article, for example, how the writer's use of pronouns helps to persuade the reader?

3 Summaries and opinions (45 minutes)

Learning intention: Listen to and summarise opinions on crime fiction, and express an opinion.

Resources: Learner's Book, Session 2.6, Activities 5 and 6

> ⬇ **Download the audioscript for Activity 5 from Cambridge GO (Track 14).**

Description: Explain that learners will be listening to a recording with three people speaking. Write the names of the three speakers on the board: Jake, Abebi and Vanessa. Ask learners to create a table or grid on paper so they can capture specific comments made by the speakers (as described in the Listening tip). Next, read Activity 5 to learners and emphasise they will need to take accurate notes of the speakers' comments in order to write their summaries. Play the recording while learners take their notes. Afterwards, give learners approximately 20–25 minutes to write their summaries.

Discuss Activity 6 as a class. Ask learners to recommend specific detective stories they have enjoyed reading (or seen as films or on TV). When a learner recommends a story, ask them to explain why they think their classmates would enjoy it and why they enjoyed it.

> **Differentiation ideas:**

- Support: For Activity 5, remind learners of the steps in writing a summary (see Session 2.2, Main teaching idea 2, support).

- Challenge: After learners have written their summaries, ask them to write a paragraph explaining their own personal opinion of detective fiction (as if they were asked for their opinion alongside Jake, Abebi and Vanessa).

> **Assessment ideas:** Ask learners to self-assess their note-taking skills. Were their notes as useful as they could have been when writing the summary? If not, how could they improve this next time?

Plenary idea

The impact of grammar and language choices (10 minutes)

Description: Ask learners to imagine a situation where a head teacher had done something wrong and had to explain themselves to the rest of the teaching staff. Then, read to learners these two possible ways the head teacher's explanation could begin:

a *My fellow teachers, I've spoken to you before on many occasions about many things. There are responsibilities in being a teacher, responsibilities shared by all of us. The commitment and loyalty of all of you maintains the good reputation of our school.*

b *Hello everyone, I've come here today to speak about what has happened. Being a head teacher is a responsibility I take seriously, an individual responsibility involving trust. I broke that trust and all of you deserve an explanation.*

Organise learners into pairs and ask them to identify specific differences in the way language is used between the two examples. Ask learners to discuss which version they prefer and why.

Homework idea

Learners should complete Workbook Session 2.6.

PROJECT GUIDANCE

This could be a broad project, so it may be useful to put learners into medium-sized groups (5–8 people). This topic can be divided into separate areas, and the various tasks allocated to different learners or sub-groups – pairs or threes. It may also help to give learners some explicit guidelines and directions for them to carry out the work. A useful way for the learner groups to approach the project could be as follows.

Stage one: discussing and planning

Learners should meet as a group and discuss what they already know about detective figures in stories. Next, learners can discuss and plan how they will carry out further research and areas where they can focus. For example, research could involve learners using:

- the internet
- libraries (encyclopedias and other reference books and tools)
- interviewing parents, relatives, friends.

Stage two: research and assembling research

Areas where learners could focus their research could include:

- pre-20th-century literature
- 20th- and 21st-century literature
- children's and young adult literature
- detective fiction from European, American, Asian and African countries.

The project asks learners to consider specific aspects of the detective's character (as below) so these could be separate parts of the research:

- issues of gender – are there typical characteristics of female and male detectives
- details of their personal lives – are they generally happy, satisfied people
- attitudes to authority – do they follow rules or do they challenge authority
- their motivations for fighting crime.

Towards the end of this stage, learners should meet and start discussing which bits of their research will be in the final presentation and which bits they will leave out.

Stage three: planning and preparing the presentation

In this stage it would be useful for learners to decide who in their group will be involved in the final presentation. Will it be everyone in the group or just one, two or three people? Also, learners can decide how they will present. Will they give a talk, use presentation software such as PowerPoint, create posters or other visual aids, or some other way of presenting?

Stage four: delivering the presentation

All that is left is to communicate to your peers all the interesting things you have found out. Try to deliver the presentation in an enthusiastic way – and try to enjoy it. Presenting can be fun!

> 3 'The Red-Headed League'

Unit plan

Session	Approximate number of learning hours	Outline of learning content	Resources
3.1 The red-headed visitor	2 hours, 30 minutes	Learners work out the meaning of unfamiliar words, interpret information in a story and explore structural events and the presentation of characters.	Learner's Book Session 3.1 Workbook Session 3.1 ⬇ Language worksheet 3.1
3.2 The assistant	2 hours, 30 minutes	Learners explore the implications of information in a detective story, improvise a conversation in character and consider developing feelings of sympathy towards a character.	Learner's Book Session 3.2 Workbook Session 3.2
3.3 The end of the League	2 hours, 30 minutes	Learners interpret details about a central character, identify and analyse information in a story and write a formal report.	Learner's Book Session 3.3 Workbook Session 3.3
3.4 Investigating the street	2 hours, 30 minutes	Learners read an unseen text aloud, discuss a series of clues and write and edit part of a mystery story involving tension.	Learner's Book Session 3.4 Workbook Session 3.4
3.5 The dark cellar	2 hours, 30 minutes	Learners consider the effect of structural choices in a narrative, explore language choices and effects, write descriptively and evaluate what makes an effective description.	Learner's Book Session 3.5 Workbook Session 3.5 ⬇ Language worksheet 3.2
3.6 The solution	2 hours, 30 minutes	Learners write a personal response to a story, compare presentation of theme in different texts and explore how context affects reader reactions.	Learner's Book Session 3.6 Workbook Session 3.6 ⬇ Differentiated worksheets 3A, 3B and 3C

BACKGROUND KNOWLEDGE

For the teacher

This unit continues to explore the detective genre. To prepare for these sessions, it would be useful to read the short story 'The Red-Headed League' by Sir Arthur Conan Doyle. You may wish to familiarise yourself with the character of Sherlock Holmes and other regular characters, such as his friend, Dr Watson. You may also wish to research how this famous detective has been depicted in different forms of media over time and why he remains an iconic character to this day.

The following grammatical and spelling concepts are covered in this unit:

- using morphology to work out word meanings
- using adjectives and similes in descriptive writing
- rephrasing unusual sentence constructions into modern English

- the difference between *imply* and *infer*
- adjectival order before nouns
- stress in speech patterns in English.

It may be useful to read up on these concepts before explaining them to learners, if you are not already confident in how they are defined and applied.

For the learner

Learners may be familiar with the character of Sherlock Holmes from modern interpretations, such as TV series and movies. They would benefit from researching the literary origins of the Holmes character, the author of the stories, Sir Arthur Conan Doyle, and when they were written. This is particularly important in helping learners understand that the language and the morality of the stories can be complex and old-fashioned.

TEACHING SKILLS FOCUS

Language awareness

By developing language awareness in learners, we aim to increase their related reading and writing skills. You can raise language awareness when examining writers' language choices and the linguistic features of texts, but an even more powerful approach is to raise learners' awareness of their own language choices. There are opportunities to do this during activities when learners write and redraft their own texts, whether this is fiction or non-fiction. Helping learners to consider why they chose particular words or sentence structures will lead to a greater awareness of how they can shape language to meet the needs of different audiences and to achieve different purposes.

Some particularly useful questions to ask in raising language awareness are in the following areas:

- Word choice – for example, *Why did you use that word? Can you think of another word (for the context, purpose, or audience)?*
- Sentence-combining – for example, *Can these two or three sentences be combined into a compound sentence? Would subordinating one of these clauses help here?*
- Purpose and audience – for example, *What words or sentence structures could you use to be clearer or more persuasive? How could you create an emotional effect here? How could this language be better aimed at this age-group?*
- Context – for example, *Should the language be more formal or more informal here? Would a more formal or informal tone help this text achieve its purpose?*

3.1 The red-headed visitor

Learning objectives	Learning intentions	Success criteria
9Rv.01, 9Rv.02, 9Rs.01, 9Ri.01, 9Ri.03, 9Ri.05, 9Ri.06, 9Ri.07	Learners will: • work out the meaning of unfamiliar words • read and interpret information in the opening of a mystery story • consider the impact of structural events • explore the presentation of characters in two texts.	Learners can: • use a variety of strategies to work out the meaning of unfamiliar words in an older text • work out the implied meaning of information in the opening of a detective story • comment on the impact of language and structure in a story • analyse how two victim figures are presented in different texts.

LANGUAGE SUPPORT

Morphology is the study of the structure of words. It is a critical tool in helping learners to decode meaning and develop their vocabulary. Some learners may need support using morphological clues to work out the meaning of unfamiliar words.

Remind learners that words can be broken into morphemes (a letter or a string of letters in a word that cannot be further divided). Morphemes are either roots, or they are prefixes or suffixes that 'morph' (change) the meaning of the root. To break a word down into morphemes and work out its meaning, learners should use the following strategy:

• identify an unfamiliar word that is blocking their understanding of the text
• break the word down into recognisable morphemes
• identify the root and any prefixes and suffixes
• work out the possible meaning based on their knowledge of the meaning of the morphemes, including similar words and cognates
• reread the word in context and check that the possible meaning makes sense.

Language worksheet 3.1 provides more practice in this area.

Common misconception

Misconception	How to identify	How to overcome
'Imply' and 'infer' mean the same thing.	Write the following sentence on the board. *'It is not cold which makes me shiver,' said the woman in a low voice.* Ask learners what the suggested or hidden meaning of this sentence might be (she is scared or ill). Did they 'infer' or 'imply' that meaning? What is the difference?	Remind learners that we imply something by what we say or write. We infer something from what somebody else says or writes. In a text, the writer can only imply. The reader can only infer (sometimes called 'making the inference' or 'reading between the lines'). In the example sentence, the writer implies that there is another reason she is shaking without revealing it. The reader infers that she might be scared or ill.

Starter idea

Picture discussion (10 minutes)

Resources: Learner's Book, Session 3.1, Getting started activity

Description: Introduce the unit by asking learners some general questions about Sherlock Holmes. What was his job? Where did he live? Who wrote the books and when? In pairs, learners should look at the pictures in their Learner's Book. What do they suggest about Sherlock Holmes and the stories he features in? Learners should have a short discussion about any more details they know, such as Holmes's friends and enemies in response to the Getting started activity. Why do they think this detective is still so popular today in TV series and films?

Main teaching ideas

1 Unfamiliar words (50 minutes)

Learning intention: Work out the meaning of unfamiliar words.

Resources: Learner's Book, Session 3.1, 'The Red-Headed League' Extract 1, Activity 1; Language worksheet 3.1; dictionaries

Description: Read the introduction to Extract 1 of 'The Red-Headed League', then ask learners to read the extract through for the first time. Ask learners to discuss what they have read in pairs. Have they understood the text fully? What is blocking their comprehension? Learners should read the text again and then share any words or phrases that they are unfamiliar with. Do not discuss their meaning yet.

Write *context*, *etymology* and *morphology* on the board. Remind learners that these are all techniques for working out the meaning of unfamiliar words. Ask learners if they can explain what the three words mean. Read the Language focus information and ensure that learners understand what context and etymology mean. Explain that they will be looking at the other skill – morphology – in detail.

Use the guidance to introduce Language worksheet 3.1. Explain that the sheet provides practice in using morphological clues to work out the meaning of words. Learners should complete the worksheet and use dictionaries to check their work. Use the Reading tip to emphasise that learners should use a combination of techniques when faced with unfamiliar words. For example, they should always check that any meaning they have arrived at using morphological or etymological clues makes sense in context.

Learners should complete Activity 1 in pairs, writing their own definitions in a glossary. Remind learners that glossaries are written in alphabetical order. Again, they should check their definitions against those in a dictionary.

Learners should complete the Reflection feature as self-assessment, then share their reflections with a partner. Discuss as a class and explore whether there is a consensus about the most or least useful techniques.

> Differentiation ideas:

- Support: Provide a list of common prefixes and suffixes and their meanings or functions, for example, *pre-* means 'before' and *-ate* means 'become'.

- Challenge: Ask learners to list any words they know that are similar to the words on the worksheet or in Activity 1. For example, in the same word family as *expression* are the words 'impression', 'compressed' and 'depressing'.

> Assessment ideas: Provide written feedback on the Language worksheets and how well learners have used morphological clues. In particular, comment on whether learners have split the words into correct morphemes and how they have used their knowledge of the meaning of those morphemes.

2 Interpreting information and events (40 minutes)

Learning intentions: Read and interpret information in the opening of a mystery story. Consider the impact of structural events.

Resources: Learner's Book, Session 3.1, 'The Red-Headed League' Extract 1, Activities 2 and 3

Description: Ask learners to reread the extract, and explain that they will now be looking at the meaning of the opening of the story and how it is structured. Write *imply* and *infer* on the board. Ensure learners understand the difference (see Common misconception). Learners should complete Activity 2, making their own notes. Discuss their responses as a class. Draw out what learners can infer about Holmes's character and skills from his observations.

Write *structural events* on the board, then read the introduction to Activity 3, outlining the three structural events at the start of the story. Learners should complete Activity 3, exploring how Jabez Wilson is presented and how a sense of mystery is created through the introduction of the advertisement. Again, learners should make their own notes before sharing these with a partner and discussing responses. They should encourage each other to use evidence from the text to justify their ideas.

Open out the discussions to the class:

- How does the author create a sense of mystery?

- How do learners feel about Jabez Wilson so far?

- How do they feel at the end of the extract?

> Differentiation ideas:

- Support: Consider putting learners into pairs that will provide suitable levels of support for each other for both activities.

- Challenge: Add a third task to Activity 2, asking learners to write an answer to the following: *What is your interpretation of the character of Sherlock Holmes? Write a paragraph giving your views. Use short quotations and refer to examples from Extract 1 to support your points.*

> Assessment ideas: Provide informal oral feedback linked to the learning intentions during both class discussions. How well are learners using inference to analyse the characters? Can they present appropriate evidence for their views? How well can they explain the significance of the structural events on meaning?

3 Sympathetic characters (45 minutes)

Learning intention: Explore the presentation of characters in two texts.

Resources: Learner's Book, Session 3.1, 'The Red-Headed League' Extract 1, Activity 4; Learner's Book, Sessions 2.4 and 2.5, *The Case of the Missing Masterpiece* extracts

Description: Ask learners to recall some details from the story *The Case of the Missing Masterpiece*. What was the name of the victim character (Sir Jasper Ryde)? Introduce Activity 4. Ensure that learners understand the meaning of 'sympathetic' in the sense of a 'sympathetic character'. Learners should complete Activity 4, making notes and choosing details from both texts to support their responses.

Draw a table on the board as below:

Jabez Wilson	Sir Jasper Ryde
How he reacts to his experience:	How he reacts to his experience:
How you react to him:	How you react to him:

Fill in sections of the table by asking learners for their responses using their notes and chosen details. Discuss the completed table. Do learners agree with each other? What makes a sympathetic character?

> **Differentiation ideas:**

- Support: Limit the amount of detail learners need to gather from both texts. For example, ask learners to write down two examples for each section of the table.

- Challenge: Ask learners to consider the following questions: *Do victims in crime stories always need to be sympathetic? What about the hero, usually a detective?* Can they think of any stories, films or TV shows where the victim or hero is not a sympathetic character (for example Professor Snape in *Harry Potter* or Magneto in the *X-Men* films, who could be considered an *anti-hero* – a central character in a story who does not have heroic qualities).

> **Assessment ideas:** Listen to learners' responses to Activity 4 in the class discussion and assess how well they have understood how characters are presented directly (stated meaning) and indirectly (implied meaning). Ask learners how confident they feel about inferring character from a text. Do they need any further clarification? Answer questions and address misconceptions.

Plenary idea

Summary checklist (5 minutes)

Description: End this session by asking learners to read through the Summary checklist. Ask them to write a number on a whiteboard to show you how confident they feel about each bullet point, where 1 is 'very confident' and 5 is 'not confident at all'. What do they think they need to learn or practise to improve? Ask learners to share their thoughts. Use responses to plan activities in future sessions to address any issues raised.

Homework idea

Learners should complete Workbook Session 3.1.

3.2 The assistant

LEARNING PLAN		
Learning objectives	**Learning intentions**	**Success criteria**
9Rs.01, 9Ri.01, 9Ri.03, 9Ra.02, 9SLs.01, 9SLp.03	Learners will: • explore the implications of information in a mystery story • consider the structural effects of introducing a new character • improvise a conversation in character • explore developing feelings of sympathy towards a character.	Learners can: • identify and understand the meaning and implications of information in a mystery story • explain the structural effects of introducing a new character at a particular point in a story • confidently improvise a conversation to express a character's feelings • listen to a dialogue between two characters and comment on how it develops feelings of sympathy.

LANGUAGE SUPPORT

The extract in this session contains examples of reporting clauses used with direct speech. However, many of these take archaic forms that may be unfamiliar to learners. It will be useful to review the use, position and structure of reporting clauses.

Remind learners that reporting clauses are not always used when dialogue is being represented in fiction, especially if the context makes it clear who is speaking. When writers do use reporting clauses they generally take forms such as *he said*, *she wrote* and *they replied*. Sometimes words are added to show *how* the words were spoke (for example *he said sadly*).

The position of the <u>reporting clause</u> may be before, after or in the middle of the direct speech:

* 'It's time to tidy up,' <u>Ruby said</u>.
* <u>Ruby said</u>, 'It's time to tidy up.'
* 'It's time,' <u>Ruby said</u>, 'to tidy up.'

When the reporting clause is in the middle or at the end of the direct speech, the writer may swap subject and verb, for example from *he said* to *said he*. This is more common in older texts such as the story in this unit:

* *'Tell me all about it,'* <u>*said I*</u>.
* *'But,'* <u>*said I*</u>, *'there would be millions of red-headed men who would apply.'*
* *'My name,'* <u>*said he*</u>, *'is Mr Duncan Ross.'*

Starter idea

Making predictions (15 minutes)

Resources: Learner's Book, Session 3.2, Getting started activity

Description: Give learners five minutes to reread Extract 1 from Session 3.1, focusing on the character of Jabez Wilson. Ask them to consider these three questions as they read: *How has Jabez Wilson become involved with the Red-Headed League? Why is he asking for help from Sherlock Holmes? What do you think will happen next and why?* Then put learners into pairs and ask them to compare their thinking as they discuss the Getting started activity together.

Main teaching ideas

1 Characters and clues (40 minutes)

Learning intention: Explore the implications of information in a mystery story.

Resources: Learner's Book, Session 3.2, 'The Red-Headed League' Extract 2, Activities 1 and 2

Description: Explain that learners are now going to discover more about Vincent Spaulding and the details of a mystery, then ask them to read Extract 2. You may wish to help learners interact with the text actively through close reading and by predicting, clarifying, questioning or summarising (see Teaching skills focus).

Write *suspicious* on the board and ask what it means (making you feel that something illegal is happening or that something is wrong or mysterious in some way). Learners should complete Activity 1 as a pair discussion before discussing as a class. List things learners find suspicious about Vincent Spaulding's behaviour on the board. Ask learners about the structural impact of the details revealed in this part of the text. What effects do these details and revelations have on the reader at this point in the story?

Ask learners to remember their thinking, predictions and discussions about Jabez Wilson during the Getting started activity. Then, introduce Activity 2, explaining how most writers choose to introduce characters when they want to develop the plot. Emphasise that in a mystery story this can mean structuring the plot and introducing characters in a way that invites the reader to use clues to work out the mystery for themselves. Before learners write their own paragraphs, ask them to discuss the implications of the 'clues' they have been given so far. For example, what is the possible significance of Vincent Spaulding being very smart and seeming to know a lot about the Red-Headed League? Learners should then complete Activity 2.

⟩ Differentiation ideas:

* Support: Before they write their paragraphs for Activity 2, ask learners to imagine the scene with Wilson and Spaulding in the Red-Headed League's office as a picture or as if it were in a film. Point out that although their imagined pictures may be different from each other, they

will all include some details about Vincent Spaulding's appearance, posture, behaviour and speech – and that something about these will act as 'clues' that tells us about his character. They should consider these details and link them to examples from Extract 2 as they write their paragraphs.

- Challenge: Ask learners to write a paragraph, about Duncan Ross and what his character adds to the mystery of the story. Tell learners to study the picture of him in the Learner's Book and link it to examples from Extract 2 as they write.

> **Assessment ideas:** Write the expression *a red herring* on the board. Ask learners what it means (in mystery fiction, a misleading or irrelevant idea). Ask learners to decide which clues they think are relevant so far and which might be a 'red herring'. Why would a writer include 'red herrings' (to distract the detective and the reader)? Use this discussion and learners' paragraphs to assess how well they can comment on the implications of information in a detective story.

2   Getting into character (40 minutes)

Learning intention: Improvise a conversation in character.

Resources: Learner's Book, Session 3.2, Activity 3

Description: Ask learners to recall what they have discovered so far about Jabez Wilson and Vincent Spaulding. Introduce Activity 3. Explain that learners will be working in pairs to do a type of performance called an improvisation. To demonstrate, start with a 'hot-seating' improvisation in the character of Jabez Wilson. You may choose to sit in the hot seat yourself or ask a volunteer to do it. Learners should then ask questions directly to the person in the hot seat about Jabez Wilson's life, up to the point reached in the story. For example: *What sort of manual labour did you do? How long were you in China? What were you doing there? What sort of writing do you do? How do you feel about the Red-Headed League?* Learners should then complete Activity 3 by improvising a conversation in character between Jabez Wilson and Vincent Spaulding. They can begin with the line suggested in the Learner's Book.

> **Differentiation ideas:**

- Support: Give learners some 'Acting Tips for Improvising':

- use your imagination – try things, anything that comes into your head

- work as a team – actors need to read, respond and react to each other to create a performance

- say 'Yes' and go with the flow – you may not like how your partner is acting but accept it and respond rather than saying 'No' and ruining the performance

- learn by doing – discover what works and does not by doing it and assessing the results.

- Challenge: Encourage learners to think about any differences between Jabez Wilson and Vincent Spaulding before they start. Remind them that they know some things about each of the men's personalities, but that there are some things they do not know, so they can use their imaginations as they experiment, play and act out their characters during the improvisation. Is one man cleverer than the other? Which behaves more suspiciously? What kind of conflict is there between them?

> **Assessment ideas:** Monitor the improvisations, but only intervene to encourage learners to remain in character. Afterwards, ask each pair to write a number from 1 (lowest) to 5 (highest) to assess how well they felt their improvisation went. What did they enjoy about it? What did they find difficult? What would they do differently in an improvisation next time?

3   Analysing and responding to character (40 minutes)

Learning intention: Explore developing feelings of sympathy towards a character.

Resources: Learner's Book, Session 3.2, Activity 4

> Download the audioscript for Activity 4 from Cambridge GO (Track 17).

Description: Tell learners they will be listening to and answering questions on an audio recording of an imagined conversation between Wilson and Spaulding. Read the Listening tip and the questions in Activity 4 as a class. Remind learners to make notes on these as they listen to the recording.

Play the audio, then give learners 15–20 minutes to write out answers to Activity 4 in complete sentences. Where possible, they should also expand on their notes with more analysis, explanations and examples. Go through the questions one by one and ask learners to share their answers, discussing each one in turn.

> **Differentiation ideas:**

- Support: Play the recording two or three times if necessary. The first time, learners could listen without making notes, the second time, they make notes. Play a third time if there is still information they feel they missed.

- Challenge: Organise your lesson timings so that after learners have shared their answers as described above there is 10–15 minutes left. In this time, learners should write new answers to questions **a–d**, incorporating new ideas they learnt from the sharing of answers. Afterwards, learners could write two or three sentences reflecting on what and how they learnt between their first set of answers and their second set of answers.

> **Assessment ideas:** Ask learners to write a paragraph self-assessing what they learnt from listening to the recording, writing their answers and listening and sharing answers with their peers. If you included the Challenge above, ask learners to reflect on what they learnt from this also and add this to their paragraph.

Plenary idea

Using words and performance to generate sympathy (15 minutes)

Description: Give learners a definition of *pathos* – pathos is a quality in the words of a text or an actor's performance (or any work of art) that creates feelings of sympathy, pity or sorrow in the reader or audience. Give some examples, such as when Ernesto poisons Hector and steals his songs in the Disney film *Coco* or when Dobby dies in *Harry Potter* or when Caesar is hurt by 'the most unkindest cut of all' from his closest friend, Brutus, in Shakespeare's *Julius Caesar*.

Put learners into pairs and ask them to discuss stories, novels, poems, TV shows, plays or films where they have felt strong sympathy for one or more characters. Emphasise that learners should discuss *how* the writer or actor created those feelings in them, that is, *how* the writer used words or what the actor did to create sympathy in them.

CROSS-CURRICULAR LINK

Drama (improvisation): In this session, learners are asked to improvise a dialogue between two characters from the story. They could use the 'Acting Tips for Improvising' in their next drama lesson, or add their own ideas to these tips and share them in a drama group. If practising improvisation in a drama session, this story could be used as the basis and the improvisation activity here used and developed.

Homework idea

Learners should complete Workbook Session 3.2.

3.3 The end of the League

LEARNING PLAN

Learning objectives	Learning intentions	Success criteria
9Rv.01, 9Ri.01, 9Ri.03, 9Ri.04, 9Ri.07, 9Ww.01, 9Ww.02, 9Ww.03, 9Wv.01, 9Wg.02, 9Wg.04, 9Wg.05, 9Ws.01, 9Ws.02, 9Wc.03, 9Wc.05, 9Wp.02, 9Wp.04, 9SLm.02, 9SLm.03, 9SLs.01	Learners will: • work out the meaning of unfamiliar words • interpret details about a central character in a story • identify and analyse information in a story • write a formal report.	Learners can: • choose appropriate strategies to work out the meaning of unfamiliar words • comment on interpretations of and reactions to a central character in a story • identify, analyse and discuss the implications of information in a story • plan and write a clear, well-structured report using appropriate features.

LANGUAGE SUPPORT

This session asks learners to write a report, so it may be useful to review the type of language and structure appropriate for reports. Learners may know that a report is an account written in chronological order of an event in the past. Here, they are asked to write an account of the history of Wilson's interaction with the Red-Headed League, but also to include their own analyses and theories.

The narrative present of the story is when Wilson is speaking with Holmes; when he recounts reading the advertisement, speaking with Spalding and

Ross, etc. it switches to the narrative past of the story. It would be logical to follow a chronological approach in the report: starting in the past when Wilson first reads the advertisement, converses with Spalding, etc., then moving towards Wilson's meeting with Holmes.

The language of reports is formal, using standard English and correct grammar, punctuation and spelling. Recap previous learning on standard English and ways of editing drafts of writing before learners begin this activity.

Starter idea

If you were a detective . . . (15 minutes)

Resources: Learner's Book, Session 3.3, Getting started activity

Description: Organise learners into pairs and allocate to each one of these roles:

• **Role A:** Victim of a burglary – this person arrives home and discovers it has been broken into.

There is broken glass, upturned furniture, etc. and possessions are missing.

• **Role B:** Detective – this person interviews the victim and asks them questions about what they saw when they arrived home.

Ask learners to role-play this interview. After 3–4 minutes, ask learners to decide which questions got the most useful information in reply and why. Then ask learner pairs to use what they discovered in their discussions for the Getting started activity.

Main teaching ideas

1 Understanding and interpreting detail (45 minutes)

Learning intentions: Work out the meaning of unfamiliar words. Interpret details about a central character in a story.

Resources: Learner's Book, Session 3.3, 'The Red-Headed League' Extract 3, Activities 1 and 2

Description: Tell learners you are going to read the next part of the story, and that they should follow in their Learner's Books. Note that they will need to find the meanings of the underlined words in the extract so they should pay close attention to the context in which those words are used.

Read the extract, then ask learners to write their glossaries for Activity 1. Remind them that they can use context, morphology and etymology where appropriate to work out the meaning of unfamiliar words.

After 15 minutes, organise learners into small groups and read Activity 2 to them. Point out that the different ways of describing Jabez Wilson contrast with one another; learners may feel that only some of them are true, or that all are true. Emphasise they should try to find supporting examples in Extract 3 for whatever descriptions they think are true. Groups then complete the activity. Remind learners to take turns in speaking, be polite, explore where they agree and disagree and give reasons/example from the text to support their views.

> **Differentiation ideas:**

- Support: For Activity 1, have some dictionaries available, but first ask learners to write their glossaries as best they can without one. When they have a first draft, allow them to check the definitions in a dictionary and correct their glossaries if needed.

- Challenge: For Activity 2, give groups 15 minutes to discuss the four descriptions, then ask groups to suggest two additional one-word descriptions for Jabez Wilson. They should find supporting evidence for these new descriptions in Extract 3.

> **Assessment ideas:** Listen to learners' group discussions and their reasoning for agreeing or disagreeing with the descriptions in Activity 2.

Specifically, assess whether learners find and use examples from Extract 3 to support their views.

2 Reporting on a mystery (75 minutes)

Learning intention: Write a formal report.

Resources: Learner's Book, Session 3.3, Activities 3–5

Description: Ask learners to reread Extracts 1–3 on their own. Then ask: *Do you find anything suspicious about the Red-Headed League?* Spend 5–10 minutes getting responses from learners and write any key words from this discussion on the board.

Read Activity 3 to learners and give them 15 minutes to generate and organise their notes. They should then pair up to compare their notes and discuss their ideas about the Red-Headed League, Spalding and Ross for Activity 4. Remind them to explore points of agreement and disagreement, and to update their notes as they improve their ideas.

Explain that learners are now going to plan and write a report based on their work in this session. Ask them to recall when they have written a report before. What structural and language features can they remember? Use the Language support feature at the start of the session to recap key features. Emphasise they should structure their report for Activity 5 in sections, and use headings, subheadings and paragraphs etc. Draw attention to the Writing tip then ask learners to write their reports.

> **Differentiation ideas:**

- Support: Provide learners with a list of formal expressions to help express their ideas. For example: *I firmly believe . . ., I am utterly convinced . . . , My suspicion is . . . , I have no doubt that . . .*

- Challenge: Encourage learners to explain their theories about the mystery in detail, using more than the 250 words specified in the activity. They should justify their ideas by explaining the details of their theories about the League as well as which things need to be investigated further and why.

> **Assessment ideas:** Learners should complete the Peer assessment feature. Before they start, ask how they might feed back to each other in a constructive way – for example, by identifying a few areas of success as well as suggesting improvements in terms of clarity, structure and language choice.

Afterwards, discuss how helpful this type of feedback is. How could they improve peer-assessment activities like this that would help them identify clearly what they need to do to improve?

Plenary idea

Reflection on interpreting information (15 minutes)

Description: Ask learners to reflect on the activities in this session using the Summary checklist.

They should identify something that held them back during the session. For example, do they feel confident about analysing and discussing the implications of information in a story? Do unfamiliar words still block their understanding? What do they think they need to learn or practice in order to improve? Ask learners to share their thoughts. Use responses to plan activities in future sessions to address any issues raised.

Homework idea

Learners should complete Workbook Session 3.3.

3.4 Investigating the street

LEARNING PLAN

Learning objectives	Learning intentions	Success criteria
9Ri.01, 9Ri.04, 9Wv.01, 9Wv.02, 9Wg.01, 9Wg.02, 9Ws.01, 9Wc.01, 9Wc.03, 9Wc.05, 9SLg.03, 9SLg.04, 9SLp.01, 9SLp.02, 9SLr.01	Learners will: • read an unseen text aloud • discuss a series of clues and make predictions • write and edit an ending to a mystery story involving tension, climax and release.	Learners can: • read an unseen text aloud confidently and accurately, using dramatic techniques for effect • explore layers of meaning in a story and use them to make predictions • plan, write and edit the ending of a story, combining various techniques for effect.

LANGUAGE SUPPORT

The first activity in this session asks learners to use their voices to bring out the drama. First, remind learners who may need extra language support that English is a stress-timed language, putting equal emphasis on content words in a sentence, such as nouns and verbs, and less emphasis on other grammatical words, such as articles, prepositions and auxiliary verbs. Learners should identify the content words that should be stressed and the grammatical words that should have less stress. This will raise awareness of natural speech patterns in English. Second, encourage learners to experiment with stressing different words in the same sentence when reading aloud, especially when reading out direct speech. Ask learners what effect stressing different words has on meaning and how it might help bring out the drama – for example:

- *'My _dear_ doctor, this is a time for observation, not for talk.'*
- *'My dear doctor, this is a time for _observation_, not for talk.'*
- *'My dear doctor, this is a time for observation, not for _talk_.'*

Common misconception

Misconception	How to identify	How to overcome
You must always use a question mark with *what*.	Write these sentences on the board: • *What happened today.* • *What a beautiful day it is.* Ask learners which punctuation marks they should use at the end of each sentence – a question mark, an exclamation mark or a full stop. Ask them to explain the difference (the first one is eliciting a response, the second does not need a reply and can be either an exclamation or declarative statement.	Ask learners to find a similar declaration in Extract 4 of 'The Red-Headed League' (*'What I expected to see'*). Ask learners if this sentence functions as a question and invites a reply (no). Draw out how this sentence ends in a full stop and not a question mark. Point out that it is in fact a statement which answers Holmes's question. Sentences like this are also called declarative statements or declarative sentences.

Starter idea

What happens next? (10 minutes)

Resources: Learner's Book, Session 3.4, Getting started activity

Description: Ask learners to work in pairs and discuss their predictions about the next part of the story. What will happen next as Holmes continues his investigation of the Red-Headed League? Remind learners to refer to their prior knowledge of events so far, and the suspicions and theories they have previously established. After five minutes ask learners to briefly discuss the Getting started activity – what other stories do they know where they used clues to predict what would happen.

Main teaching ideas

1 Make predictions about a story after reading and studying an extract (40 minutes)

Learning intentions: Read an unseen text aloud. Discuss a series of clues and make predictions.

Resources: Learner's Book, Session 3.4, Activities 1 and 2

Description: Read Extract 4 once to the class then ask them to read it again to themselves. Organise learners into groups of four and ask them to assign one of the roles listed in the bullet points in Activity 1. They should then complete the activity, reading Extract 4 aloud as a group several times.

Remind learners to experiment with varying the volume, tone and pace of their voice to make their reading more engaging for listeners. After 10–15 minutes, split groups into pairs to complete the Reflection feature.

To complete Activity 2, pairs should re-join as groups. They should start by spending a few minutes asking the learner who read Holmes's dialogue: *What did you do in this extract to try to solve the mystery?* They should make brief notes on and discuss responses. Afterwards, ask learners to write their lists and guesses for Activity 2 on their own.

> **Differentiation ideas:**

• Support: Visit groups as they read aloud. Give them coaching tips on how they can vary the volume, tone and pace of their voice for specific lines. For example, many of Holmes's lines should be spoken in a confident, authoritative or commanding tone, while Watson's dialogue should be in a tone that is less confident and at time questioning, or even confused as he tries to understand what Holmes is doing.

• Challenge: For Activity 1, ask groups to act out or role play Extract 4 as a dramatic scene. Learners should use physical actions and movement as well as their voices to bring out the drama and meaning of the scene. They should also use the dialogue from the story as if it were the lines in a script, with the narrative text functioning as stage directions.

> **Assessment ideas:** Listen to learners as they read aloud in their groups. Specifically, monitor if learners are able to: read ahead so they know when it is their turn; read accurately what is in Extract 4; and experiment confidently with changing the volume, tone and pace of their voice.

2 The mystery solved (90 minutes)

Learning intentions: Discuss a series of clues and make predictions. Write and edit an ending to a mystery story involving tension, climax and release.

Resources: Learner's Book, Session 3.4, Activities 3 and 4

Description: Read Activity 3 to learners. Explain that for the discussion they will use the same 'fishbowl' format as in Unit 1. Remind learners that in a 'fishbowl' discussion, some learners are seated inside the fishbowl and discuss a topic, while everyone else stands outside, listening carefully to the ideas presented. The learners outside the fishbowl should take notes, which they will use in their writing for Activity 4.

Ask learners to reread all four extracts of the story so far. While they are doing so, set up the classroom for the activity, with chairs in a circle for half the class and enough room round the outside for the rest to stand and listen.

When everyone is ready, complete the discussion for Activity 3 using the fishbowl format. Ask the speakers to focus their comments on the bullet points in the activity, and ensure that the listeners are making notes. After 10–15 minutes, stop the discussion and swap the class over so the listeners become the speakers and vice versa.

At the end of the discussion, tell learners to use their notes to write an ending for the story in response to Activity 4. Remind learners to use the guidance in Activity 4 and the Writing tip in planning, writing and editing their story ending.

> **Differentiation ideas:**

- Support: Suggest some sentences, in Watson's narrative voice, to get learners started on their story ending. For example: *It was midnight as I stood in the empty bank. Through the window, I saw a carriage pass and I heard the sound of horses' hooves clacking along the street. Then, in the corner a menacing shadow seemed to move towards me and grow larger.*

- Challenge: When learners have written their story ending, ask them to write a paragraph explaining which clues they used from the four extracts and how they built on these to develop the specific ending they wrote for the story.

> **Assessment ideas:** Ask learners to use the Self-assessment exercise in the Learner's Book to evaluate the effectiveness of their story ending and the language choices they made. Based on their evaluation, learners should write a second draft of their story ending adding in their improvements.

Plenary idea

What makes a good ending? (10 minutes)

Description: Point out that readers of stories and viewers of films often have strong responses to endings. Point out also that endings can be satisfying and seem to work well, or they may not seem to work at all, be a big disappointment and could even ruin the whole story!

In pairs, learners should discuss one example of a good ending and one example of a bad ending from a story or film they know. Ask learners to analyse what makes the good ending 'good' and the bad ending 'bad' and whether they considered any of these points when writing their story ending for Activity 4.

Homework idea

Learners should complete Workbook Session 3.4.

3.5 The dark cellar

LEARNING PLAN

Learning objectives	Learning intentions	Success criteria
9Rv.02, 9Rv.03, 9Rs.01, 9Ri.01, 9Wv.01, 9Wv.02, 9Wg.01, 9Wg.02, 9Wc.01, 9Wc.03, 9Wc.07, 9Wc.08, 9Wp.04	Learners will: • consider the effect of structural choices in a narrative • explore how language choices contribute to the overall effect of a text • practise writing descriptively, using aural and tactile images • identify what makes an effective description.	Learners can: • analyse the effect of structural choices in a narrative • comment on how language choices contribute to the overall effect of a text • write descriptively, using effective choices of aural and tactile imagery and other techniques • understand and comment on what makes a description effective.

LANGUAGE SUPPORT

If several adjectives are used before a noun, they usually appear in a particular order: adjectives describing opinions or attitudes come first, followed by more neutral, factual ones. Here is the most common order for adjectives.

1 opinion (e.g. beautiful)
2 size (e.g. small)
3 physical quality (e.g. thin)
4 shape (e.g. square)
5 age (e.g. old)
6 colour (e.g. red)
7 origin (e.g. Egyptian)
8 material (e.g. plastic)
9 type (e.g. three-sided)
10 purpose (e.g. cooking)

For example:

• I bought a small, new, red umbrella.
• She owns a lovely, round, wooden, jewellery box.
• The man entered the low, old, stone, hunting lodge.

Remind learners that noun phrases with multiple adjectives like this are rare and can sound clumsy. It is better to use one or two carefully chosen adjectives that convey a depth of meaning. Language worksheet 3.2 provides learners with further practice in using adjectives in descriptive writing.

Starter idea

Detective and mystery story settings (10 minutes)

Resources: Learner's Book, Session 3.5, Getting started activity

Description: Ask learners about the settings of the Sherlock Holmes story, e.g. Holmes's lodgings at 221b Baker Street and other locations in late-Victorian London. Have learners heard of Baker Street, or even visited it? It plays an important role in the stories. It is now the Sherlock Holmes museum and often has long queues of tourists outside it. Ask learners to discuss the kind of settings you find in crime stories. How do these settings add to the story?

Main teaching ideas

1 Building tension (55 minutes)

Learning intentions: Consider the effect of structural choices in a narrative. Explore how language choices contribute to the overall effect of a text.

Resources: Learner's Book, Session 3.5, 'The Red-Headed League' Extract 5, Activities 1 and 2

Description: Draw the shape of a typical story arc on the board (see Main teaching idea 2 in Session 2.5). Remind learners that this shape represents a plot structure and that different points represent sections of the story (exposition, climax, denouement, etc.). Tell them that they are going to explore these story parts further in this session and the next.

Point out to learners that they are reaching the climax of 'The Red-Headed League'. Ask them to explain what this means, then read through Activity 1 as a class. In pairs, learners should read the extract aloud, taking a sentence each in turn. Afterwards, discuss what happens in Extract 5, ensuring that learners understand what happened in the story.

Introduce Activity 2. Discuss the 'shape' of the story so far. Ask learners what happens in Extract 5 to build tension. Explain that they are now going to look at the language in the extract. Ask learners to write a list of words and phrases that help create and release the tension at this point in the story. Discuss some examples as a class. Use questioning to draw out how language choices work within the context of the whole scene not just their immediate sentence, for example, *I expect that within an hour matters will come to a head* makes readers expect that something dramatic will happen. Other words and phrases implicitly or explicitly create tension. Explain that learners should read carefully to identify these.

Read the Reading tip to learners and emphasise that for Activity 2 learners should find specific language examples and that they can also discuss *how* they have the effect of creating tension for the reader.

> **Differentiation ideas:**

- Support: Point out that certain words, phrases and story situations will create tension through implication, inference or expectation.

Give some contrasting examples to illustrate before learners complete Activity 2:

- **Word:** *I am _worried_* contrasted with *I am _terrified_* (more tension).
- **Phrase:** *I _fell quickly_* contrasted with *In a flash I was plummeting* (more tension).
- **Story situation:**

  a   Two people are talking at a café. Then there is an explosion nearby.

  b   We learn there is a bomb timed to go off near a café at 12 noon. Two friends meet at a café and begin talking. A clock shows it is 11:57 a.m. (**b** has more tension).

- Challenge: Ask learners to think of an example of another story that builds towards a climax and then consider *how* the writer has built increasing tension in the story. Give examples, such as the race to defuse a bomb in the *Mission Impossible* movies or progressing through game levels to reach boss battles in video games. Which genre of book or other media uses this technique of building more and more tension most commonly?

> **Assessment ideas:** Discuss the way tension can be created and built upon in a story as a class. Asking questions to draw out their understanding of how a writer's structural choices help create tension. For example in Extract 5:

- What role does darkness play in the scene?
- What role does quietness have?
- How does the need to wait help create tension?
- Do we learn about the physical and emotional effects of stress for any character?
- Why has the author chosen Watson and not Holmes as the narrator?

2 Write a descriptive piece and discuss effective description (75 minutes)

Learning intentions: Practise writing descriptively, using aural and tactile images. Identify what makes an effective description.

Resources: Learner's Book, Session 3.5, Activities 3 and 4; Language worksheet 3.2

Description: Write the title *Imagery* on the board and underneath the subtitles *Visual*, *Aural* and *Tactile*. Ask learners what each of the words mean and how they relate to different senses.

Introduce the Language focus feature, then give learners one minute to write their own example of aural or tactile imagery. Share examples as a class.

Use the guidance to introduce Language worksheet 3.2. Explain that this provides practice using adjectives for description in an interesting way, which is one aspect of effective description. Learners should complete the worksheet, then use dictionaries to check their work.

Check that learners understand the meaning of the first-person voice, then introduce Activity 3 by telling learners that they need to put themselves into the character of Dr Watson, waiting in the dark cellar of the bank. Emphasise that they should use imagery to create tension in the description and to portray Watson's nervousness.

Ask learners to read the learner's answer in Activity 4. They should discuss it in pairs, identifying what they found most effective about it and why. Come together as a class to share ideas.

> **Differentiation ideas:**

- Support: Provide learners with a checklist of language and grammatical elements that they should include in their writing, including first-person voice, past tense, a simile based on aural imagery, a metaphor based on tactile imagery, emphatic adjective-noun combinations (for example *absolute darkness, my nerves were worked up to the highest pitch*).

- Challenge: Ask learners to use the fact that it is so dark that Watson cannot see in an interesting way, using imagery. Even though there is nothing to see, you could suggest giving the darkness an aural or tactile quality – for example *It was so quiet I could hear the drumbeat of my pulse in my ear, The darkness was so thick it felt like a heavy blanket.*

> **Assessment ideas:** Learners should carry out the Self-assessment activity to compare their writing to the learner's answer. Encourage them to focus on their own use of aural and tactile imagery. Allow time for learners to edit and produce a final draft.

Plenary idea

Planning the climax (10 minutes)

Description: Ask learners to reflect on the part of the story told in Extract 5. Ask them to imagine they are writing a similar scene in a story of their own. From what they have learnt in this session, what two things would they include? For example, would they include a structural clue that builds tension or a simile that describes a character's fear? Finally, ask learners to recall what still needs to be explained: Why did Holmes tap the pavement and ask Ross for directions? What is the Red-Headed League and why was it formed?

Homework idea

Learners should complete Workbook Session 3.5.

3.6 The solution

LEARNING PLAN

Learning objectives	Learning intentions	Success criteria
9Rs.01, 9Ri.01, 9Ri.04, 9Ri.05, 9Ri.08, 9Ri.10, 9Ra.02, 9Ra.04, 9Ra.05, 9Wc.06, 9Wp.01, 9SLm.02, 9SLm.03, 9SLg.02	Learners will: • express a personal response to the end of a mystery story • compare the way a theme is presented in two texts • explore how readers' reactions to stories are shaped by their experiences and beliefs.	Learners can: • clearly express a personal response to the ending of a mystery story • analyse and discuss themes and moral messages in more than one text • explain how readers' reactions to stories are shaped by their experiences and beliefs.

LANGUAGE SUPPORT

In this session, learners are asked to give their opinion on ideas about morality and goodness. In activities like this, it is common for some learners to be limited in how they respond by a lack of functional language. It would help learners to know or have access to a range of functional language they can use to express their opinions clearly and add nuance to their responses. Support learners by presenting them with a selection of phrases they can use. For example:

• Expressing an opinion strongly: I firmly believe . . .   Personally, . . .   I disagree entirely with . . .
• Providing further arguments: Similarly, . . .   In addition, . . .   Furthermore, . . .
• Adding contrast: However, . . .   Despite this . . . On the other hand, . . .
• Summarising: It seems clear . . .   Overall, . . . For all these reasons . . .

Starter idea

A twist in the tale (5 minutes)

Resources: Learner's Book, Session 3.6, Getting started activity

Description: Write the expression *twist in the tale* on the board and ask learners what it means. Are they expecting a twist in the tale in this story? How do mystery stories usually end? Learners should discuss some examples they have read with a partner.

Main teaching ideas

1 Reacting to the denouement (45 minutes)

Learning intention: Express a personal response to the end of a mystery story.

Resources: Learner's Book, Session 3.6, 'The Red-Headed League' Extract 6, Activity 1; Differentiated worksheets 3A, 3B and 3C

Description: Introduce the final extract, which contains both the climax and Holmes explaining the mystery. Learners should then read Extract 6.

Write *denouement* on the board. Ask learners what language the word is from and what it means (French, meaning 'the undoing of a knot'). Remind learners how this word is used to describe the part of a detective story when any remaining mysteries are explained. Explain how the denouement is the final part of a story structure that can be represented by the pyramid they looked at in the previous session. Introduce and hand out the Differentiated worksheets 3A, 3B or 3C on Freytag's Pyramid using the guidance notes.

Learners should complete their worksheets. Discuss their responses briefly as a class and ensure learners have correctly identified each stage of the story. To compare, ask them to identify any stories they know that use the three-act structure from Activity 4 on their sheets.

Discuss what learners think about the denouement. How do they feel about the explanation? Do they like it or not? Is it a satisfactory end to the story? Learners should complete Activity 1, writing a personal response to the denouement.

> **Differentiation ideas:**

- Support: To help learners overcome any difficulties with comprehension that would affect their personal responses, you may wish to help learners interact with the text actively through close reading and by predicting, clarifying, questioning or summarising (see Teaching skills focus).

- Challenge: Learners could also write about other stages of the story and compare them with how they feel about the denouement. For example, they could compare how the story is set up and how it builds to the tension of the climax with the explanation at the end.

> **Assessment ideas:** Provide feedback on learners' Differentiated worksheets. Have they identified and defined the stages on Freytag's Pyramid correctly? Have they identified the five stages within the story?

2 Exploring moral themes (45 minutes)

Learning intention: Compare the way a theme is presented in two texts.

Resources: Learner's Book, Session 3.6, 'The Red-Headed League' Extract 6; Learner's Book, Sessions 2.4 and 2.5, *The Case of the Missing Masterpiece* Extracts 1 and 2

Description: Read Activity 2 to learners. Ask learners to think about what happens to John Clay/

Vincent Spalding in 'The Red-Headed League'. Then ask learners to consider what happens at the end of *The Case of the Missing Masterpiece* from Unit 2. Discuss as a class how the endings of both stories deal with moral themes such as good and evil, crime and punishment, and power and human behaviour.

Ask learners: *What happens to the villains in these stories? What moral message emerges from these stories about crime and punishment?* Get several responses from different learners and discuss them. Then, give learners 20 minutes to write a comparison of the two endings for Activity 2.

Introduce Activity 3, which asks learners to consider Holmes's morality. Learners should read Marcus's view in the speech bubble in the Learner's Book and discuss it in pairs. Draw attention to the Reading tip. Learners should then complete Activity 3, using their discussion to help them frame their personal responses.

> **Differentiation ideas:**

- Support: Provide learners with a range of functional language to support them in both discussing and writing their personal responses (see Language support at the start of the session).

- Challenge: Define binary or black-or-white thinking, that is, where two alternative ideas (such as hero or villain) are presented as the only possibilities that exist. Point out that thinking in this way can stop us from seeing balance, nuance or complexity in stories and story characters (as well as in real-life situations and people). Ask learners: *Are moral themes in stories more enjoyable when they are not presented as black-and-white? Do you enjoy stories that show a hero with character flaws? Do you enjoy stories that show villains with good motives?*

> **Assessment ideas:** Provide formal written feedback on learners' responses to Activity 2. Highlight where learners have successfully compared both texts and where they could improve their answer, for example, have they written a conclusion at the end of their comparison?

3 Consider different responses to a story and give your own response (45 minutes)

Learning intention: Explore how personal experiences and opinions affect responses to fiction

Resources: Learner's Book, Session 3.6, Activities 4 and 5

Description: Write when the story was written on the board (1891). Read Activity 4 to learners and ask them if they find the story old-fashioned and why. Ask learners to identify any ideas and objects that stand out as being from the past in the story, for example an English bank holding French gold coins (Napoleons).

Ask learners to read the three views of the story in Activity 4, and then to discuss them in pairs. They should consider how their personal experiences and opinions affect the points of view.

After 10–15 minutes, ask learner pairs to share points from their discussion with the rest of the class. Establish if there is a consensus with which of the three views people agree. Learners should then reflect on their discussions for Activities 3 and 4 in this session. They should use these reflections to develop and write their personal responses for Activity 5.

> **Differentiation ideas:**

- Support: For Activity 4, consider putting learners into pairs that will provide suitable levels of support for each other.

- Challenge: Open out the whole-class discussion to cover bias, objectivity and anachronistic interpretation. For example, ask learners if it is possible to read a story without bringing your personal experiences and opinions to its interpretation. Or is it right to judge older texts by today's standards? Should older texts ever be banned?

> **Assessment ideas:** Listen to learners as they discuss the three views. Provide informal, oral feedback on the quality and depth of their discussions. For example: *Do you agree with Sofia that the story is predictable? Why do think she is right or wrong about this?*

Plenary idea

Developing a personal response to a literary text (10 minutes)

Description: Explain that to give a personal response to a literary text, learners should first read it and think about the effect it has had on them. Emphasise they should always read a literary text two, three or even more times before writing about their response. Then, organise learners into pairs and ask them to discuss the following questions about 'The Red-Headed League':

- What did this story make me think about?

- How did this story make me feel?

- Were there parts of the story that stood out for me and why did these stand out?

- How did the author tell the story and use language to make me feel this way?

Homework idea

Learners should complete Workbook Session 3.6.

PROJECT GUIDANCE

A useful sequence for carrying out this project would be as follows.

1 Outline the entire project to the class. Explain what the aim is and what they need to produce and present. For example:

- collaborate in groups to write reports about story endings from different genres

- decide on which story from which genre to read

- prepare a report and present a summary on the chosen story and how it ends

- read the reports from other groups to compare.

2 Organise the class into small groups for the project. Ask each group to choose a coordinator. Explain that the coordinator's role is to help organise the group and make sure everyone's contributions are ready on time. Tell learners that you will be asking each coordinator to report to you on their group's progress as they prepare their reports.

3 Present the class with a list of story genres and an example of an age-appropriate, familiar book from each genre. Allow some class time for each group to decide which story genre they would like to report on. Ask each group to have a first choice and two reserve choices.

CONTINUED

Discuss as a class and assign each group a genre. Make sure as many genres as possible are covered and avoid repetition if possible.

4   Allow time for research, discussion and debate of possible stories to read. Remind learners that even though the focus of their reports will be on story endings, they will have to read each story in full. Ensure each group has chosen an appropriate story. Allow time for each group to read their chosen stories.

5   Ask groups to discuss their stories using the bullet points in the Learner's Book. Coordinators should then lead a discussion on what their group will include in their report, how they will structure it and how they will divide the work amongst themselves. Set a deadline for completion of the reports. Remind groups that they will also need to prepare a summary of their reports for presentation, including whether to use visual aids.

6   Before the deadline, allow some class time for coordinators to check on the progress their group is making.

7   Ask each group to present their report to the rest of the class. After the presentations, allow time for learners to read each other's reports.

Meet at least once with the coordinators during the project. Use the meeting to gauge how well their group's preparation is going. Are they on schedule? Do they need to organise themselves differently? Use dialogue and questioning to guide the coordinator in exploring any new options for managing the project. If necessary, meet each group and hold a short discussion about their progress and any obstacles to make sure that their reports and summaries are ready on time.

❯4 Time

Unit plan

Session	Approximate number of learning hours	Outline of learning content	Resources
4.1 Moments in time	2 hours, 30 minutes	Learners explore the themes and language in a poem, give a personal response to a poem and write their own.	Learner's Book Session 4.1 Workbook Session 4.1 ⬇ Differentiated worksheets 4A, 4B and 4C
4.2 Making the most of time	2 hours, 30 minutes	Learners examine the effect and meaning of a poem's language and structure, discuss personal interpretations and use genre features in their own poem.	Learner's Book Session 4.2 Workbook Session 4.2
4.3 The tribe that time forgot	2 hours, 30 minutes	Learners respond to an informative article, detect bias and write and perform a persuasive speech.	Learner's Book Session 4.3 Workbook Session 4.3 ⬇ Language worksheet 4.1
4.4 The time tornado	2 hours, 30 minutes	Learners explore genre features, story openings and verb choices. They also write a story opening.	Learner's Book Session 4.4 Workbook Session 4.4 ⬇ Language worksheet 4.2
4.5 The visitor	2 hours, 30 minutes	Learners explore how writers create mystery, discuss predictions about a story and write part of a mystery story.	Learner's Book Session 4.5 Workbook Session 4.5
4.6 Into the future	2 hours, 30 minutes	Learners explore the impact of informal and formal styles in speech. They also consider how a writer creates an informal voice and write in an informal voice themselves.	Learner's Book Session 4.6 Workbook Session 4.6

BACKGROUND KNOWLEDGE

For the teacher

For this unit, it will be useful to familiarise yourself with the language features used in the following text types:

- poetry
- informative articles
- persuasive speeches
- stories in the fantasy genre.

This unit explores metre and the patterns of stressed and unstressed syllables that create rhythm, so a secure understanding of these ideas will also be useful.

Various grammar topics are covered in this unit, but you may want to consider tense and aspect, and dynamic and state verbs in particular, before teaching the unit. Sessions 4.1 and 4.4 contain language support resources on these topics.

For the learner

Previous knowledge of the following will be helpful to learners:

- Fantasy stories and their genre features, including those in literature and from film and television.
- Informative articles – online or print.
- Poetry, rhythm in poetry and poetic themes, in particular stressed and unstressed patterns in poetry. As this unit focuses on the theme of time, familiarity with other poems on this theme may help learners.
- Persuasive language – before starting this unit, encourage learners to become more aware of both written and spoken examples of persuasive language. They might reflect on how they change their language when they want to persuade a friend or relative, or how others (friends, advertisers, newspapers, etc.) use language when trying to persuade them. They could also observe people such as politicians trying to persuade others on television.

Familiarity with language and grammar that refers to past or present time (tense) or actions that are continuous or finished (aspect) will be helpful.

TEACHING SKILLS FOCUS

Active learning

As they start new learning activities, learners bring their previous knowledge with them. This can influence *what* new knowledge they gain as they progress and *how* they gain it. Learners' understanding of a topic can be increased through activities that confront and expand their previous knowledge. If what learners discover through an activity differs from or builds on what they have learnt previously, they will compare their experiences, and their knowledge will increase as they reflect on both previous and current activities.

This resource has been structured to support the principles of active learning. For example, Starter ideas provide opportunities for teachers

and learners to judge current knowledge of a topic. The Main teaching ideas are designed to prompt learners' thinking so they can add new knowledge to their existing understanding. Many activities require participation with peers, such as paired, group and whole class discussions, as well as paired reading and writing activities. However, independent activities are emphasised too, as these also provide good opportunities for active learning. Finally, peer- and self-assessment exercises are included (alongside teacher assessments) to give learners structured opportunities to reflect on their learning experiences and increase their knowledge.

4.1 Moments in time

LEARNING PLAN

Learning objectives	Learning intentions	Success criteria
9Rv.03, 9Rg.03, 9Ri.01, 9Ri.05, 9Ri.07, 9Ri.08, 9Ri.09, 9Ri.10, 9Ri.11, 9Ra.01, 9Ra.02, 9Wv.01, 9Wv.02, 9Wg.03, 9Wc.01, 9Wc.03, 9Wc.08, 9SLm.03, 9SLp.01, 9SLp.02	Learners will: • read an unseen poem aloud • explore a poet's themes and language choices • write a poem in the style of a well-known poet • give a personal response to a writer's work.	Learners can: • read poetry aloud accurately and confidently • understand how a poet uses language and grammatical techniques to explore themes and create effects • write a short poem in a particular style, using appropriate language and structural features • write a personal response to a selection of poems by one writer.

LANGUAGE SUPPORT

Part of the focus in Activity 3 in this session is on understanding how the present tense affects our understanding of when actions happened or are happening. This can involve two areas of verb grammar: tense and aspect.

Tense refers to the way a verb changes its endings to indicate when an action takes place.

• Present tense (base form + s for third person): I/you/we/they **walk**, He/she it/**walks**.

• Past tense (base form + ed for regular verbs): I walk**ed**, I play**ed**, I laugh**ed**.

Tense is combined with aspect to form different constructions, such as past continuous or present perfect.

The continuous (or progressive) aspect indicates that actions are *in progress* at a particular time.

• Past continuous: I **was talking** with Ruby last night.

• Present continuous: Praveen **is shouting**.

The perfect aspect suggests *looking back* at actions:

• Present perfect: I **have** worked in London for years.

• Past perfect: The colour **had faded**.

The Differentiated worksheets in this session give learners further practice in identifying and commenting on the effect of different tenses and aspects.

Starter idea

Year's end (15 minutes)

Resources: Learner's Book, Session 4.1, Getting started activity

Description: Put learners into groups of four and ask them to discuss how they would like to spend New Year's Eve, for example at a party, quietly at home, in a special place or with friends or family. They should then complete the Getting started activity in their groups or pairs.

Main teaching ideas

1 Exploring a poem (25 minutes)

Learning intentions: Read an unseen poem aloud. Explore a poet's themes and language choices.

Resources: Learner's Book, Session 4.1, 'Autumn', Activities 1 and 2

Description: Organise learners into pairs and give them 10 minutes to study the Reading tip in the Learner's Book, and then to read the poem 'Autumn' aloud to each other for Activity 1. Remind them to use the glossary if there are words they are not familiar with.

Afterwards, ask learners to discuss Activity 2 together, making brief notes. Come together as a class to share notes and ideas about whether the poem is optimistic.

> **Differentiation ideas:**

- Support: Point out that writers may use autumn to symbolise some of the following: change, maturity, ripening, beauty or sadness at an approaching end. Learners can then consider these meanings during their discussion.

- Challenge: Explain that writers often use the seasons in a symbolic way, then pose this additional question to share with the class at the end: *What is symbolised by the season of autumn in this poem?*

> **Assessment ideas:** Assess the quality of learners' notes as they share these with the class. Evaluate whether learners give their opinion on whether the poem is optimistic or not, provide reasons for their opinion and refer to lines of the poem to support their opinion.

2 Comparing two poems (40 minutes)

Learning intention: Explore a poet's themes and language choices.

Resources: Learner's Book, Session 4.1, 'The Turning Year', Activity 3; Differentiated worksheets 4A, 4B and 4C

Description: Read the Language focus information to learners and discuss any questions or misunderstandings. Use the Language support feature at the start of the session to explain further the concepts of tense and aspect, and how these can be used to form constructions such as past perfect or present continuous. Hand out the Differentiated

worksheets and give learners 15–20 minutes to complete them.

Organise learners into pairs and ask them to read the poems 'Autumn' and 'The Turning Year', then compare them using the bullet points in Activity 3 to structure their discussion.

> **Differentiation ideas:**

- Support: Give learners some examples from both poems for each of the bullet points in Activity 3. For example:

  - the narrator's feelings about time passing: *Nothing remains, tonight I do not enjoy life to the full*

  - words connected with disappearance and cold: *fading, white with frost, Nightfall, pure and cold*

  - images connected to the natural world: *water lilies, summer, leaves, frost, oranges, clouds, sky*

  - use of the present tense alongside speculation about the future in the last two lines: *are, remains, is, will be.*

- They can base their discussion and comparison on these language examples, and any others they find.

- Challenge: Ask learners to work in pairs to write a paragraph summarising their comparison. They should comment on each of the bullet points in Activity 3.

> **Assessment ideas:** Assess whether learners comment on the use of the present tense in both poems and describe the effects of this – for example, the reader experiences the poems' events as 'happening now' rather than 'already happened' or 'finished' if the past tense had been used.

3 Writing a poem (25 minutes)

Learning intention: Write a poem in the style of a well-known poet.

Resources: Learner's Book, Session 4.1, Activity 4

Description: Read Activity 4 and the Writing tip as a class. Make some positive suggestions to encourage and inspire learners, such as noting that 4–8 lines is not much but with well-chosen words they can say a lot! Explain that the time of year could be a season, a festival, a birthday or anniversary and that nature is constantly providing us with imagery (sky, clouds, rain, wind, sunshine, flowers, birds, fruit, snow, daytime, mornings, dawn, sunrises, evening, sunsets, etc.). Learners should then write their poems independently.

> **Differentiation ideas:**

- Support: Point out to learners that they can emphasise the present and refer to the future in their poems by using present tense *to be*, the present tense verb (for example *fade/fades*, not *fad<u>ed</u>*), present continuous aspect (*fad<u>ing</u>*) or future forms.

- Challenge: Ask learners to write their poem emphasising the present tense, then to create a second version by changing the present tense and continuous forms to past tense and perfect forms. They could conclude by briefly explaining which they prefer and why.

> **Assessment ideas:** Ask learners to swap their poem with a partner and use the questions in the Peer assessment feature to give each other feedback.

4 Responding to poetry (35 minutes)

Learning intention: Give a personal response to a writer's work.

Resources: Learner's Book, Session 4.1, 'The End of the Year', Activities 5 and 6

Description: Ask for a volunteer to read Activity 5 to the class. Emphasise that they are being asked to consider themes and voice in the poems. Remind them that themes are the main ideas in a text, which may be expressed directly or indirectly, and that voice is the distinctive way a writer uses language, style and point of view to distinguish characters, as well as the tone and attitude of their writing.

Organise learners into pairs or small groups and give them 10–15 minutes to read 'The End of the Year', and to reread 'The Turning Year' and 'Autumn' and discuss the questions in Activity 5. They should then write their paragraph for Activity 6 independently.

> **Differentiation ideas:**

- Support: For Activity 6, provide an outline structure as below (each paragraph can be 30–60 words):

  - Paragraph 1: Explain how you feel as you read 'Autumn'.

  - Paragraph 2: Explain how you feel as you read 'The Turning Year'.

  - Paragraph 3: Explain how you feel as you read 'The End of the Year'.

  - Paragraph 4: Summarise and explain what you think all three poems have in common, and how you feel about the three poems as a collection.

- Challenge: Ask learners to include one or more paragraphs in which they analyse Su Tung P'o's language choices (for example, use of the present tense) and explain their effects on them as a reader.

> **Assessment ideas:** Evaluate learners' personal responses by looking for: language that identifies enjoyment or specific emotional attitudes (for example *sad, happy, positive, optimistic, pessimistic, negative, uplifting*), comments on specific parts of any poem and why these stand out and what they feel Su Tung P'o is saying or why they like the voice in which he writes.

Plenary idea

Summing up Su Tung P'o (10 minutes)

Description: Write these two quotations about poetry on the board and explain that Frost and Coleridge were poets.

> *Poetry is when an emotion has found its thought and the thought has found words.*
>
> Robert Frost
>
> *Prose = words in their best order; poetry = the best words in the best order.*
>
> Samuel Taylor Coleridge

Organise learners into small groups and ask them to decide whether or not these quotations could be used to describe Su Tung P'o's poems.

Homework idea

Learners should complete Workbook Session 4.1.

4.2 Making the most of time

Learning objectives	Learning intentions	Success criteria
9Rv.02, 9Rv.03, 9Rs.01, 9Rs.02, 9Ri.01, 9Ri.09, 9Ra.01, 9Ra.02, 9Ra.04, 9Ra.05, 9Wv.01, 9Wv.02, 9Wv.03, 9Wg.04, 9Ws.01, 9Wc.01, 9Wc.03, 9Wc.04, 9SLg.02, 9SLg.03, 9SLp.01	Learners will: • explore the effect of images and language choices in a poem • consider how a poem's structure can be used to convey meaning • discuss how personal beliefs can affect interpretations of a poem • write a poem using genre features.	Learners can: • explain the effect of images and language choices in an older poem • analyse how structure is used to convey a poem's meaning • contribute effectively to a discussion about personal responses to a poem • write a poem incorporating specific features of the genre.

LANGUAGE SUPPORT

Many older poems contain archaisms – words and structures that are more common to an earlier form of English. Archaisms include words (for example *ye, thou, thee, thine, thy, methinks*), prefixes and suffixes such as *a-* (for example *a-flying, a-getting*), *-est* (for example *knowest*) and *-eth* (for example *goeth*) and grammatical forms (for example *would that I could*, meaning 'I wish I could' or *we must away*, meaning 'we must leave').

In the poem in this session, learners may notice the following archaisms:

- several uses of the word *ye*
- use of the *a-* prefix to verbs in *a-flying* and *a-getting*
- the words *coy* and *tarry*, which are still used today, but sound old-fashioned.

Modern poets often rearrange normal grammatical structures to create rhythm, but older poetry may have archaic grammatical forms as well as altered grammar for rhythmic reasons.

Starter idea

Idioms about life (10 minutes)

Resources: Learner's Book, Session 4.2, Getting started activity

Description: Remind learners that an idiom is a phrase that has a meaning that cannot be understood from the individual words, for example, to be *over the moon* means you are extremely happy. Idioms communicate their meaning metaphorically rather than literally.

Write the following idioms on the board and point out that they express positive, negative or mixed attitudes towards situations in life:

- Every cloud has a silver lining.
- Turn over a new leaf.
- Once bitten, twice shy.

Organise learners into pairs or small groups and ask them to decide what each idiom means before they complete the Getting started activity.

Main teaching ideas

1 Exploring metaphorical meaning in a poem (30 minutes)

Learning intention: Explore the effect of images and language choices in a poem.

Resources: Learner's Book, Session 4.2, 'To Make Much of Time', Activities 1 and 2

Description: Tell learners they will be exploring the imagery and metaphors in the first two stanzas of a poem. Ask a volunteer to read these two stanzas aloud slowly, pausing briefly where needed and placing stress on key words and syllables. Then allow two minutes for all learners to read the stanzas again silently to themselves and reflect on the language and meaning.

Organise learners into pairs to complete Activities 1 and 2, making notes as they do so. Explain that they will be sharing these notes with the rest of the class later. Remind learners to look at the picture and read the learner's notes in the Learner's Book, along with the activity instructions.

Monitor how well learners are working. Help any pairs that might have stalled in their discussion by asking questions: *Flowers grow from buds then age over the seasons, and the sun rises and sets in a day – what do these images communicate about time? What metaphors would you use to show that time is precious and often seems to pass too quickly, especially as we age?*

Afterwards, ask learners to share their notes on Activities 1 and 2 with the class. Discuss the similarities and differences between learners' notes.

> **Differentiation ideas:**

- Support: Draw some diagrams on the board to show the connections between time, flowers and the sun. For example, a linear process might be shown as:

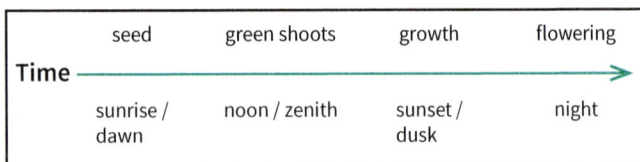

	seed	green shoots	growth	flowering
Time				→
	sunrise / dawn	noon / zenith	sunset / dusk	night

Or repeating cycles may be shown as:

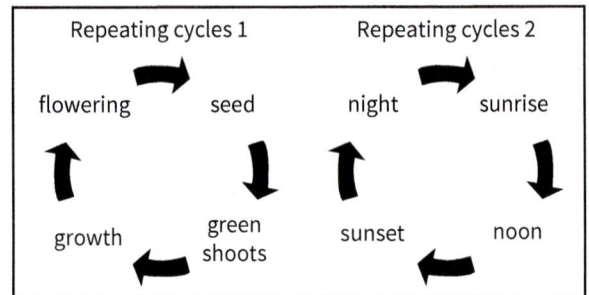

- Challenge: Add the following task to Activity 2. Create a list of metaphors that show the passing of time as instructed, then ask learners to list two or three metaphors that show opposite ideas about time, such as eternity, infinity, endlessness, agelessness or changelessness. These metaphors could be shared during class feedback. You could then discuss how the metaphors about passing time differ from those about timelessness.

> **Assessment ideas:** Listen closely to learners as they share their notes with the rest of the class. Do they:

- connect the ageing of flowers to the ageing of people (from youth to old age)
- connect the idea of enjoying the beauty and freshness of flowers with the beauty and energy of youth
- express ideas about the title of the poem or the first line (for example, 'make the most of time' can mean not to waste time but also to use the time we have well, which could be one interpretation of the first line).

2 Understanding poetic structure and language (40 minutes)

Learning intentions: Explore the effect of images and language choices in a poem. Consider how a poem's structure can be used to convey meaning.

Resources: Learner's Book, Session 4.2, 'To Make Much of Time', Activities 3 and 4

Description: Read the last two stanzas of the poem as a class. Explain that learners should use short quotations to support their answers to Activity 3. Remind them to use the Glossary in the Learner's Book to help them explore the meaning of the poem. They should then complete the activity on their own.

Next, point out that 'To Make Much of Time' uses end rhyme and has a regular repeating ABAB rhyme scheme. There is also a repeating pattern of unstressed and stressed syllables. Some people might hear 'extra' syllables, depending on how a reader pronounces specific words, for example, *a-fly-ing* (three syllable) versus *afly-ing* (two) or *to-mor-row* (three) versus *t'mor-row* (two).

Organise learners into pairs and give them 10–15 minutes to read the poem aloud to each other and make notes in response to Activity 4.

> **Differentiation ideas:**

- Support: Show learners how to use short quotations to support their answers to Activity 3 by writing an example on the board: *In these stanzas, the poet advises that young people should make the most of their 'prime', 'best' and first time before it is 'lost', 'spent' or used up. In other words, his advice is that people should use their time well when they are young, when 'youth and blood are warmer', before they get too old.*

- Challenge: Give learners 10 minutes to make notes on their answers to Activity 3, then another 10 minutes to write two paragraphs in answer to this question: *Do you see the poem 'To Make Much of Time' as a warning to young people or a celebration of youth? Give reasons for your answer and refer to specific language the poet uses.*

> **Assessment ideas:** Ask learners to swap answers with a partner and feed back on their explanations. Could learners' answers be improved? If so, how?

3   Interpreting meaning (25 minutes)

Learning intention: Discuss how personal beliefs can affect interpretations of a poem.

Resources: Learner's Book, Session 4.2, '*Carpe diem* poetry: inspiring the young?', Activity 5

Description: Read the introductory text and the extract about *carpe diem* poetry to the class. Point out that *carpe diem* is often translated as 'seize the day', but it can also be translated as 'plucking the day', as in plucking and gathering ripening fruits or flowers. Both translations highlight the importance of the present time, either for taking action (to prepare for an uncertain future) or for the enjoyment of opportunities (which might not come again).

Organise learners into groups to discuss the three bullet points in Activity 5. Remind them that all group members should contribute to the discussion and that they should explore in detail any points of disagreement.

> **Differentiation ideas:**

- Support: Write a list of good discussion practices on the board to refer to, such as taking turns, listening respectfully, asking questions and ensuring everyone has an opportunity to contribute.

- Challenge: Ask learners to write a short summary of the discussion, focusing on points of agreement and disagreement.

> **Assessment ideas:** Assess learners' active learning progress by listening carefully to their talk and seeing how well their discussion skills have developed. For example, have any learners increased in confidence in terms of guiding a discussion and ensuring other group members get a chance to contribute?

4   Writing a poem about time (35 minutes)

Learning intention: Write a poem using genre features.

Resources: Learner's Book, Session 4.2, Activity 6

Description: Ask learners to recall the metaphors describing the passing of time they created for Activity 2 and explain that they may wish to use these in the last activity in this session. As a class, read the Writing tip and the instructions for Activity 6. Emphasise that learners' poems should be no longer than 16 lines, but that they can experiment with rhyme and rhythm. They then write their poems.

> **Differentiation ideas:**

- Support: Remind learners that metaphors suggest shared qualities between two different things. Give the following examples:

  - *stealing time* or *thief of time* (we can steal someone's possessions or money because they are tangible objects, but time is not an object so these metaphors suggest time is a thing we can get more of, like money)

  - *time slipping through my fingers* (time cannot be held on to physically any more than water can).

- Challenge: Ask learners to write their poems using the same structure as 'To Make Much of Time': a rhyme structure of ABAB, a repeating pattern of unstressed and stressed syllables and alternating lines of eight and six syllables (with some variations if needed).

> **Assessment ideas:** Learners should complete the Self-assessment in the Learner's Book to reflect on their writing.

Plenary idea

Language and meaning (10 minutes)

Description: Write out an annotated first line of 'To Make Much of Time' on the board, noting the stressed and unstressed syllables:

/ ˘ ˘ / ˘ / ˘ /
Gather | ye rose | buds while | ye may

Point out that the language of this line can be analysed in several ways:

- Grammar: *Gather* is an imperative verb, making this an imperative sentence (a sentence that gives an order or command).

- Sound: The poem starts a stressed/unstressed syllable pattern (*GATHer*) rather than an unstressed/stressed pattern like the rest of the poem.

- Imagery: A 'rosebud' is a baby flower and a flower has a short life.

Organise learners into pairs and ask them to reread the whole poem before discussing how the poet has created meaning through language choices related to grammar, sound and imagery.

> ### CROSS-CURRICULAR LINK
>
> Science (organisms and the environment): In this session, learners have explored how a poem metaphorically represents time using imagery from nature, for example flowers and the sun. Learners could research the timings of natural processes, such as the carbon cycle or atmospheric change over millions of years. After researching these processes, learners could use diagrams, charts, graphs and text to present their findings in class.

Homework idea

Learners should complete Workbook Session 4.2.

4.3 The tribe that time forgot

LEARNING PLAN		
Learning objectives	**Learning intentions**	**Success criteria**
9Ri.02, 9Ri.04, 9Ri.07, 9Ra.02, 9Wc.03, 9Wc.04, 9Wc.05, 9SLm.01, 9SLm.03, 9SLm.04, 9SLm.05, 9SLp.04, 9SLp.05	Learners will: • give a personal reaction to an informative article • identify meaning and bias in a text • justify their opinions on a topic • write and perform a persuasive speech.	Learners can: • give a personal response to an informative article • identify and interpret meanings and bias in a non-fiction article • justify their opinion in a discussion • write and perform an effective speech using a range of persuasive techniques.

LANGUAGE SUPPORT

The article in this session uses commas to add information and clarify meaning. It may benefit learners to recap the use of commas for these purposes.

Begin by writing the following sentence from the article on the board without the commas, then add them in to show how they clarify meaning:

- *Members of the inner zone of about 800 people, or 40 families, dress in white, as opposed to the black attire worn in the outer zone, and they follow the Baduy traditions much more strictly.*

You can describe the use of commas in this sentence in the following ways:

- Bracketing phrases: *Members of the inner zone of about 800 people (or 40 families) dress in white (as opposed to the black attire worn in the outer zone) and they follow the Baduy traditions much more strictly.*

- Indicating extra information about the subject of the clause. The <u>subject</u> and the essential ideas of the sentence are linked as follows: <u>*Members of the inner zone of about 800 people*</u> *dress in white and they follow the Baduy traditions much more strictly.*

Language worksheet 4.1 offers further practise with commas.

Starter idea

Technology – good or bad? (15 minutes)

Resources: Learner's Book, Session 4.3, Getting started activity

Description: Write the following list on the board: *access to information, isolation from other people, entertainment, connection to other people, wasting time / distraction, cyberbullying, emergencies, addiction, accidents, videos and photos.*

Organise learners into small groups and give them five minutes to decide which items in the list are benefits and which are disadvantages of mobile phones. Afterwards, ask groups to share their decisions with the rest of the class. After completing the pair discussion in the Getting started activity, discuss as a class whether the impact of mobile phones is good, bad or both.

Main teaching ideas

1 Discuss bias and meaning in an article (40 minutes)

Learning intentions: Give a personal reaction to an informative article. Identify meaning and bias in a text.

Resources: Learner's Book, Session 4.3, 'The tribe that time forgot', Activities 1 and 2

Description: Give learners five minutes to describe their typical day with the person sitting next to them. In their description, they should emphasise every time they use technology (or things made using

technology), such as phones, televisions, computers, the internet, hot water, heating, air conditioning, transport, packaged food/snacks, microwave oven/electric or gas cooker, clothing/footwear, etc.

After the discussions, ask learners: *What do you think it would be like living without any of the technology you typically use?* Take a few responses.

Read the article 'The tribe that time forgot' to the class, then ask learners to complete Activity 1 on their own. Remind them to use the Glossary in the Learner's Book as they reread the article and make notes.

After 15–20 minutes, organise learners into pairs. Before they work on Activity 2, recap the concept of bias. Write the following questions on the board to help them while responding to the activity.

- Is the writer biased or not?

- If the writer is biased, what are they biased towards or against?

- What specific examples of language that shows bias can you find?

- Do you agree with the writer or not?

> **Differentiation ideas:**

- Support: Point out some language from the article that shows bias and give learners some explanations and follow-up questions. For example, you could highlight *forbid*, *long list of taboos* and *Baduy who break the rules are banished* and explain that these words and phrases have strong negative connotations of living under restrictive rules. Ask whether the writer agrees or disagrees with the rules and how they know this.

- Challenge: For Activity 2, ask pairs to write a paragraph together explaining whether the writer is biased or not. They should use short quotations from the article to support their views.

> **Assessment ideas:** Activity 2 requires learners to carefully read the article with sensitive awareness of the language used. In the paired discussions, listen for whether learners refer to specific language as evidence of bias, and assess whether the example they refer to supports their views or not.

2 Explaining opinions (25 minutes)

Learning intention: Justify opinions on a topic.

Resources: Learner's Book, Session 4.3, Activity 3

Description: Set up this discussion topic by giving some examples of technology/inventions that you would like to 'uninvent', for example, something small could be the annoying door entry chimes in shops and something big could be vehicles that pollute the air. Point out that by 'uninventing' them, your intention would be to remove the negative effects of these things from the world. Emphasise that learners should create their lists of eight items by considering technology/inventions that have negative effects.

Organise learners into pairs and give them 15–20 minutes to complete Activity 3. In the last five minutes, ask learners to share the invention/technology they would 'uninvent' with the rest of the class.

> **Differentiation ideas:**

- Support: Write a list on the board of technology/inventions that could be 'uninvented' that learners can discuss. Small things could be door chimes, video games, chewing gum or pop-up adverts on web pages. Big things might be plastic packaging, fossil fuels, etc. Allow them to focus their discussion on why they would 'uninvent' one of these ideas.

- Challenge: Put learners into groups of four and explain that for Activity 3 they should discuss a list of eight items and collectively agree why one of those items should be

'uninvented'. Afterwards, ask groups to share which item they would uninvent with the class and explain the group's reasons.

> **Assessment ideas:** Assess whether learners give *reasons* for why they would 'uninvent' a specific technology/invention. Also, assess the thinking behind learner's reasoning:

- Has the learner used logical or rational thinking in considering negative effects (such as saying getting rid of fossil fuels would help reduce global climate warming)?

- Even for the smaller items, has the learner used humour intelligently to get their point across (such as saying that in a world without video games children would have more time to spend with their parents – but is that a good thing or a bad thing!).

3 Writing and delivering a speech (60 minutes)

Learning intention: Write and perform a persuasive speech.

Resources: Learner's Book, Session 4.3, Activities 4 and 5; Language worksheet 4.1

Description: Using the Language support feature at the start of the session, remind learners about the use of commas. To consolidate their understanding, ask learners to complete Language worksheet 4.1.

Explain what makes speeches powerful: skilful use of language (stylish words or simple, easily understood words and phrases that people strongly relate to), memorable phrases or slogans (well-known speeches are often remembered because of key phrases) and connecting with the audience (people respond when you speak about what is important to them).

Next, give learners some examples of the persuasive techniques mentioned in the Learner's Book:

- Hyperbole: *He's so rich money pours out from his pockets.*

- Rhetorical questions: *If we rid the world of this evil, would it not be a better world?* (Note also the repetition of *world* and emotive language with strong negative connotations, such as *rid* and *evil*.)

- Statistics: 'The United States is home to 5 per cent of the world's population, but 25 per cent of the world's prisoners.' These words and statistics were used by US President Barak Obama to persuade people of the need to reduce numbers in American prisons.

- Triples and repetition: *I came, I saw, I conquered*; *tough on crime, tough on the causes of crime*.

- Emotive language and words with strong positive or negative connotations: freedom, peace, life, liberty, happiness, war, sickness, disease, poverty.

- Figurative language: *Our land will be a land of milk and honey*. (This example also uses repetition of *land* and emotive language with positive connotations in *milk* and *honey*.)

- Direct address and pronouns: *Think about that*. Also, remind learners they can use 'you' to speak to everyone in the audience directly and 'we' and 'us' to make it seem that they and the audience are on the same side.

- Imperatives: *Think about that* is also an imperative or command to the audience.

Give learners 15–20 minutes to write and rehearse their two-minute speech using some of these persuasive techniques.

For Activity 5, learners should rehearse their speeches, using gestures and tone of voice. They should then perform their speeches to the class. When all learners have given their speeches, ask for a show of hands to vote on which technology/invention they would 'uninvent'.

> **Differentiation ideas:**

- Support: Give learners an outline for writing their speech. For example:

  - Say what technology/invention you believe is negative/evil (use emotive words and figurative language).

  - Say why it harms and damages the world – describe all the reasons and lead up to the most convincing reason (use rhetorical questions, direct address and imperatives).

  - Say how the world will be better when it is 'uninvented' (use direct address, imperatives, pronouns, emotive words and figurative language).

- Challenge: Ask learners to use at least one example of every persuasive technique listed in the Learner's Book in their speech.

> **Assessment ideas:** Learners should use the Reflection questions to self-assess their writing and delivery of their speech.

Plenary idea

Thinking independently (10 minutes)

Description: Point out that language is being used to persuade us more often than we might realise, for example by friends and family, advertising to make us buy things, newspapers to influence our opinions and politicians giving speeches so we will support them. Encourage learners to recognise the two ways in which we experience the persuasive techniques listed above – that is, when we use them to persuade others and when others use them to persuade us.

Explain that it can be useful to be open to being persuaded and changing one's mind – but it can also be useful to defend yourself against being persuaded when you do not want to be, such as resisting advertising when you do not need or want that product.

Organise learners into pairs and ask them to discuss how they might remember the persuasive techniques so they can recognise when they are being used (or recognise opportunities for using them on other people!).

Homework ideas

Learners should complete Workbook Session 4.3.

4.4 The time tornado

LEARNING PLAN

Learning objectives	Learning intentions	Success criteria
9Rv.02, 9Rg.03, 9Rs.01, 9Ri.01, 9Ri.07, 9Ww.01, 9Ww.03, 9Wg,03, 9Wc.01, 9SLs.01	Learners will: • discuss genre features in relation to a story • explore the structure and effect of a story opening • consider how verb choices convey action, pace and atmosphere • write an effective story opening.	Learners can: • make notes on the features of a genre, then identify those features in a story opening • analyse the effect of a story opening • understand how verb choices can convey action and establish a change in mood and pace • write an effective story opening using structural and grammatical features to show a shift in pace.

LANGUAGE SUPPORT

In this session, learners are asked to examine verbs that convey action. Verbs can be categorised in two groups: dynamic and state verbs. Distinguishing between these types will help learners understand their different effects.

Dynamic or event verbs express physical actions (*jump*, *leap*, *dance*). They also include mental actions (*think*) and the activity of our senses (*see*, *hear*, *taste*, *watch*, *listen*, *savour*).

State or stative verbs express states of being in which there is no obvious action (*possess*, *believe*, *know*, *understand*).

Some verbs can function in both categories:
• I can smell something wonderful. (dynamic)
  Sour milk smells awful. (state)
• I have dinner at 7 p.m. every evening. (dynamic)
  I have a cold. (state)

The important thing to note is the contrast in meaning:
• states are described as permanent, semi-permanent or unchanging situations
• events are described as dynamic actions, showing change or drama.

Language worksheet 4.2 gives learners more practice in dynamic verbs.

Common misconception

Misconception	How to identify	How to overcome
State verbs cannot express a dynamic meaning.	Write the following examples on the board and ask learners if they describe states or events: • *You're being difficult.* • *We're having a celebration.* Discuss learners' responses.	Point out that the verbs *be*, *being* and *have* are often categorised as state verbs, but in these examples they have a dynamic meaning – that is, they describe: • someone acting in a 'difficult' way • the event of a party/celebration.

Starter idea

Getting to grips with story openings (15 minutes)

Resources: Learner's Book, Session 4.4, Getting started activity

Description: Organise learners into groups of three and give them 5–10 minutes to discuss the Getting started activity. They should first write a list of the story openings their group likes best then write another list of the reasons why they, as readers, enjoy these openings. Come together at the end to briefly share ideas as a class.

Main teaching ideas

1 Identifying genre (40 minutes)

Learning intention: Discuss genre features in relation to a story.

Resources: Learner's Book, Session 4.4, *Tanglewreck* Extract 1, Activities 1 and 2

Note: Please note that the *Tanglewreck* extracts have been abridged in order to lower the language level.

> ⬇ **Download the audioscript for Activity 1 on Cambridge GO (Track 29).**

Description: Tell learners they will be making notes as they listen to a recording of someone describing features of the fantasy genre. Before playing the audio, read the Listening tip to learners and list the tips included there, and any others you think may be useful, on the board for learners to refer to. You could suggest some words that would signal key information, such as *fantasy, genre, features, real, strange, magical, opening, ending, themes* and *morals*). Then play the audio and ask learners to make their notes for Activity 1.

Organise learners into pairs and ask them to read Extract 1 of *Tanglewreck*, thinking about the features of fantasy stories that they have just heard about. They should complete Activity 2 together, making comparisons between their notes from Activity 1 and Extract 1 so they can successfully identify genre features in the extract.

> **Differentiation ideas:**

• Support: Before playing the audio, ask learners to write down the following headings and leave space underneath them for taking notes: *Events, ideas and characters*; *Types of worlds*; *Openings*; *Endings*; *Journeys and time*; *Morals*; *Good versus evil*. Remind learners to listen for key words and, when they hear one, to make a note under the appropriate heading or sub-heading.

• Challenge: For Activity 2, ask learner pairs to write a 150–200-word summary (in paragraphs) of the genre features of fantasy stories.

> **Assessment ideas:** Check learners' notes from Activity 1 to ensure they have used an appropriate note-taking method. Assess whether their method helped them to capture key information about fantasy stories: strange or magical events, ideas, objects and people that are not possible in the real world; journeys; characters who learn about themselves; time being played with; openings involving an immediate conflict; themes of good and evil.

2 Analysing a fantasy story opening (25 minutes)

Learning intention: Explore the structure and effect of a story opening.

Resources: Learner's Book, Session 4.4, *Tanglewreck* Extract 1, Activity 3

Description: Ask a volunteer to read Extract 1 to the class. Then read the instructions for Activity 3 to learners. Emphasise that story openings are very important in story structure, and that in the opening, writers usually establish plot and themes, set the scene and atmosphere and introduce characters. Learners should then write the answers to Activity 3 independently.

> **Differentiation ideas:**

- Support: Outline the PEA technique to learners for them to use in their response to Activity 3:

  - **P**oint: Make a point about the text or the language.

  - **E**vidence: Refer to a specific part of the text or use a short quotation as evidence.

  - **A**nalysis: Analyse and explain the effect of the evidence on the reader (for example how the text or language functions, their effect on the reader or how they show the writer's purpose).

- Challenge: Ask learners to write two or three sentences analysing how the extract uses description and imagery to explore ideas about time.

> **Assessment ideas:** Assess if learners have identified specific examples of 'mysterious events' in Extract 1 and how clearly they have explained the effects of these on the reader.

3 Writing fantasy (60 minutes)

Learning intentions: Consider how verb choices convey action, pace and atmosphere. Write an effective story opening.

Resources: Learner's Book, Session 4.4, Activities 4 and 5; Language worksheet 4.2

Description: Read the Language focus information as a class, then discuss dynamic and state verbs using the Language support feature at the start of the session. Write the examples on the board if necessary, and emphasise the contrast between a dynamic meaning and stative meaning in verb use. Learners should then complete Language worksheet 4.2.

Ask learners to reread Extract 1 and give them 15 minutes to write their analysis for Activity 4.

Introduce Activity 5 by listing some tips for good writing on the board:

- Help readers picture the scene – use imagery that appeals to the senses.

- Create and establish a setting.

- Show *when* the action is happening – past, present or future, or time on another world, the season and time of day.

- Use state verbs to describe semi-permanent situations and dynamic verbs to describe action and dramatic events.

Emphasise that learners need to include a 'Time Tornado' in their story opening. They should then complete Activity 5 on their own.

> **Differentiation ideas:**

- Support: Give learners an outline they can follow for their story opening:

  1 Show the place and time (setting) and the characters doing something that seems ordinary – then dramatically introduce some strange or unusual event.

  2 Vividly describe the strange event, focusing on the use of dynamic verbs to show action, drama and change.

  3 Show the effects of the unusual event on your characters (use imagery that appeals to the senses).

  4 End with an unanswered question, a mystery or puzzle.

- Challenge: As well as using dynamic verbs, ask learners to include verbs in the present tense, considering what effect this has on their story.

> **Assessment ideas:** Learners should swap story openings with a partner and use the Peer assessment feature in the Learner's Book to give each other feedback.

Plenary idea

The language of action (10 minutes)

Description: Read the following story opening to learners: *The match scratched noisily across the rusted metal of the corrugated iron shed, fizzled, then burst into a sputtering pool of light, the harsh sound and sudden brilliance alike strangely alien in the stillness of the desert night.*

Then read this plainer version: *The match struck across the rusted metal of the corrugated iron shed, then it came alight, the sound and sudden brightness of both seemed strange in the stillness of the desert night.*

Organise learners into pairs and ask them to discuss the differences in language use between the two versions. Why would most readers prefer the original version?

Homework idea

Learners should complete Workbook Session 4.4.

4.5 The visitor

Learning objectives	Learning intentions	Success criteria
9Rg.03, 9Rs.01, 9Ri.01, 9Ri.03, 9Ri.06, 9Ri.09, 9Ra.02, 9Ww.02, 9Ww.03, 9Wv.01, 9Wg.03, 9Ws.01, 9Wc.01, 9Wc.08, 9Wp.01, 9Wp.04, 9SLm.03, 9SLg.02, 9SLg.03, 9SLg.04	Learners will: • consider the effect of withholding information from readers • explore the methods a writer uses to portray a mysterious character • discuss how a story might develop based on events so far • write a chapter containing mysterious events.	Learners can: • understand the effect of withholding information in a story • analyse the techniques a writer uses to make a character seem mysterious • contribute effectively to a discussion on what might happen next in a story • write a chapter of a mystery story using appropriate structural, language and grammatical features.

LANGUAGE SUPPORT

The extract in this session breaks with standard rules for nouns by capitalising the words *Now* and *Then*. To understand the purpose and effect of this deliberate choice, it may be useful to recap the standard rules in English for capitalising nouns, then consider why the writer has 'broken' them.

Common nouns refer to general things. They can be concrete (*house*, *tree*, *door*, *apple*) or abstract (*happiness*, *trust*, *love*, *truth*). Both concrete and abstract nouns can be further subdivided into countable and uncountable nouns. Countable nouns have plural forms, that is, they can be counted. Uncountable nouns have no plural form.

Some nouns can be countable and uncountable (*light*, *glass*).

Proper nouns usually refer to a unique person, place or thing and begin with a capital letter (*Albert Einstein*, *New York*, *Malaysia*, *the Taj Mahal*).

Learners may recall from reading 'The Selfish Giant' that the author capitalised some common nouns such as the Hail, the Snow, the Frost. He did this to personify the weather and make these things unique characters in the story. In *Tanglewreck*, the writer uses a similar technique to make the reader question their ideas about how time functions – a strong theme in the story.

Starter idea

What makes a character mysterious? (10 minutes)

Resources: Learner's Book, Session 4.5, Getting started activity

Description: On the board, list some mysterious characters from books, comics and films, such as Captain Ahab in *Moby-Dick*, Miss Havisham in *Great Expectations*, Sherlock Holmes, Batman, the Joker, Boba Fett from *Star Wars* or Rorschach from *Watchmen*. Then organise learners into small groups and ask them to discuss these and other mysterious characters they know as they complete the Getting started activity.

Main teaching ideas

1 Creating mystery using language and structure (25 minutes)

Learning intentions: Consider the effect of withholding information from readers. Explore the methods a writer uses to portray a mysterious character.

Resources: Learner's Book, Session 4.5, *Tanglewreck* Extract 2, Activities 1–3

Description: Start by explaining the ideas in the Reading tip to learners. Emphasise that a writer's choices of language and grammar are often connected to their purpose, themes, characterisation and the effect they want to create.

Ask a volunteer to read Extract 2 aloud. After the reading, point out that Activities 1, 2 and 3 ask learners to analyse the effects of the writer's use of language when: referring to time (Activity 1), creating mystery through both giving and withholding information about character and setting (Activity 2) and deepening the reader's impressions of Abel Darkwater (Activity 3). Learners should then complete the three activities in pairs.

> **Differentiation ideas:**

- Support: Ask learners questions to get them thinking about specific language choices and their effect: *What are the effects of describing Abel Darkwater as* never late *and his watch* never wrong? Tanglewreck *is called a* great house *with* gates *and a* long ragged driveway – *why has the writer described the house in this way? How is the reader's impression of Abel Darkwater and Tanglewreck deepened by* the house was telling him the beginning of its own past?

- Challenge: Ask pairs to work together to write a paragraph that summarises their analysis and answers to Activities 1, 2 and 3.

> **Assessment ideas:** Listen to learners' discussions to assess how closely they analyse the language of Extract 2. They should refer to specific examples from the text and use precise terms to describe the writer's language choices, such as use of figurative language, capital letters, characterisation, punctuation, repetition and sentence structure.

2 Investigating a mysterious character (25 minutes)

Learning intention: Explore the methods a writer uses to portray a mysterious character.

Resources: Learner's Book, Session 4.5, Activity 4

Description: Read Activity 4 to learners and use the Key word definition to ensure they understand what 'connotations' are. To prepare for the activity, give learners some notes and prompt questions that link to each of the bullets:

- Connotations: Abel sounds like 'able', Darkwater is like 'dark water'. What are the separate connotations of these three words and how do they combine to give his name an overall meaning?

- His ability to understand time: He is *never late*, his watch is *never wrong*, he has *all the time in the world*, and he knows *all time is always present* – what does all this mean?

- What you know about the Age-Gauge: Note that it is capitalised; it indicates the year 1588; it works on *echoes of time*; and Abel's pocket watch has an extra *fourth hand* with a special function. What uses might these special devices have?

- Language and grammatical patterns: What effects are created by the semi-colon, colon and dash (–), and the writer's use of 'and' as well as 'but' as coordinators?

Learners should then write their answers to Activity 4 on their own.

> **Differentiation ideas:**

- Support: Explain to learners that the coordinating conjunction 'but' is used to introduce a contradiction, and that semi-colons, colons and dashes (–) can all be used to introduce surprises or contrasts. Ask learners to find specific examples of these in Extract 2 and write about the effect they have on them as readers in their answer to Activity 4.

- Challenge: Ask learners to write one paragraph that focuses on the first three bullet points of Activity 4 plus two further paragraphs that analyse and explain the effects of language and grammar in the extract (two paragraphs on the fourth bullet point).

> **Assessment ideas:** Assess whether learners' paragraphs refer to specific language examples in Extract 2 and explain their effects on readers.

For example, do learners mention the connotations of *dark* as suggesting something 'unclear', 'unknown' or 'mysterious' and link this to creating the impression of a mysterious character? Do they refer to the use of 'but' to introduce a contradiction and then link this to creating mystery and raising questions that will keep a reader interested the story?

3 What might happen next? (20 minutes)

Learning intention: Discuss how a story might develop based on events so far.

Resources: Learner's Book, Session 4.5, Activity 5

Description: In small groups, give learners 5–10 minutes to come up with one sentence describing what they think will happen next in the story in response to Activity 5. Emphasise that everyone should contribute, take turns and speak respectfully when they have different views.

After the discussion, ask each group to read out their sentence and write these on the board. Groups should then spend the remaining time discussing which of the suggestions is the most likely way for the story to continue, and why.

> **Differentiation ideas:**

- Support: Point out that the *face at the window* could be either a friend or an enemy (antagonist) to Darkwater and suggest that they use this idea of a potential source of conflict as the basis for their prediction about the story.

- Challenge: After listing suggestions on the board, ask groups to pick two of them – the ones they think are *most* and *least* likely to happen next – and discuss their reasons for these choices.

> **Assessment ideas:** Learners could self-assess their participation in the small group discussion using the following questions:

- Did I communicate my ideas clearly so that my peers could easily understand them? If not, how could I communicate my ideas more clearly in future?

- Did I listen carefully to what my peers were saying? If I did not understand them, did I ask helpful questions to help me understand them better? If not, how can I remember to do this in future?

4 Writing and editing a text (60 minutes)

Learning intention: Write a chapter containing mysterious events.

Resources: Learner's Book, Session 4.5, *Tanglewreck* Extract 2, Activities 6 and 7

Description: Read Activity 6 as a class. List some of the language techniques learners have explored in this session on the board: using connotations and giving characters and setting suggestive names; using figurative language; capitalisation of unexpected words; inventing fantasy devices; creating mystery through both giving and withholding information; use of punctuation to create surprise or drama; using coordinating conjunctions such as 'but' to introduce a contradiction.

Give learners 30 minutes to reread Extract 2, then draft the next part of the story for Activity 6.

In the last 10–15 minutes of the lesson ask learners to complete Activity 7 on their own, editing and improving their writing.

> **Differentiation ideas:**

- Support: Offer some suggestions for what might happen next in the story for learners to use in their writing: the *face at the window* is a grey-haired, wrinkly old man with a mysterious-sounding name; he tells Darkwater he knows when and where the next Time Tornado will be; he gives Darkwater a new device and asks him to stop the Time Tornado; after Darkwater leaves he wonders to himself whether he can trust the old man.

- Challenge: Tell learners they must use at least one example of every technique listed on the board in their writing for Activity 6.

> **Assessment ideas:** Learners should complete the Peer assessment feature in the Learner's Book.

Plenary idea

Evaluating other people's work (10 minutes)

Description: After Activity 7, ask learners to swap their newly edited version with a partner. They should use the statements in the Summary checklist in the Learner's Book to assess each other's writing – does their chapter show evidence that they can do all the things listed? They should offer positive and constructive feedback.

Homework idea

Learners should complete Workbook Session 4.5.

4.6 Into the future

LEARNING PLAN

Learning objectives	Learning intentions	Success criteria
9Rv.02, 9Rg.02, 9Rg.03, 9Rg.04, 9Ri.02, 9Wv.01, 9Wg.01, 9Wg.02, 9Wg.05, 9Wc.07, 9SLg.01, 9SLg.02, 9SLg.03, 9SLg.04, 9SLm.01, 9SLm.02, 9SLm.03, 9SLm.05, 9SLr.02	Learners will: • explore the impact of variations in speech • practise group work and discussion skills • consider how a writer creates an informal voice • write in an informal voice.	Learners can: • understand how variations in speech have a different impact on audiences • work effectively in a group, contributing ideas and listening to others • explain the methods a writer uses to create a particular voice • use language, punctuation and grammatical techniques to write in an informal voice.

LANGUAGE SUPPORT

The text in this session uses several contractions to create an informal tone. Contractions are abbreviated and short forms. They are formed by omitting syllables or parts of a word. Some of the main contractions learners will come across in written English are:

• *'s*: he's (he is/has), she's (she is/has), it's (it is/has – not to be confused with possessive *its*)

• *n't*: don't (do not), can't (cannot), won't (will not), shouldn't (should not), wouldn't (would not)

• *'ll*: I'll (I will), he'll (he will), she'll (she will), they'll (they will), it'll (it will)

• *'re*: we're (we are), they're (they are)

• *'ve*: I've (I have), we've (we have), they've (they have)

• *'d*: I'd (I had/would), he'd (he had/would), she'd (she had/would), they'd (they had/would).

Starter idea

Predicting the future (15 minutes)

Resources: Learner's Book, Session 4.6, Getting started activity

Description: Tell learners that people have always tried to make predictions about the future – sometimes the predictions come true, but often they do not. Give some examples of accurate and inaccurate predictions:

• In 1865, Jules Verne imagined a man landing on the moon in his novel *From Earth to the Moon* (the first moon landing was in 1969).

• In 1909, Nikola Tesla speculated that wireless messages from handheld devices would be possible (such as wi-fi and mobile phones).

• In 1932, Albert Einstein thought that nuclear energy would be too difficult to obtain (he changed his mind later when he saw new evidence).

• 20th-century economists predicted a super-efficient 'leisure society', in which people would only work 15 hours a week in the early 21st century.

Put learners into pairs and give them 5–10 minutes to discuss the Getting started activity. Then share ideas as a class.

Main teaching ideas

1 Exploring differences in spoken language (25 minutes)

Learning intention: Explore the impact of variations in speech.

Resources: Learner's Book, Session 4.6, 'Ways of speaking', Activity 1

Description: Read the introductory paragraph under the 'Ways of speaking' heading as a class, then ask two learners each to read one of the transcripts. Outline some language concepts that learners should consider when they discuss the transcripts (you could do this verbally or on the board). These might include the following:

- Audience: Language choices are normally influenced by who we are speaking to.

- Purpose: Speakers alter their language to entertain, inform, persuade, etc.

- Non-fluency vs. fluency: In formal contexts such as giving a speech, speakers aim for fluency; in informal contexts pauses and hesitations are more common.

- Word choice: Some words sound more formal or informal. Using a person's title (Mr, Ms etc.) is formal, *yes* is more formal than *yup*, *uh-huh*, etc.

- Contractions: These can be used in formal speech but too many will sound informal.

- Content: Personal or subjective examples will sound more informal than objective and impersonal examples.

- Tone: Friends may use lots of humour and an exclamatory tone, which would be inappropriate when talking to someone in authority.

Organise learners into pairs and ask them to complete Activity 1 together.

> **Differentiation ideas:**

- Support: Point out one or two of the language differences between the two transcripts. Ask learners to find additional examples and connect them to the concepts outlined above. You could note that Abeed is a friend, while Mr Ganem is a teacher (audience), that Ahmed uses *Er . . .* when speaking with Abeed (non-fluency) or that *yeah* and *kids* are informal

word choices compared to *I think* and *students* in the second transcript.

- Challenge: Ask pairs to write one paragraph analysing the effects of the language differences in the two transcripts.

> **Assessment ideas:** Listen to learners discuss the language differences between the two transcripts and note if they: identify specific examples, link these examples to the language concepts you have outlined and describe the effects the language examples have.

2 Making predictions (40 minutes)

Learning intention: Practise group work and discussion skills.

Resources: Learner's Book, Session 4.6, 'The future is bright', Activities 2 and 3

Description: Tell learners they will be discussing some fun and interesting predictions for the future, choosing which they would most like to come true, then explaining why to the class.

Organise learners into groups and give them 25 minutes to discuss Activity 2. Suggest they spend five minutes deciding roles (for example scribe, chairperson), five minutes discussing each prediction, and then five minutes planning how to present the group's ideas to the class. Remind learners to read the activity instructions and the Speaking tip carefully before they start their discussions.

After 25 minutes, move on to Activity 3 and ask each group to present their ideas to the class according to the roles they planned. Before the groups start presenting, ask learners to make notes on the differences they observe in how their peers speak when in small groups compared to speaking to the whole class.

> **Differentiation ideas:**

- Support: Give learners some questions to help them assess each prediction:

  - How likely is the prediction? Does it seem like a possible development from the present or something unbelievable or impossible?

  - If the prediction came true what effects would it have? Would positive effects outweigh negative effects?

  - Which prediction do you personally find the most appealing even if it seems unbelievable? Why do you find this prediction so appealing?

- Challenge: Ask groups to present their ideas on all three predictions, that is, to outline the advantages and disadvantages of each, to say if it would improve the world or not, to rate the three predictions in order of preference (1 for the best) and explain why they gave each prediction that rating.

> **Assessment ideas:** Learners should complete the Reflection feature to self-assess their performance in the discussion and when speaking to the class.

3 Analysing informality (60 minutes)

Learning intentions: Consider how a writer creates an informal voice. Write in an informal voice.

Resources: Learner's Book, Session 4.6, Activities 4 and 5

Description: Read Activity 4 as a class, then ask learners to create headings in their notebooks from the bullet points in Activity 4: *Punctuation*, *Pronouns*, *Sentence types*, *Repetition*.

Give learners 20 minutes to find language examples from the text to go under each heading. They should also write notes analysing and explaining the effect of each language example on the reader. Emphasise that they should explain *how* the language is helpful in creating a feeling or tone of informality.

Next, read Activity 5 and the Writing tip to learners. Explain that they should use punctuation and pronouns, variation in sentence types, and repeated words, phrases and structures in a similar way to the text in order to create an informal tone in their own writing. Remind learners that their audience is readers of their own age.

Allow 30 minutes for learners to complete Activity 5 on their own. When they have finished, ask for volunteers to read their writing aloud to the class.

> **Differentiation ideas:**

- Support: Write some language terms and examples (in random order) on the board as hints for what learners can look for (for example *'No more'*, *minor sentences*, *'you'*, *'your'*, *rhetorical questions*, *exclamations*, *ellipsis*) before they continue the analysis on their own.

- Challenge: For Activity 5, ask learners to spend 15–20 minutes writing an informal version, then move on to writing a second version with more formal language. Afterwards, they should reflect on the specific changes they made between the informal and formal versions and what effects these have.

> **Assessment ideas:** Assess learners' writing for Activity 5 by checking if they have used similar techniques to those present in 'The future is bright' text:

- punctuation: rhetorical questions, exclamations and ellipsis

- pronouns: second person pronouns 'you' and 'your'

- sentence types: minor sentences (*No more teachers.*)

- repetition of key words or phrases (*No more . . .*).

Plenary idea

Modifying language for audience and context (10 minutes)

Description: Draw the following 'formality scale' on the board:

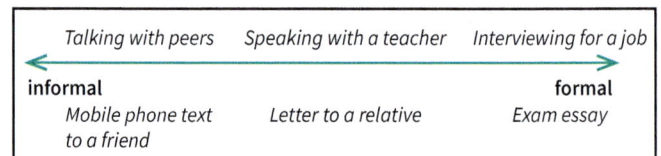

Talking with peers	Speaking with a teacher	Interviewing for a job
←		→
informal		**formal**
Mobile phone text to a friend	Letter to a relative	Exam essay

Organise learners into small groups and ask them to discuss how they would use language differently when interviewing for a job compared to talking to a friend, and writing in an English exam compared to texting a friend.

Homework idea

Learners should complete Workbook Session 4.6.

PROJECT GUIDANCE

This project invites learners to use their imagination, envisage how the world could be better and say what they think is important in life and to the world. You could introduce this project with a talk outlining some of the areas learners could consider and providing them with positive, encouraging suggestions about how to approach the tasks. Outline some general categories that affect the lives of ordinary people so that learners consider a wide range of ideas.

Technology and inventions

Although it would be useful for learners to consider non-technological things that could improve the world, they will naturally consider possible improvements in technology and new inventions. You could point out some inventions from the past that revolutionised society, and emphasise that technology can have far-reaching social effects beyond simple convenience. Examples might include the wheel, the printing press, sewers and indoor plumbing, the telegraph, the automobile (internal combustion engine), aeroplanes, space flight, the internet and smartphones.

Changes in society

Point out that there have been many political changes in history. For example, in the past, many societies were ruled by kings and queens. Democracy and voting came later and then not always to everybody equally. Sometimes only landowners were allowed to vote and later only men. Women only got the vote in the 20th century in many parts of the world.

The environment

Finally, learners could consider things that have an environmental impact, such as a car that does not cause pollution or some change to how society is organised such as political methods to reduce wealth inequality or a shift to homeworking to reduce pollution from transport. Point out to learners that many things can have combined technological and social effects.

Suggested approach:

- Discussing and planning: Learners meet as a group and discuss how they will carry out further research.

- Research and assembling research: Learners meet and discuss which research will be in the final presentation.

- Creating the presentation: Learners plan and write their talk and presentation. This should include: why they have chosen these four things; how they will benefit people; how you could make it happen. Learners should aim for a 10-minute talk and decide whether to use visual aids or not.

- Delivering the presentation: Ask learners to try to show their peers why the things they have chosen would make the world a better place!

> 5 That's entertainment

Unit plan

Session	Approximate number of learning hours	Outline of learning content	Resources
5.1 Leaving Jamaica	2 hours, 30 minutes	Learners read a drama script, explore the features and importance of performance in comedy and consider how character is conveyed.	Learner's Book Session 5.1 Workbook Session 5.1
5.2 Arriving in England	2 hours, 30 minutes	Learners perform a comedy scene, explore how contrast is used to create humour, respond to familiar situations and stereotypes and write their own comedy scene.	Learner's Book Session 5.2 Workbook Session 5.2 ⬇ Differentiated worksheets 5A, 5B and 5C
5.3 *The Boy Who Harnessed the Wind*	2 hours, 30 minutes	Learners consider the importance of titles, explore the structure of autobiographies, consider how figurative language adds meaning and effect and write a first-person account.	Learner's Book Session 5.3 Workbook Session 5.3
5.4 K-pop	2 hours, 30 minutes	Learners explore two texts on similar themes, consider features of non-fiction and analyse how context affects responses.	Learner's Book Session 5.4 Workbook Session 5.4
5.5 Animals and entertainment	2 hours, 15 minutes	Learners react to a persuasive text, identify political language and explore how contexts affect interpretations.	Learner's Book Session 5.5 Workbook Session 5.5 ⬇ Language worksheet 5.1
5.6 The benefits of zoos	2 hours, 45 minutes	Learners read an opinion article, compare arguments in two related texts, explore language, punctuation and grammar choices, and write a discursive response.	Learner's Book Session 5.6 Workbook Session 5.6 ⬇ Language worksheet 5.2

BACKGROUND KNOWLEDGE

For the teacher

This unit uses some entertaining and engaging texts to explore issues through comedy, fiction and debate. To prepare for these sessions, it would be useful to read the play *Small Island* and read the novel by Andrea Levy, or watch the film of *The Boy Who Harnessed the Wind* by William Kamkwamba and Bryan Mealer. You may also wish to research the cultural phenomenon of K-pop from South Korea and read up on arguments for and against zoos.

CONTINUED

The following grammatical and spelling concepts are covered in this unit:

- standard and non-standard English, including dialects
- past perfect tense
- modal verbs to express obligation
- rhetorical questions
- adverbs of manner and degree.

It may be useful to read up on these concepts before explaining them to learners, if you are not already confident in how they are defined and applied.

For the learner

Any familiarity with *Small Island* and the novel or film version of *The Boy Who Harnessed the Wind* will be of use.

Learners may be familiar with some of the issues in the second half of the unit, such as the pros and cons of zoos and K-pop, and they may have strong opinions on such issues. This unit encourages them to consider different viewpoints, debate their own views and their own contexts and write in a balanced way. It may help to provide support for the functional language learners may need for these activities.

The grammatical and spelling concepts in this unit should build on learners' prior knowledge – for example, learners will know about modal verbs and adverbs; however, they will be asked to develop that knowledge by considering the nuance in meaning of different types of modal verbs and adverbs. Encourage learners to use their knowledge of expressing a personal response and writing persuasively to help them contribute to a debate.

TEACHING SKILLS FOCUS

Skills for life

It is the role of teachers to prepare learners so that they can succeed in a fast-changing world. So, how can you give learners the skills and competencies they need to succeed through all the levels of their education and then into the world of 21st-century work? These skills and competencies have been grouped into the following six main areas, which can be successfully delivered through your teaching: creativity, collaboration, communication, critical thinking, learning to learn and social responsibilities. The activities and project in this unit focus on collaboration and communication.

Learners will have the opportunity to develop the following three key competencies of collaboration:

- taking personal responsibility for their own contribution to a group task

- listening respectfully and responding constructively to others' contributions
- managing the sharing of tasks in a project.

They will also focus on the following key competencies within the area of communication:

- using appropriate language/register for context
- managing conversations
- overcoming one's own language gaps
- participating with confidence and clarity
- supporting others to communicate successfully
- structuring content
- using language for effect.

5.1 Leaving Jamaica

LEARNING PLAN

Learning objectives	Learning intentions	Success criteria
9Rv.02, 9Rs.01, 9Ri.01, 9Ri.03, 9Ri.04, 9SLs.01, 9SLp.01, 9SLp.02, 9SLp.03	Learners will: • read an unseen drama script • identify features of the comedy genre • explore the importance of performance in creating comedy • consider the way asides are used to convey character and situation.	Learners can: • read an unseen dramatic comedy accurately, reading ahead when necessary • understand the genre features of comedy • explain how comedy is conveyed through words and actions in a dramatic performance • explain how asides are used to convey character and create effects in drama.

LANGUAGE SUPPORT

Learners may need support understanding the construction and meaning of the non-standard language in the playscript. You may wish to review learners' understanding of the difference between standard language (for example British English, American English, Indian English, etc.) and non-standard language (e.g. regional dialects). Remind learners that standard varieties differ in terms pronunciation, but there are not many grammatical differences. In contrast, non-standard varieties tend to differ more from each other. Example of non-standard language from Extract 1 of the play involve missing words, incorrect pronouns and verbs that do not agree with subjects.

GILBERT	*You seen how much it cost?* (<u>Have</u> you seen how much it <u>costs</u>?)
GILBERT	*I think me ears playing a trick on me.* (I think <u>my</u> ears <u>are</u> playing a trick on me.)
GILBERT	*How I ever be a lawyer if I stay here?* (How <u>will</u> I ever be a lawyer if I stay here?)
HORTENSE	*No one will feel sorry for I.* (No one will feel sorry for <u>me</u>.)

Common misconception

Misconception	How to identify	How to overcome
You should never use non-standard English in writing.	Ask learners which of these sentences is 'incorrect'? • I don't have any money. • I don't have no money. Learners will probably identify the second sentence. Ask learners why they think it is incorrect. Ask learners which of these sentences is 'incorrect'? • So, you are come at last. • So, you have come at last. Learners will probably identify the first sentence. Ask learners why they think it is incorrect. Explain that the first sentence was written by Jane Austen using a standard English tense form from her time.	Explain that neither standard nor non-standard English are incorrect. Simply put, non-standard English is exactly what it says it is: it is not standard English! There is not a single form of non-standard English. In addition, as language is always evolving, standard English does not always stay the same. Learners should be taught the difference and when standard English and formal language are required to suit the purpose and audience of their spoken or written work.

Starter idea

What makes you laugh? (10 minutes)

Resources: Learner's Book, Session 5.1, Getting started activity

Description: Ask learners to discuss the books, plays and films that make them laugh and to identify what it is about them they find funny. Is it the characters? Is it the setting? Is it the plot? Is it a mix of all of three? Discuss learners' ideas briefly as a class and list any genres of comedy that come up (for example sitcoms, satire, black comedy, slapstick).

Main teaching ideas

1 Performing a comedy scene (35 minutes)

Learning intention: Read an unseen drama script.

Resources: Learner's Book, Session 5.1, *Small Island* Extract 1, Activity 1

Description: Introduce the play *Small Island* and explain that it is a dramatic comedy. Ask learners what they would expect a dramatic comedy to be like. Introduce the characters of Gilbert and Hortense and the scene's physical and historical settings. Briefly discuss anything learners know about the 'Windrush generation'.

Learners should read through the whole extract in pairs for the first time, reading the dialogue and stage directions aloud. Refer learners to the Speaking tip. Ask if they noticed any examples of non-standard language as they were reading. Were there any words or phrases that blocked their understanding? One of the key competencies of communication in skills for life is overcoming one's own language gaps. Ask learners to reread the extract on their own to identify anything that is blocking their understanding (this could be standard or non-standard English). They should then discuss this with their partner to see if they can work out the meanings together. Ask learners to share anything they still cannot understand, in particular any non-standard words or phrases.

Learners should complete Activity 1 in pairs. Following a discussion on how to bring out the humour, learners should perform the extract a second time and experiment with different ways of performing the line they have identified.

> **Differentiation ideas:**

• Support: Use the Language support and Common misconception above to help learners identify and understand the difference between standard and non-standard language.

- Challenge: Ask learners to write down any dialect phrases from their country or region – for example: in Indian English, 'I have a doubt' meaning 'I suspect'; in South African English, 'now-now' meaning sometime later.

> **Assessment ideas:** Listen to the pairs as they read the extract aloud. This will allow you to assess learners' accuracy, fluency and expression. Ask questions to improve their performance: *How do you think Gilbert is feeling at this point? What tone would he use? What do you think Hortense thinks of Gilbert? What does she want? How would that affect how she speaks to him?*

2 What makes comedy? (60 minutes)

Learning intentions: Identify features of the comedy genre. Explore the importance of performance in creating comedy.

Resources: Learner's Book, Session 5.1, Activities 2 and 3

> **⤓ Download the audioscript for Activity 2 from Cambridge GO (Track 36).**

Description: Introduce Activity 2 and explain that learners will be listening to an interview with two people talking about the features of the comedy genre. Play the audio for the first time and ask learners to make brief notes on those features as they listen.

Share the Listening tip. Allow learners some time to organise and refine their notes before playing the audio again. Learners should take brief notes again and then combine them with their organised notes from before. If necessary, play the audio for a third time while learners make and then refine their notes. Ask learners to share and discuss their notes with a partner, then discuss as a class.

Ask learners to discuss which features from their notes they can find in Extract 1, then to recall how you defined the genre of *Small Island* at the start of this session (a dramatic comedy). How does this fit with what they have learnt about the features of the comedy genre?

Now ask learners to join with their partner from Activity 1 and perform the scene again in response to Activity 3. This time they should focus on bringing out the humour in the lines and the situation.

> **Differentiation ideas:**

- Support: Limit the amount of information learners need to gather from the interview. For example, ask learners to write down three features.

- Challenge: Ask learners to find other features of the comedy genre that have not been identified so far in the audio or the play extract. What else makes something funny in their opinion?

> **Assessment ideas:** Monitor and discuss with learners how they are going about taking and refining their notes. Are they identifying the genre features successfully from the audio? What do they find hard about it? How are they organising their notes? Are they using the ideas in the Listening tip or other methods? Are they omitting notes when they refine them? Why?

3 Asides and dramatic irony (35 minutes)

Learning intention: Consider the way asides are used to convey character and situation.

Resources: Learner's Book, Session 5.1, Activity 4

Description: Write the terms *aside* and *dramatic irony* on the board. Introduce the Language focus feature and discuss how asides are used and how they link to dramatic irony. Ask learners to read the examples about Mahsa and Darab. Ask questions to gauge their understanding and address any misconceptions. What do learners think of asides? Are they realistic? What must the audience do for asides to work (suspend their disbelief that the other characters cannot hear them)?

Learners should complete Activity 4, writing an analysis of the use and effect of asides.

> **Differentiation ideas:**

- Support: Learners may need help writing their analyses for this activity. Consider providing a sheet with sentence starters to help them organise their writing. For example: *Hortense's asides reveal . . . , Gilbert's asides show . . . , The asides help the audience . . . , The playwright uses dramatic irony to . . .*

- Challenge: Ask learners to think of other examples of dramatic irony they have come across before in plays (or films or TV shows) – for example, in Shakespeare's *Romeo and Juliet*, the audience knows Juliet is only asleep but Romeo thinks she is dead and kills himself.

> **Assessment ideas:** Provide written feedback on learners' analyses in line with the success criteria. Have learners commented on the role of asides as a genre feature of comedy? Have they included references to how asides reveal characterisation and create dramatic irony?

Plenary idea

Session reflection (10 minutes)

Description: Ask learners to read the Summary checklist. They should give themselves a score out of 10 for each bullet point to indicate how well they think they have achieved the success criteria. Learners could share their scores with a partner and identify where the difference in their scores for one criteria was the greatest. The learner with the higher score should then ask the learner with the lower score what it was they found difficult and explain or address any misconceptions if they can. If possible, the pair should find a further criteria to discuss where they swap roles.

CROSS-CURRICULAR LINK

History (the Windrush generation): Learners could find out more about the Windrush generation and how and why people emigrated from the Caribbean to the United Kingdom in the 1950s and 1960s. The Windrush generation has also been back in the news recently in the UK. Learners could look at recent accounts of people's experiences and the political and societal issues involved.

Homework idea

Learners should complete Workbook Session 5.1.

5.2 Arriving in England

LEARNING PLAN

Learning objectives	Learning intentions	Success criteria
9Rs.01, 9Ri.01, 9Ra.01, 9Ra.02, 9Wv.01, 9Ws.01, 9Wc.01, 9Wc.04, 9Wc.07, 9SLp.02, 9SLp.03	Learners will: • read and perform a comedy scene • explore how contrast is used to create humour • respond to familiar situations and stereotypes in a play extract • write their own comedy scene.	Learners can: • understand and perform a comedy scene from a play • understand how playwrights use contrast to create humour • discuss and explain their reaction to stereotypes in a scene from a play • write an effective comedy scene, using contrast and dialogue for effect.

LANGUAGE SUPPORT

In this session, learners perform a scene from a comedy. The Speaking tip advises them to vary their voice to show a character's feelings and emotions. Discuss how learners could vary their volume, pace and tone to convey this. Some learners may find this challenging, so it is useful to practise features of pronunciation, such as asking questions. Point out that in spoken English different question types require different intonation (the rise and fall of someone's voice as the speak).

In general:

- Questions that require a yes/no answer and statements as questions have rising intonation at the end of the question: *Are you going out? You've finished your homework?*

- Choice questions use rising then falling intonation: *Would you like tea or coffee?*

- Question-word questions have falling intonation at the end of the question: *What did you think of that meal?*

Provide learners with similar types of questions and model the intonation to build their confidence of this feature of spoken English.

Starter idea

Pairs of characters (5 minutes)

Resources: Learner's Book, Session 5.2, Getting started activity

Description: Ask learners to think about famous 'comedy duos' in film or literature. They should write a brief list, then discuss the questions in the Getting started activity in pairs.

Main teaching ideas

1 Performing a comedy scene (40 minutes)

Learning intention: Read and perform a comedy scene.

Resources: Learner's Book, Session 5.2, *Small Island* Extract 2, Activity 1

Description: Introduce the next scene from the play and explain that the setting has changed. Ask learners to skim read the extract and share anything they notice about it (there are lots of stage directions, no asides, etc.).

Learners should complete Activity 1 in pairs. Make sure they take their time to understand the stage directions and how they link to the dialogue that follows. Draw attention to the Speaking tip. Learners should then perform the scene as instructed.

Write the following question on the board: *Is this a comedy scene?* Ask for a show of hands to see who thinks it is and who disagrees. Ask pairs to discuss and then open up the discussion to the class. Explore their responses by asking further questions:

If it is not funny, how would you describe it? Is there anything funny about it? How could you make it funny without changing a word? How does this scene fit with the genre (dramatic comedy)? How does it fit with the idea from the last session that comedy must involve some sort of 'suffering'?

Ask learners to perform the scene to the rest of the class. If they have completed the Challenge idea, they can perform the scene in the two different ways.

> Differentiation ideas:

- Support: Support learners' performances by asking them to describe exactly how the characters are feeling when they say each line – for example, how would they describe Gilbert's feelings when he says, *But . . . that is it?* (embarrassed, worried).

- Challenge: Ask learners to perform the scene in two different ways. First, they should perform it to bring out the comedy. Then they should change how they speak and move to make the scene sad and serious. In addition, another of the key competencies of communication is supporting others to communicate successfully. Ask learners who are more confident with this activity to help learners who are less confident before or during their performances in a sensitive way. They could ask if a partner needs help with pronunciation, expression or emphasis.

> Assessment ideas:
Learners should complete the Self-assessment feature to evaluate how they performed the scene.

2 Contrast in comedy (40 minutes)

Learning intention: Explore how contrast is used to create humour.

Resources: Learner's Book, Session 5.2, Activity 2; Workbook, Session 5.2, Focus and Practice sections

Description: Ask learners what the word *contrast* means. Introduce Activity 2 and explain that contrast is a device that writers use to structure a piece of writing (other examples include flashbacks, shifts of focal character, circular narratives, etc.). Ask learners to list the contrasts in the play extracts so far (setting, physical appearance, attitude).

Learners should first complete the Focus and Practice sections in their Workbooks, then move on to Activity 2 in the Learner's Book, where they should base their analysis on Extract 2.

> **Differentiation ideas:**

- Support: Learners may need help understanding the non-standard English and implied meaning of the extra scene in the Workbook Practice section. Ask questions to check learners' understanding: *What does Gilbert mean in the last line? How is the audience likely to react to it? What do you think 'caan' means in this context?*

- Challenge: Ask learners to include the extra scene from the Workbook Practice section in their analysis, as well as Extract 2.

> **Assessment ideas:** Review learners' written responses to Activity 2 to assess how well they are meeting the success criteria. Provide formal or informal feedback to help learners understand the next steps they can take to improve their skills.

3 Writing a comedy scene (60 minutes)

Learning intentions: Respond to familiar situations and stereotypes in a play extract. Write a comedy scene.

Resources: Learner's Book, Session 5.2, Activities 3 and 4; Differentiated worksheets 5A, 5B and 5C

Description: Introduce Activity 3. In pairs, learners should discuss their reactions to the stereotypes listed. Discuss ideas briefly as a class.

Tell learners that they will now be exploring the role of different types of characters in more detail. Use the worksheet guidance to introduce and distribute the Differentiated worksheets on archetypes, stock characters and stereotypes.

Explain that learners are now going to write their own comedy scene with two contrasting characters. Introduce Activity 4 and draw attention to the Writing tip. Learners should then write their own scenes.

> **Differentiation ideas:**

- Support: Provide learners with a checklist of features they should try to include in their writing, such as contrasting characters, quickfire dialogue, asides, stage directions that involve humorous actions and an embarrassing situation. You could also provide a planning sheet with prompts, such as *How do your characters differ from one another? What is the conflict between them? What are they really thinking?*

- Challenge: Ask learners to edit their scripts to maximise the overall effect of the techniques they have used. Pose questions to prompt improvements: *Could you add a further stage direction to make it clear how the other character is reacting? Could you edit that line to make the character's tone clearer?*

> **Assessment ideas:** Ask learners how confident they are at identifying stereotypes in writing, giving a score from 1 (very confident) to 5 (not at all confident). If learners give a 4 or 5, ask them to think about what they need to know to make them more confident. If learners give a 1, 2 or 3, ask them to think about what they need to practise to improve this skill. Take questions and address any misconceptions at this point.

Plenary idea

Peer assessment (5 minutes)

Resources: Completed playscripts

Description: In terms of skills for life, two of the key competencies within the area of communication are structuring content and using language for effect. Ask learners to swap books and share their scripts with a partner and to comment constructively on each other's scripts basing their feedback on these two key competencies.

Homework idea

Learners should complete the Challenge section of Workbook Session 5.2.

5.3 *The Boy Who Harnessed the Wind*

LEARNING PLAN

Learning objectives	Learning intentions	Success criteria
9Rv.02, 9Rv.03, 9Rs.01, 9Rs.02, 9Ri.02, 9Ri.07, 9Wv.01, 9Wv.02, 9Ws.02, 9Wc.07	Learners will: • consider the importance of titles • explore structural patterns in an autobiography • consider how figurative language adds layers of meaning and effect • write a first-person account in a specific voice.	Learners can: • explain the purpose and effect of story titles • analyse the effect of language and structural patterns in an autobiographical account • explain the layers of meaning and effect created by figurative language • write a first-person account in a particular voice and structure.

LANGUAGE SUPPORT

The extract from *The Boy Who Harnessed the Wind* is written in the past tense. However, the narrator also writes about memories of past events that occurred earlier in his life. It may be useful to remind learners of the construction and usage of the past perfect tense.

The past perfect tense is used to describe an action completed in the past before another action is completed. It is formed using the auxiliary verb <u>had</u> and the **past participle**. Here are some examples from the extract:

• *News of my work <u>had</u> **spread** far and wide.*

• *These same men <u>had</u> **teased** me from the beginning.*

Some learners may find it hard to identify this tense because the auxiliary verb *had* is often abbreviated. Here are some examples:

• *I'<u>d</u> barely **slept** the night before.*

• *They'<u>d</u> **closed** up their shops.*

Support learners in avoiding the use of *has/have* instead of *had*. The present perfect is formed using *has/have* and the **past participle** to describe actions started in the past and continuing into the present. For example: *News of my work <u>has</u> **spread** far and wide.*

Starter idea

Book titles (5 minutes)

Resources: Learner's Book, Session 5.3, Getting started activity and Activity 1

Description: Ask learners to discuss the titles of some books they have read recently. Were the titles straightforward or unusual? Was it the title that attracted them to the book? What expectations did they have of the book from the title? What makes an interesting title and why?

Introduce the extract and explain that it is the prologue from an autobiography. Write the title of the book *The Boy Who Harnessed the Wind* on the board, then ask learners to complete Activity 1 in pairs. Briefly discuss ideas as a class.

Main teaching ideas

1 Structural patterns (45 minutes)

Learning intention: Explore structural patterns in an autobiography.

Resources: Learner's Book, Session 5.3, Activities 2 and 3

Description: Ask learners to read the extract themselves (you may wish to repeat the communication skills activity of overcoming language gaps from Session 5.1).

Introduce Activity 2 and read through the bullet points. Learners should complete the activity, writing a summary of these patterns in the extract and the effect they have on the reader.

Ask learners to list some of the genre features of an autobiography (for example first person, past tense, chronological order, specific people and dates). Introduce Activity 3 and briefly discuss the overlap between non-fiction and fiction in autobiographies. Remind learners that the extract is the prologue to the book. It reveals the moment when William successfully 'harnessed the wind'. Why does the writer start the book with this revelation? Does it ruin the suspense to know the ending? Ask learners to complete the activity, discussing the bullet points in pairs.

> **Differentiation ideas:**

* Support: Use the Language support at the start of the session to help learners identify and understand the difference between the past tenses used in the extract.

* Challenge: Ask learners whether they think the rest of William's autobiography would be a comedy. What evidence is there from the prologue to back up their opinions? Does it 'sound' like a comedy to them? Encourage learners to think about the tone as much as the content.

> **Assessment ideas:** Provide written feedback on learners' writing. Make sure comments focus on the success criteria, particularly on how well learners have identified and commented on the structural patterns in the extract.

2 Structural choices and figurative language (30 minutes)

Learning intention: Consider how figurative language adds layers of meaning and effect.

Resources: Learner's Book, Session 5.3, Activity 4

Description: Ask learners to recall what they know about figurative language. What is it? What different types can they name? Emphasise that one of the roles of figurative language is to make comparisons. Ask learners to read and discuss the Language focus feature. Answer any questions about it and address any misconceptions.

Learners should then complete Activity 4 on their own. Make sure they understand that they need to comment on the *layers of meaning* in the figurative language and the effect these have.

> **Differentiation ideas:**

* Support: Learners should use the Language focus information as a useful model for what to write: it describes some layers of meaning and then comments on their effect.

* Challenge: Ask learners to find further examples of figurative language in the extract, such as *as hard as green fruit* or *the soft wood groaned*. They could add an example to their analysis, commenting on layers of meaning and their effect.

> **Assessment ideas:** Provide written feedback on learners' analyses. Highlight where learners have successfully identified layers of meaning created by the figurative language and ensure they have also commented on their effect. Prompt learners to think of other layers of meaning they might have used to answer more fully. For example: *You were right to say that 'reborn' suggest a new start. What else does it suggest?* (escape, hope, etc.)

3 Writing a villager's account (60 minutes)

Learning intention: Write a first-person account in a specific voice.

Resources: Learner's Book, Session 5.3, Activity 5

Description: Ask learners to imagine they are William. They are just about to climb the tower but first they have to go through the crowd that has gathered. How do they think William feels at that moment? To explore this, create a 'thought tunnel'. Split the class in two and line them up facing each other. Leave a space for a learner to walk down the middle. Ask the learners on one side to imagine all the negative/doubtful thoughts William might be having (*I hope this works*). Ask the learners on the opposite side to imagine the positive thoughts William might be having (*I know the science is*

Resources: Learner's Book, Session 5.4, 'How to be a K-pop idol', Activity 1

Description: Ask learners what they know about K-pop and have a brief class discussion before learners read the extract. You may wish to repeat the communication skills activity of overcoming language gaps from Session 5.1.

Ask learners to identify any modal verbs in what Noh Young-joo says in the last three paragraphs of the article (*must*, *have to* and *should*). What is the function of most of these modal verbs (expressions of obligation)? Explore the difference between the types of modal verbs of obligation (see Language support).

Ask learners to discuss Activity 1 in pairs. They will need to refer back to the extract in Session 5.3 as well as refer to the K-pop article. Tell pairs to divide a page into three columns and make some notes in response to the three bullet points in the activity.

Afterwards, discuss learners' responses as a class. What do the two boys have in common? What is different about their experiences?

> **Differentiation ideas:**

- Support: Learners may need help identifying modal verbs, so ask questions to prompt their recall: *What is the job of a modal verb? In terms of word order, where might you find a modal verb? 'Could' is a modal verb; can you think of another?*

- Challenge: Ask learners to summarise their comparison. Are there more similarities or differences between the two young men's experiences? What do both texts say about success?

> **Assessment ideas:** Monitor how learners are taking notes. Are they identifying the key facts from both texts? Listen to the complexity of their discussions to assess the depth of their understanding, for example how well are they inferring meaning about the personalities of the two young men? This will give you some idea of learners' inferential skills before they complete Activity 3.

2 Features of an article (30 minutes)

Learning intention: Consider the effect of organisational features in non-fiction.

Resources: Learner's Book, Session 5.4, Activity 2

Description: Explain that learners are now going to look at the how the article is structured and organised. Ask them to briefly discuss the following questions:

- Where do you think the article is from?

- What do you think the purpose of it is?

- Who do you think it is aimed at?

Introduce Activity 2 and explain the source of the article, its purpose and audience as outlined. Learners should then complete the activity, writing an evaluation of the structure and organisation of the article based on the key features in the bullet points.

> **Differentiation ideas:**

- Support: Consider putting learners into pairs that will provide suitable levels of support for each other and asking them to discuss Activity 2 before they write their evaluations.

- Challenge: Encourage learners to use both abstract nouns and the adjectival equivalents when describing personal qualities, attitudes and differences. For example: *What is the adjectival form of 'resilience'? What is the abstract noun form of 'determined' or 'diligent'?*

> **Assessment ideas:** Ask learners to share their evaluations from Activity 2 as a class. Give oral feedback suggesting ways in which learners could improve their answers, for example, by quoting explicit evidence from the text or using connective words and phrases to contrast or draw links between the two texts (*On the one hand . . . on the other hand*; *similarly*).

3 Inference and personal responses (45 minutes)

Learning intention: Discuss a range of responses to a text.

Resources: Learner's Book, Session 5.4, Activities 3 and 4

Description: Ask learners what 'reading between the lines' means (making inferences). Introduce Activity 3 and ask learners to organise themselves into groups of three or four. In terms of skills for life, one of the key competencies of collaboration is listening respectfully and responding constructively to others' contributions. As they discuss the questions in the bullet points as a group, encourage learners to take turns and listen to one another's opinions carefully. Explain that after the discussion, to check that they have been listening to each other, you will be asking for opinions on each of the bullet points. However, learners will not be able to give their own contributions, only those of someone else in the group. After the discussion, model an example by repeating a contribution you heard a learner make. Ask learners to share each other's contributions in a similar way.

Tell learners that in the next activity they will be free to express their own opinions about the article. Learners should then read the Writing tip and complete Activity 4 on their own, writing a personal response that includes quotations.

> **Differentiation ideas:**

- Support: Assign, or ask learners to assign, a chairperson to ensure that all group members are given a chance to contribute fairly.

- Challenge: You may decide not to reveal that learners will be expressing someone else's opinion instead of their own. However, this may reduce the quantity and quality of the responses if learners are not used to this approach, so allow extra time for pairs of learners to express their opinions to each other and then retry.

> **Assessment ideas:** Ask learners to think about their group discussions. How successful were they? Did each member have enough opportunity to speak? Did people listen carefully? Did all group members have a chance to ask questions or challenge opinions? Was their discussion controlled or chaotic and what effect did that have? How might they organise themselves differently next time?

4 Personal context (25 minutes)

Learning intention: Analyse how learners' own context affects their response to a text.

Resources: Learner's Book, Session 5.4, Activity 5

Description: Ask learners to hold up their hands if they know any K-pop music, and then if they like or dislike it.

Read the introduction to Activity 5, then in pairs learners should discuss how their own attitudes, likes and dislikes influenced them when they read the article and during their group discussion. Did they have any preconceived ideas about K-pop that made them feel positively or negatively about the article?

Learners should complete the activity by writing a paragraph describing what influenced their response.

> **Differentiation ideas:**

- Support: Ask learners to try to articulate their ideas to the key question (*What influenced your reaction to the article?*) out loud to you first. Consider providing a planning sheet or a writing frame to scaffold learners' responses, and a list of key functional language phrases beyond *I think . . .* (for example *In my view . . . , Personally. . . , I believe . . .*).

- Challenge: Extend the activity by asking learners to comment on whether their attitude changed after reading the article. Do they feel more positively or more negatively towards the article, Jeon and K-pop? Learners could also comment on how their group discussion influenced their opinion and whether it strengthened their beliefs or changed their mind in any way.

> **Assessment ideas:** Provide some written feedback on learners' paragraphs. How well do the paragraphs demonstrate the learner's ability to understand and analyse their own context and reactions?

Plenary idea

Analysis skills (5 minutes)

Description: Ask learners to discuss and list the different ways they have analysed the texts in this and the previous session (they have looked at organisational features, used inferential skills and considered their own contexts). Emphasise that using a range of ways like this helps them reach a deeper understanding of a text, its purpose, audience and effect.

End the session by asking learners to review the Summary checklist. Ask them to write down a number to show you how confident they feel about each bullet point, where 1 is 'very confident' and 5 is 'not confident at all'. They should make a note of the areas where they feel least confident for future reference.

Homework idea

Learners should complete Workbook Session 5.4.

5.5 Animals and entertainment

LEARNING PLAN

Learning objectives	Learning intentions	Success criteria
9Rv.02, 9Rv.03, 9Ri.02, 9Ri.04, 9Ri.07, 9Ri.10, 9Ra.02, 9Ra.04, 9Ra.05, 9Wv.01, 9Wc.04, 9SLm.03	Learners will: • discuss their reaction to a persuasive text • consider the effect of political language in an article • explore how different contexts affect interpretations of a text • consider their own context and analyse its effect on their response to a text.	Learners can: • express a personal response to a persuasive text • identify political language in a text and explain its effects • understand how different types of context affect interpretations of a text • explain their own context and how it influences their response to a text.

LANGUAGE SUPPORT

The article in this session contains numerous rhetorical questions. It may help learners to recap the function and formation of rhetorical questions so that they can try using them in their own writing in Activity 3. Ensure that learners understand that rhetorical questions do not require an answer: they are a stylistic device used to make a reader think about a point that is being made. You may wish to provide learners with some rhetorical question stems.

For example:

Did you ever wonder . . . ?
Have you ever considered . . . ?
How would you feel if . . . ?

Isn't it time that . . . ?
What if . . . ?
Isn't the real issue . . . ?

Is it really worth . . . ?
Should we really accept . . . ?
What would happen if . . . ?

Starter idea

How to persuade someone (10 minutes)

Resources: Learner's Book, Session 5.5, Getting started activity

Description: Ask learners to read the Getting started activity, and to discuss in pairs when someone tried to persuade them to do something. They should consider the persuasive techniques that person used and how effective those techniques were. Ask pairs to create a list of any persuasive words or phrases they can recall.

Main teaching ideas

1 The case against animals for entertainment (50 minutes)

Learning intentions: Discuss their reaction to a persuasive text. Consider the effect of political language in an article.

Resources: Learner's Book, Session 5.5, 'Why we shouldn't use animals for entertainment', Activities 1 and 2; Language worksheet 5.1; dictionaries and thesauruses

Description: Tell learners that they will be reading a persuasive text written from a biased point of view. What type of features and language do they expect to find?

Introduce the article, 'Why we shouldn't use animals as entertainment'. Learners should read it on their own and make some brief notes on its structure and features. Then, in pairs, they should complete Activity 1 by discussing their reactions to the views and their counterarguments. Briefly discuss ideas as a class.

Introduce Activity 2 and the link between political language and power. Ensure learners understand the meaning of the four bullet points. Explain that they will now be exploring in detail how emotive language can be used to assert, persuade and grab attention.

Use the guidance to introduce Language worksheet 5.1 on language to assert, persuade and grab attention, then ask learners to complete the activities on it. You may wish to allow some time to discuss their responses.

Learners should then read the Reading tip and complete Activity 2. They should make brief notes and find relevant quotations to write their summaries of the political language in the article. Remind learners to comment on the *effect* the language has on the reader.

> **Differentiation ideas:**

* Support: Learners may need help 'translating' the tabloid-style words and headlines on the worksheet. Provide access to dictionaries and thesauruses, and pose your own questions to help learners work out the meanings.

* Challenge: Ask learners to describe the overall tone of the article. For example: *The tone of the article is forceful and demanding. The questions force you to consider your own attitudes and the imperatives demand you change your behaviour.*

> **Assessment ideas:** Review learners' responses to both the worksheet and Activity 2 to assess how well they are meeting the learning intentions. Provide formal or informal feedback to help learners understand the next steps they can take to improve their skills.

2 Extend a persuasive argument (30 minutes)

Learning intention: Consider the effect of political language in an article.

Resources: Learner's Book, Session 5.5, Activity 3; thesauruses

Description: Introduce Activity 3. Ask learners to read the article again. They should identify one paragraph where they think they can extend the view by writing some extra sentences. Emphasise that the aim is to write in the same style, using emotive language to persuade and assert.

> **Differentiation ideas:**

* Support: Encourage learners to use a thesaurus to help them choose emotive vocabulary.

* Challenge: Ask learners to use a range of devices to try to match the voice of the article, not just emotive vocabulary (questions, imperatives, assertions).

> **Assessment ideas:** Ask learners to swap their sentences with a partner and complete the Peer assessment activity. Tell each pair to feed back something they really liked about each other's writing and why, and something they thought was less effective and why.

3 Contexts of production and reception (45 minutes)

Learning intentions: Explore how different contexts affect interpretations of a text. Consider their own context and analyse its effect on their response to a text.

Resources: Learner's Book, Session 5.5, Activities 4–6

Description: Write the title *Context* on the board and then two subheadings, *Production* and *Reception*. Remind learners how in the previous session they thought about their own context when reading the K-pop article (how their own attitudes influence their reaction to something). Explain to learners that they will now be looking at other forms of context.

Introduce Activity 4 and give learners the context of production for the online article in this session. Learners should complete Activity 4 as a discussion in pairs.

Introduce Activity 5 and the meaning of the 'context of reception'. Explain that they read the K-pop article in the previous session within their own contexts of reception. Learners should complete the activity in their pairs, discussing how each of the readers might respond.

Tell learners that they are now going to write a paragraph about the article, explaining how their own context of reception affected their reaction. Introduce Activity 6. Ensure that learners understand they should comment on their reaction to both the point of view and the style of the article. Remind learners that they are *not* writing a counterargument to the point of view in the article; they are analysing what they bring to a text before they even read it. Learners should complete the activity on their own.

> **Differentiation ideas:**

- Support: Provide a planning worksheet to help learners organise their writing in Activity 6. It could be split into sections with the following headings: *My personal attitude to zoos, Attitudes in my country or culture, What I find persuasive* and *What I do not find persuasive.*

- Challenge: Extend the activity in the same way as Activity 5 in Session 5.4: ask learners to comment on whether their attitude had changed after reading the article. Did they dismiss the article when they saw the title, but have now been persuaded? Did they agree with the title, but were put off by the style? Did their context of reception mean they were unlikely to be persuaded for or against the article?

> **Assessment ideas:** Ask learners to share their paragraphs with the class. This will help you assess how well they have addressed the success criteria and plan next steps.

Plenary idea

Persuade me (5 minutes)

Description: Ask learners to work in pairs for two minutes to think of ways of persuading you to release them from class a few minutes early. Discuss as a class and say how much or little you are persuaded by their different arguments. You may wish to finish by saying your own context of reception is that it is against the rules to let them out of class early, so you are not persuaded!

Homework idea

Learners should complete Workbook Session 5.5.

5.6 The benefits of zoos

LEARNING PLAN		
Learning objectives	**Learning intentions**	**Success criteria**
9Rv.02, 9Rg.01, 9Rg.03, 9Rg.04, 9Ri.02, 9Ri.04, 9Ri.08, 9Ra.02, 9Ra.05, 9Ww.01, 9Ww.02, 9Ww.03, 9Wg.04, 9Wg.05, 9Ws.01, 9Wc.04, 9Wc.05, 9SLm.01, 9SLm.02, 9SLm.03, 9SLg.01, 9SLg.02, 9SLg.03, 9SLg.04	Learners will: • discuss an opinion article, considering its context • compare the arguments made in two related texts • explore the effect of language, punctuation and grammar choices • write a balanced discursive response.	Learners can: • read and discuss an opinion article, including contextual information • compare the arguments made in two different texts on a similar topic • identify and analyse the effect of language, punctuation and grammar choices • write a discursive response, using a range of information and viewpoints.

LANGUAGE SUPPORT

Some learners may need support understanding the function and positioning of adverbs of manner and degree.

Adverbs of manner answer the question 'How?'. They are usually formed from adjectives and used to modify verbs. Many take the suffix -ly and usually go after the verb they are modifying. For example:

He walked <u>briskly</u>.   *She spoke <u>loudly</u>.*
They won <u>easily</u>.

There are some irregular adverbs of manner, such as *hard, fast, early, late, well, straight,* etc.

Adverbs of degree answer the question, 'How much?'. They not only modify verbs but also adjectives and other adverbs. They usually come before the word they are modifying. For example:

- *I <u>almost</u> fainted.* (modifying the verb 'fainted')
- *The film was <u>really</u> funny.* (modifying the adjective 'funny')
- *How did you do that <u>so</u> quickly?* (modifying the adverb 'quickly')

Common misconception

Misconception	How to identify	How to overcome
When writing a discursive response, you always have to be objective and should avoid stating your own view.	Ask learners what the word 'objective' means when you are talking about a point of view. What is the opposite (subjective)? Ask learners whether the articles they have read about zoos are objective or subjective. Do learners think a piece of writing that covered both views in a balanced way would be objective or subjective? What if the writer included their own view on the topic?	Explain that discursive writing allows you to write about a topic from a range of views in an objective way. However, it is expected that the writer will conclude the piece of writing in a way that sums up their view on the topic when all of the views have been taken into account. Therefore, discursive writing should be objective, but it should also include the writer's view in the conclusion.

Starter idea

Effective persuasion (10 minutes)

Resources: Learner's Book, Session 5.6, Getting started activity

Description: Ask learners to think back to a time they have had a debate before, either in groups or as a class. Ask learners to write a list of skills and rules for holding a successful debate and share them with the class. Encourage learners to note down any new good ideas they hear that they might use themselves.

Main teaching ideas

1 The case for zoos (30 minutes)

Learning intentions: Discuss an opinion article, considering its context. Compare the arguments made in two related texts.

Resources: Learner's Book, Session 5.6, 'Why zoos are good', Activities 1 and 2

Description: Explain to learners that they will be reading about zoos again, but from a different point of view. Introduce the newspaper opinion article and the two pieces of contextual information.

Learners should complete Activity 1 as a discussion in pairs before coming together as a class to briefly discuss ideas.

Ask learners to read the article a couple of times and make some brief notes about its structure and organisation. Then instruct learners to divide a page in half and write the titles of the two articles at the top. Learners should then complete Activity 2 in pairs, making bullet points about the differing arguments, as well as how persuasive and biased they are. Discuss learners' responses as a class, focusing on which article they found most convincing and the level of bias in each. Avoid discussing the pro- and anti-zoo arguments at this stage as learners will be debating this in a later activity.

> **Differentiation ideas:**

- Support: Organise learners into pairs that will provide suitable levels of support for each other. Ensure that less confident learners are given the opportunity to contribute equally to Activity 2. Encourage their partners to support them by asking questions about their ideas rather than just suggesting their own.

- Challenge: Ask learners which article is more biased (the article in Session 5.5). Draw out the distinction between a different point of view (as found in the second article) and bias by asking: *The second article takes the opposite view, but is it biased?* Draw attention to the Reading tip. Ask learners to find examples in the newspaper article of 'subtle' bias.

> **Assessment ideas:** In Activity 2, check learners' pair work to ensure they identify the differing arguments. Then monitor the class discussion to assess how well learners are commenting on how persuasive and biased the articles are. Listen out for examples from the texts that support their comments.

2 Article analysis (25 minutes)

Learning intention: Explore the effect of language, punctuation and grammar choices.

Resources: Learner's Book, Session 5.6, Activity 3

Description: Read Activity 3 as a class. Explain that learners need to give examples and comment on their effect. Ensure learners understand the meaning of the language, punctuation and grammatical terms in the bullet points. Refer them to the Key word definitions if necessary. Learners should then complete Activity 3 independently.

> **Differentiation ideas:**

- Support: Learners may need reminding of the form and function of some of the punctuation and grammatical features they need to identify and comment on. Ask questions to draw out prior learning:

  - *What are you likely to find in parentheses?* (extra information in a phrase or clause)

  - *Apart from brackets, what other punctuation marks are used for parentheses?* (dashes, commas)

  - *Where in a sentence are parentheses found?* (in the middle or the end).

  See Language support at the start of the session for further details on adverbs of degree and manner.

- Challenge: Ask learners to consider how the overall effect would be different if the writer had not used the pronouns 'we' and 'I'. Would the article feel more or less persuasive? Why?

> **Assessment ideas:** Provide written feedback on learners' analyses in line with the success criteria. Have learners found examples of language, punctuation and grammatical features? Have they commented on their overall effect?

3 Group debate (35 minutes)

Learning intentions: Discuss an opinion article, considering its context. Compare the arguments made in two related texts.

Resources: Learner's Book, Session 5.6, Activity 4

Description: Write the following statement on the board: *This House believes that the disadvantages of zoos outweigh the advantages of zoos.* Explain that learners will now debate the statement (the 'motion'). Ask for a show of hands for who at this stage agrees with the statement ('for the motion') and who at this stage disagrees with it ('against the motion').

Introduce Activity 4. Divide the class into groups of around four so that each group contains learners who are for and against the motion. Ask learners to think back to when they have had group discussions in the past. Ask them for suggestions on how to ensure their discussion is focused and involves everyone in the group. Encourage groups to appoint a chairperson and allow two minutes for groups to establish their ground rules (for example the chairperson must be neutral, you must raise your hand to speak) before starting their debate.

Learners should debate the motion. At the end, the chairperson should decide whether their group was for or against the motion. Ask each chairperson to report back to you on their group's decision and tally the scores to generate an overall result for the class.

> **Differentiation ideas:**

- Support: One of the key competencies of communication (skills for life) is using appropriate language and register for the context. You may wish to provide learners with a list of functional language to help them contribute in a persuasive way. For example: *I firmly believe . . . , It is my firm opinion . . . , I disagree entirely . . . , It seems very clear . . . , You may not agree, but . . .*

- Challenge: More confident learners may dominate group debates. Give each group member a set of three objects (for example building blocks or toy coins). Tell learners that each time they contribute they must put one of their objects in the middle. When the learner has used their three objects, they can no longer contribute. This encourages learners to think before they speak and use their turns in a more thoughtful way.

> **Assessment ideas:** Monitor the group debates, but let learners control them as far as possible. You may find it helps to intervene in order to question whether a group is sticking to its ground rules or to question the appropriateness of their language.

4 Writing a discursive response (50 minutes)

Learning intention: Write a balanced discursive response.

Resources: Learner's Book, Session 5.6, Activity 5; Workbook, Session 5.6, Focus and Practice sections; Language worksheet 5.2

Description: Introduce Activity 5 and discuss the features of a discursive response. Tell learners that they are going to do two tasks before they write their discursive responses.

The Focus and Practice activities in the Workbook support the planning for this activity, so ask learners to complete these sections first. Explain that they can also use other 'for' and 'against' arguments generated in the debate in this last activity.

Second, they will be practising writing a possible opening sentence to their response. Use the guidance to introduce Language worksheet 5.2 and ask learners to complete the activities on it. You may wish to allow some time for learners to share their favourite opening lines. Allow time for learners to plan further and then write their discursive responses.

> **Differentiation ideas:**

- Support: Provide a planning sheet to help learners structure their writing. For example: a page divided into four boxes with headings: *Introduction and opening sentence*; *The benefits of zoos*; *The disadvantages of zoos*; *Conclusion* (including learners' own view; see Common misconception).

- Challenge: Following on from the worksheet, ask learners to edit their opening sentence to make sure they start their discursive responses in an interesting, impactful way.

> **Assessment ideas:** Provide written feedback on learners' discursive responses. Highlight areas where their writing is successful and where a further improvement could be made. For example, you could highlight where a learner has expressed three benefits of zoos in a paragraph and suggest that the paragraph could be improved if they included more connectives to link and strengthen the arguments (for example *in addition, moreover*). If possible, allow time for learners to make the improvements.

Plenary idea

Unit reflection (10 minutes)

Description: Ask learners to look back through their books at the Summary checklist at the end of each session. They should choose one success criteria from each list with which they feel they have made significant progress. Next, they should choose one from each list where they feel they need more help or practice. Ask learners to make a note of the success criteria where they need more help and practice. Collate their responses and use them to inform your planning and next steps.

Homework idea

Learners should complete the Challenge section of Workbook Session 5.6.

PROJECT GUIDANCE

A useful sequence for carrying out this project would be as follows.

1   Outline the entire project to the class. Explain what the aim is and what they need to produce and present. For example:

    •   collaborate in groups to plan and present a marketing campaign for a new music star

    •   'design' a music star

    •   produce a range of promotional materials

    •   give a launch presentation to the rest of the class.

2   To develop learners' life skills, this project gives them the opportunity to practise two of the three key competencies of collaboration: managing the sharing of tasks in a project and taking personal responsibility for one's own contribution to a group task. It also focuses on several of the key competencies of communication: using appropriate language/register for context; participating with appropriate confidence and clarity; supporting others to communicate successfully; structuring content; and using language for effect.

3   Organise the class into small groups for the project. Share the key competencies of collaboration and communication above. This means that they will not be appointing a group leader for this project. Explain that they will have to collaborate as a group to plan, prepare and present, especially making sure that their own contributions are ready on time. Tell learners that you will not be checking on each group's progress as they prepare their launch presentations.

4   Allow some class time for each group to 'design' their music star, their appearance, music style and audience. Ask groups to decide how best to promote their star and to draw up a list of the promotional materials they will need to produce. They should divide the work of preparing the materials equally between them. Remind learners that each person in a group must contribute to the presentation and that they should decide how to organise and deliver their launch presentation between them. Set a date for the launch presentations.

5   Ask each group to deliver their launch presentations to the rest of the class. After the presentations, ask the class to take a vote. They should vote for the group who has given the best marketing campaign.

6   As a follow-up, discuss how well each group thought they collaborated and communicated. What would they do next time to improve their collaboration? What would they change about how they organised themselves or the process of preparing their presentations? How well did they support each other? How would they change their presentations to improve its structure and language?

> 6 A sense of place

Unit plan

Session	Approximate number of learning hours	Outline of learning content	Resources
6.1 The city sings	2 hours, 30 minutes	Learners explore language and structural choices in descriptive fiction, respond to a descriptive text and create a vivid description.	Learner's Book Session 6.1 Workbook Session 6.1 ⬇ Language worksheet 6.1
6.2 A love letter to the Grand Canyon	2 hours, 30 minutes	Learners explore structure and meaning in travel writing, consider how humans' relationship with nature is presented and write their own descriptive text.	Learner's Book Session 6.2 Workbook Session 6.2
6.3 Chasm	2 hours, 30 minutes	Learners explore dialogue in a metaphorical setting, consider the effect of using a focal character and explore the meaning of a spatial metaphor.	Learner's Book Session 6.3 Workbook Session 6.3 ⬇ Differentiated worksheets 6A, 6B and 6C
6.4 In the desert	2 hours, 45 minutes	Learners identify meaning in a poem, consider the effect of irony and contrast, explore sonnets and analyse the setting of a poem.	Learner's Book Session 6.4 Workbook Session 6.4 ⬇ Language worksheet 6.2
6.5 Pastoral poetry	2 hours, 15 minutes	Learners explore a modern sonnet, learn about pastoral literature and using poetic structures for effect, and compare the use of couplets.	Learner's Book Session 6.5 Workbook Session 6.5
6.6 Returning home	2 hours, 15 minutes	Learners respond to audio and written texts, consider the effect of pathetic fallacy and non-chronological features, and write a sentimental account.	Learner's Book Session 6.6 Workbook Session 6.6

BACKGROUND KNOWLEDGE

For the teacher

This unit looks at a range of texts in which setting is a central feature. To prepare for these sessions, it may be helpful to read a summary of the novel *If Nobody Speaks of Remarkable Things* by Jon McGregor, and the poems 'Ozymandias' by Percy Shelley and 'Vermont' by Phillip Whidden. You may need to revisit the two travel writing articles about Coober Pedy in Learner's Book Sessions 1.5 and 1.6.

The following grammatical and spelling concepts are covered in this unit:

- the imperative form
- personal pronouns, including archaic forms
- types of irony
- perfect and imperfect rhyme
- literary devices in poetry and prose

- iambic pentameter
- writing better dialogue.

It may be useful to read up on these concepts before explaining them to learners, if you are not already confident in how they are defined and applied.

For the learner

Learners are unlikely to be familiar with the range of texts in this unit. It would benefit them to make a list of any books, poems or plays they have read in the past where the setting was memorable or which had a significant impact on the events, characters or meaning of the text. They should revisit any prior learning about poetic form, especially the technical language used to describe it (stanza, verse, rhyme, rhythm, repetition, figurative language, line breaks, etc.). This will help learners understand the more complex poetic form of the sonnet in this unit.

TEACHING SKILLS FOCUS

Assessment for Learning

Assessment for Learning (AfL) is not about testing your learners more frequently, but rather about creating successful feedback for both learners and teachers. It helps learners become more involved in the learning process and in understanding what they are expected to know and to what standard. As a teacher, you will gain insights into a learner's level of understanding of a particular concept or topic, which helps you to support their progression. AfL focuses on both the teacher and learner understanding three key things:

- where the learner is going, for example by sharing success criteria
- where the learner is now, for example through effective questioning

- how can the learner get there, for example by giving formative feedback.

The notes on this unit include suggestions for using AfL strategies, in particular, purposeful, informal feedback; this can be oral, written or peer assessment. It is important that such feedback is accurate, easy to understand and focused on the learning intentions and success criteria. Just as importantly, the suggestions in these notes provide opportunities for your learners to react to such feedback and put their learning into practice. This will help you maximise the feedback process (teacher to learner and learner to teacher) to optimise learning and guide next steps.

6.1 The city sings

LEARNING PLAN

Learning objectives	Learning intentions	Success criteria
9Rv.02, 9Rv.03, 9Rg.01, 9Rg.02, 9Rg.03, 9Rs.01, 9Ri.01, 9Ra.01, 9Wv.01, 9Wv.02, 9Wg.01, 9Wc.01, 9Wc.08, 9SLp.01	Learners will: • read and perform a descriptive text • explore the effect of language and structural choices in descriptive fiction • write a response to a descriptive text • create a vivid description of their own.	Learners can: • read, discuss and create sound effects for a distinctive city description • analyse the effect of language and structural choices in a description • write a response to a text, commenting on the effect of language and expressing their own reaction • use language, structure and grammatical features to create a vivid description.

LANGUAGE SUPPORT

Ensure learners understand the function of the imperative, and how it is formed. The imperative is used to give orders or instructions, or to suggest advice or make offers. It is formed using the base form of the verb. Importantly, an imperative clause contains no grammatical subject (even though the subject is the second person singular or plural 'you'). For example:

• *Close your eyes.* (instruction)
• *Don't worry, be happy.* (advice)
• *Have a cup of tea.* (offer)
• *Come home immediately.* (order)

Using 'Do' before the imperative can add emphasis:

• *Do hurry up!* (emphasis on urgency)
• *Do take a seat.* (emphasis on politeness)

Using 'Don't' or 'Do not' before the imperative makes it negative:

• *Don't go that way.*
• *Do not enter.*
• *Don't forget to do your homework.*

Starter idea

Spelling noises (5 minutes)

Resources: Learner's Book, Session 6.1, Getting started activity

Description: Explain to learners that this unit involves thinking about sounds and rhythms and how they are conveyed in writing. Ask them to read and complete the Getting started activity, trying to put into words the sounds listed in the bullet points. Briefly share ideas as a class.

Main teaching ideas

1 Describing of a city (50 minutes)

Learning intention: Read and perform a descriptive text. Explore the effect of language and structural choices in descriptive fiction.

Resources: Learner's Book, Session 6.1, *If Nobody Speaks of Remarkable Things*, Activities 1–3; Language worksheet 6.1

Description: Start with Language worksheet 6.1, as it follows on directly from the Getting started activity. Use the guidance to introduce the worksheet. Learners should complete the worksheet and share some of their responses.

In pairs, learners should read the extract aloud, taking it in turns to read the words and make the sounds described (Activity 1).

Learners should then move straight into Activity 2, discussing the effects of grammatical and structural features in their pairs. Use the Language support feature to support learners with identifying imperatives.

Ask learners to define what a metaphor is. Have they spotted an extended metaphor in the text (song)? What similes can they find that create this extended metaphor? Draw attention to the Reading tip and then ask learners to discuss the two similes in Activity 3 before completing the written task on their own.

> **Differentiation ideas:**

- Support: Join in with pairs as they discuss the similes in Activity 2. Ask questions to focus their discussions on the positive and negative connotations of the comparisons in the similes: *What do the alarms sound like? How would you characterise the sound? Do you think the sound of the loose drains is adding to or spoiling the atmosphere of the city?*

- Challenge: Ask learners to extend their analysis to comment on the effect and meaning created by other literary devices in the text, for example, the sibilance in the paragraph that starts, *All of these things sing constant . . .*

> **Assessment ideas:** Monitor learners' discussions to gauge the depth of their responses to the learning intention. Listen in particular for the grammatical, structural and language features learners are picking out as evidence of the writer's purpose and the effect he is creating.

2 Responding to a description (40 minutes)

Learning intention: Write a response to a descriptive text.

Resources: Learner's Book, Session 6.1, Activity 4

Description: Introduce Activity 4. Draw attention to the Writing tip. Make sure learners understand that they should express their own views, supported by quotations and examples from the text. You may wish to recap how learners should embed quotations correctly in their writing.

> **Differentiation ideas:**

- Support: Allow extra time for learners to complete Activity 4. Offer your own questions to help them find evidence from the texts and structure their response: *How do you think the writer feels about the city overall? How will you organise your writing? Can you show me a quote from the text to support your point?*

- Challenge: Ask learners to add depth to their responses by including counterpoints with evidence to their own arguments, rather than arguing that the city is definitely threatening or that it is the opposite.

> **Assessment ideas:** Use AfL techniques to provide purposeful written feedback for this activity. Such feedback should only relate to the relevant success criteria and activity instructions – it should not focus on learners' grammar, spelling, syntax, etc. Highlight three 'successful' sentences or phrases in their work in one colour and one sentence or phrase in another colour where a change would improve the learner's response. Write a short instruction or question to guide the learner in how to make the improvement. Allow time at the beginning of the next session for learners to write their improvements.

3 Writing a description (45 minutes)

Learning intention: Create a vivid description of their own.

Resources: Learner's Book, Session 6.1, Activity 5; thesauruses

Description: Refer learners back to the bullet points in the Getting started activity. Tell them they can use those ideas or anything else they can think of when writing their own vivid descriptions for Activity 5.

Read the activity instructions as a class. Discuss how the 50-word limit means they need to choose their words carefully and make the link with poetry. Discuss the bullet-point list of language and stylistic features learners may want to include and ensure everyone is clear on these features.

Ask learners to start by noting down some initial ideas, such as possible comparisons or a few alliterative words. They should draft their paragraphs and then edit them to improve their writing. Remind learners to check that every word counts, and to edit out anything that does not add to the overall effect they are trying to convey.

> **Differentiation ideas:**

- Support: Ask learners to focus on one of the listed features that may be simpler to use, for example, long sentences with commas for listing. Encourage learners to use a thesaurus to help them choose vivid vocabulary.

- Challenge: In a further link to the poetry at the end of this unit, encourage learners to think about the rhythm of their words, for example, to convey the movement of a train passing, learners may wish to use a regular, repeating rhythm.

> **Assessment ideas:** Ask learners to swap books and read each other's paragraphs aloud. Learners should then complete the Peer-assessment feature and give each other oral feedback as detailed in the bullet points. Monitor the feedback the learners give each other.

Plenary idea

Sharing descriptions (10 minutes)

Resources: Completed paragraphs from Activity 4

Description: Ask for volunteers to share their paragraphs with the rest of the class. You may wish to give your own oral feedback on how successfully learners have used language, structure and grammatical features to create a vivid description.

Homework idea

Learners should complete Workbook Session 6.1.

6.2 A love letter to the Grand Canyon

LEARNING PLAN

Learning objectives	Learning intentions	Success criteria
9Rv.02, 9Rs.01, 9Ri.02, 9Ri.04, 9Ri.05, 9Ri.06, 9Ri.07, 9Ri.08, 9Wc.01, 9Wc.02, 9Wc.03, 9Wp.01, 9SLm.02, 9SLm.03, 9SLg.03	Learners will: • read and discuss the structure of a piece of travel writing • explore meanings in two pieces of travel writing • consider how humans' relationship with nature is presented in literature • write their own descriptive text.	Learners can: • comment on the structure of a piece of travel writing • compare and contrast meaning and ideas in two pieces of travel writing • analyse how humans' relationship with nature is presented in literature • use language and structural techniques to write a vivid description of nature.

LANGUAGE SUPPORT

This session includes discussions about theme and meaning so it may be useful for learners to understand the vocabulary associated with these ideas. You could make a display of this language or ask learners to make and keep their own records for reference.

Vocabulary that learners may need support with: theme, big ideas, message, motif, notion, aspect, topic, subject, significance, key question, main concern, trope, essence, substance, thrust, argument, issue.

Learners should learn to recognise that questions that contain such vocabulary are likely to require them to focus on wider meaning rather than on the language and structure, for example: *To what extent does the author's depiction of his childhood experiences match the trope of nature in Romantic literature?* They should also know that such questions are also judged on the quality and strength of their argument, as there are no right or wrong answers.

Starter idea

Special places (10 minutes)

Resources: Learner's Book, Session 6.2, Getting started activity

Description: Read the Getting started activity as a class. Ask learners to think of a place that is special to them and to consider why that is. In pairs, learners should describe these places to one another and explain what is special about them. How do the places make them feel? Challenge them to think of three adjectives that sum up the nature of the places.

Main teaching ideas

1 Travel writing (30 minutes)

Learning intention: Read and discuss the structure of a piece of travel writing.

Resources: Learner's Book, Session 6.2, 'A love letter to the Grand Canyon', Activities 1 and 2

Description: Tell learners they are about to read a piece of travel writing. What genre features would they expect to find in this type of writing (non-fiction, first person, past tense, etc.)?

Ask learners to read the extract. Discuss how it details the writer's changing feelings about the Grand Canyon before asking learners to complete Activity 1.

Introduce Activity 2 by discussing how the writer has structured the text. Learners should use their notes from Activity 1 to complete Activity 2.

Ask learners to imagine the writer had used flashback as a structural device instead of contrast (that is, starting in the present, recounting a memory from the past, then returning to the present). Discuss the difference in effect as a class.

> **Differentiation ideas:**

- Support: Activity 1 asks learners to use the most appropriate reading strategies to locate some relevant locations. Ask learners what strategies they could use (skimming and/or scanning the text). Which one do they think is appropriate for this task (scanning)? What key words should they look out for (references to years, time periods or his age)?

- Challenge: The writer uses contrast as a structural device in the extract. Challenge learners to write down as many other structural devices as they can (flashbacks and flashforwards, shifts of focus in terms of character or place, repetition and patterns, changes of pace, circular narratives, etc.).

> **Assessment ideas:** Learners should share their paragraphs in pairs or small groups and give each other informal feedback about how well they have commented on the writer's use of contrast and its effect.

2 Comparing travel writing (40 minutes)

Learning intention: Explore meanings in two pieces of travel writing.

Resources: Learner's Book, Session 6.2, Activity 3; Learner's Book, Sessions 1.5 and 1.6, Coober Pedy Extracts 1 and 2

Description: Ask learners what they remember about Coober Pedy from earlier sessions. Where is it? What is it like? Can learners remember what the writer learnt from their experience of visiting Coober Pedy?

Introduce Activity 3 by discussing the 'big ideas' in the bullet points. Ask learners to organise themselves into small groups. Ask each group to appoint a spokesperson and a scribe/note taker. Learners should discuss the similarities and differences in the 'big ideas' arising from the Coober Pedy and the Grand Canyon articles. Draw attention to the Reading tip and support learners in their discussions by using the suggestions in the Language support feature at the start of the session.

Ask each spokesperson to report back on their group discussion using their notes, focusing on questions such as: *What were the 'big ideas' and main points the two writers were exploring? How did the articles differ from each other in that regard?*

> **Differentiation ideas:**

- Support: Organise the groups and assign roles in advance, for example, it may be a good idea to have groups where learners will provide suitable levels of support for each other and to ensure that more confident learners are appointed as their group's spokesperson.

- Challenge: Extend the discussion by asking learners to think about any 'big ideas' that have arisen from the own experiences, especially of places they have visited or that are special to them. What have they learnt about the wider world or human nature from their experience?

> **Assessment ideas:** Monitor each group in turn. Draw learners' attention to the success criteria in the Summary checklist. Avoid suggesting ideas yourself and use the opportunity to listen to how well learners articulate the themes and meanings they think arise from the texts.

3 Humans and nature in literature (60 minutes)

Learning intentions: Consider how humans' relationship with nature is presented in literature. Use language and structural techniques to write a vivid description of nature.

Resources: Learner's Book, Session 6.2, Activities 4 and 5

Description: Read the introduction to Romantic literature in the Learner's Book and discuss the photograph as a class. Elicit the type of feelings the photo conveys in terms of humans and nature.

Emphasise that the extract 'A love letter to the Grand Canyon' is a type of modern form of Romantic literature. Then ask learners to read and complete Activity 4, focusing on finding lines from the text about the writer's feelings towards nature and what he 'learns' from nature about life in general.

Discuss what learners think about nature themselves, especially landscapes. You may wish to show some examples of landscape photography that also include human subjects. What experiences have learners had in similar environments (a feeling of awe or wonder, a feeling of isolation, a feeling of being a significant or insignificant part of the natural order, a sense of timelessness, etc.)?

Introduce Activity 5 and tell learners they should try to capture those experiences and feelings in their writing. Draw attention to the Writing tip and briefly discuss personification and other figurative language learners could use. Learners then complete the activity on their own.

> **Differentiation ideas:**

- Support: Give learners a list of different types of figurative language with examples to help them convey a sense of scale and beauty (similes and metaphors based on visual imagery, personification, alliteration, etc.).

- Challenge: Ask learners to use at least three different types of figurative language in their descriptions. In addition, challenge learners to use an extended metaphor (like the metaphor of song in the previous session) as a cohesive device that amplifies the effect they are trying to create.

> **Assessment ideas:** Use AfL techniques to provide purposeful written feedback for learners' descriptions. Such feedback should focus on how well learners have used language and structural techniques to write a vivid description of nature. Write a short instruction or question to guide the learners in how to make the improvement to their answers. Allow time at the beginning of the next session for learners to write their improvements.

Plenary idea

Favourite lines (10 minutes)

Resources: Completed descriptions from Activity 5

Description: Ask learners to swap books and choose a favourite line from their partners' descriptions to share with the class. Ask learners to explain why they chose those particular lines.

> **Assessment ideas:** Ask learners how confident they are about using a range of structural and language techniques to write a vivid description, giving a score from 1 (very confident) to 5 (not at all confident). If learners give a low score, ask them to share what they need to know or practice to improve their confidence. Address questions or misconceptions.

> ### CROSS-CURRICULAR LINK
>
> **Geography:** Learners could study the physical geography and the history of the formation of the Grand Canyon in northern Arizona, USA. They could find out about other large canyons around the world – for example, the Colca Canyon in southern Peru or the Tiger Leaping Gorge in south-west China.

Homework idea

Learners should complete Workbook Session 6.2.

6.3 Chasm

LEARNING PLAN

Learning objectives	Learning intentions	Success criteria
9Rv.03, 9Rs.01, 9Ri.01, 9Ri.04, 9Ra.02, 9SLg.02, 9SLp.01, 9SLp.03	Learners will: • predict the plot of a story from its title • explore the dialogue in a story with a metaphorical setting • consider the effect of using a focal character • explore the meaning of a spatial metaphor.	Learners can: • understand the significance of a title and can predict possible plot ideas based on it • interpret a story with a metaphorical setting, including the dialogue • explain the effect of using a focal character in a story and give a personal response • analyse the different meanings of a spatial metaphor in a short story.

LANGUAGE SUPPORT

Some learners may need reminding of the difference between the first, second and third person. One of the best ways to identify this is to look at the personal pronouns used in a text. Ensure learners know the correct subject pronouns associated with each of these points of view:

Person	Singular	Plural
First	I	we
Second	you (thou*)	you (ye*)
Third	he/she/it	they

Note that in Session 6.4, learners will also encounter the pronoun *ye*. This is an archaic form of the second person plural pronoun in the subjective class. The singular form of *ye* was *thou*. Learners may also come across *ye* used to mean *the*. This usage is often used to make things sound older than they are, especially the names of shops – (Ye Olde Sweete Shoppe).

Common misconception

Misconception	How to identify	How to overcome
Metaphor is a type of figurative language that compares one thing directly with another, for example *The moon is a silver dollar*.	Ask learners to give some examples of a metaphor. What is the purpose of a metaphor? Ask learners whether they have heard the word metaphor used in any other sense apart from as figurative language. Refer learners back to the metaphor of song as a cohesive device in the previous session. Have they heard of a novel or film with a metaphorical theme or setting? (for example, the rise of Stalin in *Animal Farm* by George Orwell and the contrasting living conditions of the Eloi and the Morlocks in *The Time Machine* by H. G. Wells).	In this session, learners will explore how a setting can be used as a metaphor for the wider themes of a piece of writing. Explain how, in the extract in this session, the way Adrian and Janice view Milford Sound is a spatial metaphor for the distance ('the chasm') that exists between the way they view the world and their feelings for one another. Ask learners if they can think of any other spatial or thematic metaphors from books or films.

Starter idea

Unsympathetic characters (10 minutes)

Resources: Learner's Book, Session 6.3, Getting started activity

Description: For the Getting started activity, learners should discuss unsympathetic characters from books and films they know. Ask learners to list the qualities an unsympathetic character might have (narcissism, selfishness, shallowness, pessimism, etc.). Can an unsympathetic character still be a hero? What are such characters called (anti-heroes)?

Main teaching ideas

1 Exploring titles and dialogue (60 minutes)

Learning intention: Read and explore the dialogue in a story with a metaphorical setting.

Resources: Learner's Book, Session 6.3, 'Chasm', Activities 1 and 2; Differentiated worksheets 6A, 6B and 6C

Description: Write some young adult book titles on the board, for example *The Curious Incident of the Dog in the Night-Time, The Hunger Games, One of Us Is Lying, The Book Thief, The Fault in Our Stars,*

Darius the Great is Not Okay. Ask learners how important they think titles are. What is the job of a book or story title? What meaning do the titles on the board convey to them?

Introduce the next extract, which is set in Milford Sound in New Zealand. Write the title of the story, 'Chasm', on the board and discuss its literal meaning. Learners should then complete Activity 1 on their own. Learners should share their ideas with the class. What are their expectations of the story based on this single word?

Read the Reading tip as a class, then ask learners to read the extract on their own, using the glossary to help with any words that might be unfamiliar.

In pairs, learners should complete Activity 2, discussing the relationship between Adrian and Janice and then reading it aloud as instructed.

Share the second Reading tip and then, using the guidance notes, introduce and hand out Differentiated worksheets 6A, 6B and 6C, which focus on writing dialogue. Learners should complete the activities on the worksheets.

Finally, ask learners to read and complete the Reflection feature in the Learner's Book, making their own notes in response to the questions.

> **Differentiation ideas:**

- Support: The dialogue contains a lot of implied meaning (e.g. when Janice first speaks, she says, *We don't need words.*) These words are loaded with possible meaning. Ask learners questions to help them make inferences as they read and discuss the text: *Why do you think she says this? What is she really saying? What does this say about their relationship?*

- Challenge: Extend the worksheet activity by asking learners to write a continuation of the second version of the dialogue once they have rewritten the first.

> **Assessment ideas:** End the session by asking learners to share their rewritten dialogues (Dialogue 2 Version 2). Ask them to feed back on what they like about each other's responses. This will allow you to assess how well learners have used dialogue to convey character, tension and mood.

2 Focal characters (45 minutes)

Learning intention: Consider the effect of using a focal character.

Resources: Learner's Book, Session 6.3, Activity 3; Workbook, Session 6.3, Focus and Practice sections

Description: Ask learners what 'person' or 'voice' the extract is written in (third person, see Language support at the start of the session). Who is the 'main' character (Adrian)? How do we know (we hear his inner thoughts and therefore his point of view more prominently)? Is 'main' character the correct way of describing him? Or is Janice just as important in this scene?

Introduce Activity 3 and briefly discuss the concept of a focal character, another example of a structural choice a writer makes. Ask learners to complete Activity 3 as a pair discussion, then share ideas as a class:

- Which statements from the activity (if any) do they agree with?

- Why does the writer make Adrian the focal character?

Explain that learners will now compare two accounts of the same event, but with different focal characters to see how it changes the meaning. Learners should complete the Focus and Practice sections of Workbook session 3.2, then share their responses to both activities as a class.

> **Differentiation ideas:**

- Support: Organise learners into pairs that will provide suitable levels of support for each other and ask them to discuss the Workbook activities before they write their responses.

- Challenge: Extend the workbook activities by asking more confident learners to rewrite the extract, making Melanie the focal character.

> **Assessment ideas:** Join each group in turn during Activity 3. Listening to how learners discuss the statements and express their opinion will help you gauge how well they have understood the learning intention of this session. Give oral feedback on how learners have performed.

3 Spatial metaphors (30 minutes)

Learning intention: Explore the meaning of a spatial metaphor.

Resources: Learner's Book, Session 6.3, Activity 4

Description: Read Activity 4 to the class and briefly discuss the meaning of spatial metaphor, using the Key word definition if necessary. Address any misconceptions about how metaphors can be more than just figurative language (see Common misconception at the start of the session). Talk briefly about the difference in the feelings and attitudes that Adrian and Janice have to the setting. Learners should then complete their analysis for Activity 4 on their own.

> **Differentiation ideas:**

* Support: Provide a planning worksheet to help learners organise their analysis. It could be split into sections with the following headings: Adrian's feelings; Adrian's attitude to the chasm; Janice's feelings; Janice's attitude to the chasm; The status of their relationship; The physical appearance of the chasm.

* Challenge: Ask learners to think of other physical locations that might be suitable settings as spatial metaphors, for example, an erupting volcano could be a metaphor for a relationship crisis, or a locked room with a lost key could be a metaphor for writer's block.

> **Assessment ideas:** Use AfL techniques to provide purposeful written feedback for Activity 4. Highlight three 'successful' sentences or phrases in their work in one colour and one sentence or phrase in another colour where a change would improve the learner's response. Write a short instruction or question to guide the learner in how to make the improvement. Allow time at the beginning of the next session for learners to make their improvements.

Plenary idea

Reflecting on metaphors, dialogue and character (5 minutes)

Ask learners to reflect on the activities in this session using the Summary checklist.

* Do they feel more confident about writing dialogue?

* Do they know how to identify the focal character in a text?

* Can they make up their own example of a spatial metaphor?

* What do they think they need to learn or practise in order to improve?

They should try to identify something that held them back during the session. Ask learners to share their thoughts. Use their responses to plan activities in future sessions to address any issues raised.

Homework idea

Learners should complete the Challenge section of Workbook Session 6.3.

6.4 In the desert

LEARNING PLAN

Learning objectives	Learning intentions	Success criteria
9Rv.02, 9Rs.01, 9Ri.01, 9Ri.03, 9Ri.04, 9Ri.07, 9Ra.02	Learners will: • identify information and layers of meaning in a poem • consider the effect of irony and contrast • explore the conventions of a sonnet • write an analysis of the significance of setting.	Learners can: • identify information and explore layers of meaning in a poem • comment on irony and contrast and the effect these have in a poem • understand the conventions of a sonnet, including structure and theme • analyse the significance of setting in a poem, considering language and structural choices.

LANGUAGE SUPPORT

Learners may benefit from support in identifying and understanding different types of irony. There are three main types they should be aware of, in order to comment on them.

Verbal irony is when someone expresses something in speech that is the opposite of what they mean. For example someone might say, 'Guess it's my lucky day!' when they suffer a string of unfortunate events one after another.

Situational irony is the difference between what is expected to happen and what actually happens.

For example, in Shelley's poem 'Ozymandias', the reader understands that the arrogant king believed his statue would stand forever, but in fact it now lies forgotten and half-buried in the desert.

Dramatic irony is when a reader or audience is aware of something that the characters in a book or play are not aware of. For example in Shakespeare's *Macbeth*, the audience knows that Macbeth behaves loyally to King Duncan while at the same time plotting to kill him.

Starter idea

Poem predictions (10 minutes)

Resources: Learner's Book, Session 6.4, Getting started activity

Description: Ask learners to read the bullet-point list of things in the poem they are about the read. Ensure that learners understand the meaning of 'bragging' (boasting). Learners should discuss the list. Where do they think the poem might be set? What might the poem be about?

Main teaching ideas

1   A statue in the desert (40 minutes)

Learning intentions: Identify information and layers of meaning in a poem. Consider the effect of irony and contrast.

Resources: Learner's Book, Session 6.4, 'Ozymandias', Activities 1 and 2

Description: Introduce the poem 'Ozymandias', by the Romantic poet Percy Bysshe Shelley. Explain that Shelley was inspired to write the poem because of the archaeological discoveries being made in Egypt in the late 18th century. The 'traveller' in the poem is a reference to the Roman historian Diodorus Siculus, who wrote a description of a statue of Rameses II and translated the inscription on it.

Ask learners to read the poem on their own and then to read it aloud in pairs, taking alternate lines. Learners should then complete Activity 1, making brief notes about the content and meaning based on the bullet points. Discuss their responses as a class and make sure learners identify the arrogant, bragging tone of the words on the pedestal.

Ask learners what it means if you say something is ironic and to give some examples of irony. Have they heard of different types of irony (see Language support at the start of the session)? Read Activity 2 then ask learners to read the poem again before writing their paragraphs about the situational irony in the poem.

Write *hubris* on the board and ask learners if they can define it (excessive pride). Discuss how the ruined, forgotten statue can be seen as symbolic of Ozymandias's hubris.

> **Differentiation ideas:**

- Support: Some learners may find some lines of the poem hard to interpret because of their unusual phrasing, for example *Tell that its sculptor well those passions read*. Guide learners in using synonyms and changing the word order to make the meaning of such lines clearer, for example 'Show that the sculptor of the statue understood the subject's emotions well'.

- Challenge: Provide learners with Diodorus's translation of the actual inscription: 'I am Osymandyas, king of kings; if any would know how great I am, and where I lie, let him excel me in any of my works.' Ask learners to consider its meaning and the difference between this inscription and the words on the pedestal in the poem. What effect is Shelley creating (he is exaggerating the boastfulness and hubris)?

> **Assessment ideas:** Learners should share their paragraphs from Activity 2 as a class. Give oral feedback, suggesting ways they could improve their answers, for example by quoting explicit evidence from the text or referring to contrast or hubris.

2 Interpreting poetry (15 minutes)

Learning intention: Identify information and layers of meaning in a poem.

Resources: Learner's Book, Session 6.4, Activity 3

Description: Write the following on the board: *Political language is concerned with . . . ?* Ask learners for suggestions to finish the sentence (power). Remind learners of how they looked at this in Session 5.5.

Introduce Activity 3 and highlight the two issues the poem explores: the nature of power and the passage of time. Ask for volunteers to read each of the students' interpretations aloud. Then learners should complete the activity, discussing the descriptions of the poem and finding evidence for their interpretations in pairs.

> **Differentiation ideas:**

- Support: Read the first sentence of the first interpretation. Ask learners to raise their hands if they agree with the sentence you have just read and why, or why not. Ask for the word or phrase from the poem that makes them think as they do. Repeat with the second sentence. Read a third sentence if necessary before learners continue with the activity.

- Challenge: After their discussion, ask learners to write down their own 50-word interpretation of the poem, like the ones they have been talking about.

> **Assessment ideas:** During the discussions, circulate around the class, listening to pairs speak. Assess the following:

- Are learners showing good discussion skills, taking turns and listening to each others' ideas?

- Are they using evidence from the poem to support each interpretation?

3 The poetic form of a sonnet (40 minutes)

Learning intention: Explore the conventions of a sonnet.

Resources: Learner's Book, Session 6.4, Activity 4; Language worksheet 6.2

Description: Introduce sonnets, using the instructions for Activity 4. Ensure learners understand the technical terms in the bullet points and explain that they will be looking at iambic pentameter in more detail. Use the guidance to introduce Language worksheet 6.2 about iambic pentameter, then ask learners to complete the worksheet and share some of their lines.

Return to Activity 4. Learners should complete the activity as a paired discussion of the conventions Shelley has used in the poem. Open the discussion to the class. List on the board where conventions have been included, adapted or omitted and discuss what effect these convention choices have.

> **Differentiation ideas:**

- Support: As iambic pentameter is said to mimic the natural cadence of spoken English, some learners may find it difficult to know which words are naturally stressed and unstressed. Remind learners of some basic conventions – for example, content such as verbs and nouns are stressed, whereas articles, prepositions and auxiliary verbs are unstressed. Note that such conventions would only apply to single-syllable words in iambic pentameter.

- Challenge: Ask learners to write four lines of iambic pentameter where the lines follow on from one another. Challenge learners to use one of the following rhyming patterns too: ABAB or ABBA.

> **Assessment ideas:** Provide written feedback on the worksheets. Make a note of any misconceptions, which you will be able to address in Session 6.5 when learners study another sonnet.

4 Analysing themes and setting in a poem (50 minutes)

Learning intentions: Consider the effect of irony and contrast. Write an analysis of the significance of setting.

Resources: Learner's Book, Session 6.4, Activities 5 and 6

Description: Introduce Activity 5 and briefly discuss the idea that sonnets are usually about love. Ask learners to repeat the discussion exercise from Activity 3 using the two new learner interpretations

of the themes and poetic form. Again, learners should find evidence to support their ideas and share them with the class.

Explain that the statue on which Shelley's poem is based was not actually found in the middle of the desert; it was at the entrance to an ancient temple. Shelley adjusted the setting for effect. Ask learners why he might have done this and discuss ideas as a class.

Introduce the first sentence of Activity 6, then read the Writing tip. Ensure learners understand the purpose of the writing and what it should include. Learners should then complete their analyses for Activity 6.

> **Differentiation ideas:**

- Support: Provide learners with a checklist of key terms that they should try to use in their analyses, for example setting, contrast, situational irony, hubris, sonnet, iambic pentameter, theme, conventions and effect.

- Challenge: Ask learners to include their interpretation of why Shelley chose to change the setting for the poem in their analysis. How does this link with the poet's rewording of the statue's inscription?

> **Assessment ideas:** Use AfL techniques to provide purposeful written feedback for Activity 6. Use one colour to highlight three 'successful' times where learners have made a point about the setting and supported it with a reference from the poem. Highlight one sentence or phrase in another colour where a change would improve the learner's response. Write a short instruction or question to guide the learner in how to make the improvement. Allow time at the beginning of the next session for learners to write their improvements.

Plenary idea

Ozymandias today (15 minutes)

Resources: A photograph of the statue of the head and upper body of Rameses II from the British Museum website

Description: Explain that the statue the poem is based on is currently on display in the British Museum (a well-known museum in the UK). It was found in Egypt and taken to the UK. Ask learners:

- *If you were Shelley writing a sonnet about the statue today, what theme might you choose instead of the nature of power and time* (for example theft of cultural artefacts)?

- *How would you present Ozymandias instead of as a hubristic figure* (for example a great ruler longing to return home)?

Discuss ideas as a class.

CROSS-CURRICULAR LINK

History (ancient Egypt): Learners could research the history of Rameses II 'the Great', one of the most famous and successful pharaohs of ancient Egypt. This could include what happened after his rule and how it fits with the theme of the poem.

Homework idea

Learners should complete Workbook Session 6.4.

6.5 Pastoral poetry

LEARNING PLAN

Learning objectives	Learning intentions	Success criteria
9Rv.02, 9Rv.03, 9Rs.01, 9Ri.01, 9Ri.07, 9Ri.08, 9Ri.09, 9Ri.10, 9Ws.01, 9Wc.01, 9Wc.03	Learners will: • explore the structure and language of a modern sonnet • learn about the conventions of pastoral literature • use poetic structures for effect • compare the use of couplets in two related texts.	Learners can: • describe and analyse the effects of structure and language in a modern sonnet • understand and identify the conventions of pastoral literature • write some lines of poetry using structural features for effect • compare the way ideas are presented in couplets in two related texts.

LANGUAGE SUPPORT

In this session, learners are asked to consider rhyming couplets that use perfect and imperfect rhymes, and to consider the effect this has on meaning. It may help to remind learners about these types of rhyme in English: perfect rhyme and imperfect rhyme (also called half rhyme, near rhyme or slant rhyme).

In perfect rhyme, the words have the same final vowel and consonant sound – for example from the poem 'Vermont': *trees* and *ease, sun* and *done.*

Imperfect rhyme uses different vowel sounds with the same final consonants, or the same vowel sounds with different final consonants – for example 'bud' and 'bed' and 'must' and 'stuff'. Here is an example from literature from William Blake's poem, 'The Tiger':

> What immortal hand or <u>eye</u>
> Could frame thy fearful <u>symmetry</u>?

Common misconceptions

Misconception	How to identify	How to overcome
You must always follow the rules of the poetic form you are writing.	Ask whether learners think that poets ever break the rules. For example, does a couplet (see Language focus) always have to rhyme? What if the poet used an imperfect rhyme? What if a poet used an extra syllable in a poem otherwise written in iambic pentameter? Ask why poets might break the rules.	Discuss the difference between perfect and imperfect rhyme. Use the example from the Language focus feature in this session: *My child is grown and I am sad they've gone* *Away, now I must face life on my own.* Ask learners what effect writing a couplet like this with imperfect rhyme has. Emphasise that writers often bend the rules of poetic form to draw attention to the effect they are trying to achieve. For example, a rhyming couplet conveys a sense of completion; a couplet with imperfect rhyme might emphasise the opposite.

Starter idea

Rural settings (10 minutes)

Resources: Learner's Book, Session 6.5, Getting started activity

Description: Ask learners to think about the countryside. What do they see? What do they hear, smell or taste? Where do they get these impressions from? Are they from their own experiences of through representations in books and other media? Ask learners to discuss the questions in the Getting started activity for a few minutes, then share ideas as a class.

Main teaching ideas

1 A modern sonnet (30 minutes)

Learning intention: Explore the structure and language of a modern sonnet. Learn about the conventions of pastoral literature.

Resources: Learner's Book, Session 6.5, 'Vermont', Activities 1 and 2

Description: Ask learners what they know about New England, an area in north-eastern USA (the incredible colours of the autumn leaves). Introduce the poem 'Vermont' and explain that the setting and the time in the poem are both important.

Before learners read the poem, ask them what they can remember about the poetic form of sonnets. Learners should read the poem and then work on their own to make notes in response to Activity 1. Afterwards, ask learners to feed back from their notes to the rest of the class, commenting on the structure and language features of the poem. What overall impression of Vermont does the poem give?

Write *pastoral literature* on the board and read the introduction to this next section in the Learner's Book. Ask learners to reread the poem, looking for features of pastoral literature in response to Activity 2. Discuss as a class how much learners feel the poem is an example of pastoral literature: *How much do the setting and the time count towards this? What about the sonnet form?*

Ask learners to support their answers with examples from the text.

> Differentiation ideas:

- Support: Learners may need support following and interpreting lines 4–7 of the poem, which contain multiple clauses. Ask learners to write these lines out as a single sentence and experiment with covering up different phrases (*done / With heavy summer*) to 'declutter' the sentence and help with interpretation of the meaning.

- Challenge: Ask learners to think back to the poem 'Ozymandias' in Session 6.4. The setting is central to the meaning of the poem. Does it have any features of pastoral literature? Is there anything sentimental about the setting? Could it be described as anti-pastoral?

> Assessment ideas: Provide informal, oral feedback during the discussions. Focus your comments on how well learners are referencing the structure and language of the poem and the conventions of pastoral literature.

2 Structure and meaning in a poem (45 minutes)

Learning intention: Use poetic structures for effect.

Resources: Learner's Book, Session 6.5, Activity 3

Description: Write *enjambment* and *caesura* on the board. Explain that they are other structural features used in poetry. Introduce Activity 3 and review the example from 'Vermont'. Ask learners to discuss the explanation of how the poet uses enjambment and caesura. Discuss any difficulties and misconceptions as a class.

Ask learners to recall from the previous session how iambic pentameter works. Again, discuss to address any misconceptions. Tell learners that they will now be writing a couple of lines of pastoral poetry themselves in iambic pentameter, including enjambment and caesura. Read the Writing tip together, then ask learners to draft their lines using one of the two bullet points as a prompt. Encourage learners to experiment with the structure and language.

Learners should then complete the Peer-assessment feature in pairs. Tell learners to use the feedback they have received to redraft their lines to improve them. Ask learners to comment on each other's lines a final time (see Assessment ideas below). Finally, ask learners to share some of their redrafted lines with the rest of the class.

> Differentiation ideas:

- Support: To encourage a flexible approach, ask learners to draw a 'topic web' of words they associate with the prompts (for example colours, verbs to do with movement) so that they have plenty of ideas to experiment with. Suggest learners match words that they could combine for alliteration and use marks to note the stressed and unstressed syllables in their words.

- Challenge: Extend this activity by asking learners to write some lines for both of the bullet-point prompts. Discourage learners from writing more: the priority for this activity should be to draft and then work at improving their lines – that is, quality rather than quantity.

> Assessment ideas: As an AfL peer-assessment exercise, ask learners to show their redrafted lines to their partner. In turns, they should explain one improvement they have made and why they made it. Learners could also share a change they have made but are not satisfied with. Their partner should try to suggest an alternative improvement. Allow a few minutes for learners to make any final changes to their redrafted lines.

3 Final couplets (45 minutes)

Learning intention: Compare the use of couplets in two related texts.

Resources: Learner's Book, Session 6.5, Activity 4

Description: Ask learners what they know about couplets in poetry. Discuss whether a couplet should always rhyme (see Common misconception). Introduce the Language focus feature and discuss both couplet examples, their types of rhyming and how this might affect their meaning.

Read Activity 4 and the Writing tip as a class. Emphasise that the purpose of the writing is to compare the structure and language of the two couplets. Learners should then complete the activity independently.

> Differentiation ideas:

- Support: Give learners a list of functional language for writing a comparison texts, for example linking phrases (*in addition, furthermore*) and contrasting phrases (*in contrast, on the other hand*).

- Challenge: Extend Activity 4 by asking learners to explain which of the two couplets they prefer and why.

> Assessment ideas: Use AfL techniques to provide purposeful written feedback for learners' analyses. Such feedback should focus on how well learners have compared the two couplets. Have they started with a summary statement? Have they used linking phrases and analysed each couplet in turn? Write a short instruction or question to guide the learner in how to make an improvement to their analysis. Allow time for learners to write their improvement at the start of the next session.

Plenary idea

Finish the couplet (10 minutes)

Description: Write the following line of iambic pentameter on the board: *The moon ascends, a silver coin of light.* Ask learners to work in pairs to complete the couplet. They should discuss the effect they wish to achieve and to choose a perfect or imperfect rhyme. Ask learners to share their couplets with the class.

Homework idea

Learners should complete Workbook Session 6.5.

6.6 Returning home

LEARNING PLAN

Learning objectives	Learning intentions	Success criteria
9Rv.03, 9Rs.01, 9Ri.02, 9Ri.03, 9Ri.07, 9Ww.01, 9Ww.03, 9Wv.02, 9Wg.04, 9Ws.01, 9Wc.07, 9Wc.08, 9SLs.01	Learners will: • respond to audio and written texts about returning home • consider the effect of pathetic fallacy • consider the effect of non-chronological features • write a sentimental account.	Learners can: • respond confidently to ideas in spoken and written texts • understand the meaning and effects of pathetic fallacy • comment on the effect of non-chronological features in a piece of autobiographical writing • write an imaginative account in a particular voice, creating deliberate emotions and effects.

LANGUAGE SUPPORT

To help learners develop skills for life, one of the key competencies of collaboration is listening respectfully and responding constructively to others' contributions. In this session, learners may struggle to understand Martika's thoughts and feelings if their listening skills are not effective. Support learners by discussing what makes listening difficult (speed of speech, unfamiliar language, colloquialisms, abbreviations, idioms, slang, acronyms, etc.). Discuss strategies for effective listening (for example, make predictions about the possible content and its structure; recognise that meaning comes not only from words but also from stress, intonation and rhythm; use your own knowledge to fill in gaps).

Starter idea

What does 'home' mean to you? (5 minutes)

Resources: Learner's Book, Session 6.6, Getting started activity

Description: Write *home* on the board. Explain that this short word can mean different things to different people and can be loaded with meaning. Ask learners to respond to the Getting started activity, discussing what they associate with the word 'home'. Is it a building? Is it a place or country? Is it about people? They should list three words each that they associate with the word.

Main teaching ideas

1 Martika returns home (30 minutes)

Learning intention: Respond to audio and written texts about returning home.

Resources: Learner's Book, Session 6.6, Activity 1

> ⬇ **Download the audioscript for Activity 1 from Cambridge GO (Track 48).**

Description: Explain that learners will be listening to a woman from Germany talk about returning home to Germany in her old age. They will need to make notes on Martika's *thoughts* and *feelings* about her experience – not the whole audio. Read the Listening tip as a class.

Play the audio two or three times to ensure all learners have adequate time to make their notes. Ask if they have any questions about the audio and address any issues or misconceptions.

Organise learners into pairs and ask them to use their notes to discuss what they thought of Martika's experience. What emotions or sentiments does Martika express? How do they feel towards her? How would they feel in the same situation?

> **Differentiation ideas:**

- Support: Discuss learners' expectations of the content and structure before listening. What voice will the audio be in (first person)? What tenses will be used (past)? What sort of things might she talk about (memories, places, family)? You could also provide a transcript of the audio for learners to follow.

- Challenge: Ask learners to choose three emotions that Martika expresses most strongly (sadness, regret and nostalgia) and to identify what type of word these are (abstract nouns).

> **Assessment ideas:** Examine learners' individual notes to gauge how well they have identified Martika's feelings from the audio. Identify any issues or misconceptions and explain these to the learners to help them improve their ability to identify such information. Discuss other issues that make listening difficult (see Language support) and strategies to overcome them.

2 Pathetic fallacy (50 minutes)

Learning intention: Consider the effect of pathetic fallacy.

Resources: Learner's Book, Session 6.6, *Tales from the Riverbank*, Activities 2 and 3; photographs of a silver birch tree in different seasons

Description: Introduce the extract from *Tales from the Riverbank*. Display the pictures of a silver birch tree in different seasons and explain that this tree is an important feature in the extract they are going to read.

Learners should then read the text and complete Activity 2 as a discussion in pairs. Open the discussion to the whole class. What is the significance of the birch trees? What is the writer trying to express by referring to the difference in the leaves?

Write *pathetic fallacy* on the board and ask learners if they know what this term means. Read the first paragraph of the Language focus feature, then ask learners to read and discuss their understanding of the rest. Discuss as a class and address any misconceptions.

Ask learners to further discuss the significance of the trees in the extract using the information about pathetic fallacy. *Whose* feelings and *what* feelings do the silver birch trees reflect? Learners should then complete Activity 3 independently.

> **Differentiation ideas:**

- Support: Give learners a prepared sheet for Activity 3 to help them organise their writing, containing sentence starters such as: *The author uses the scenery to . . .* or *The use of pathetic fallacy draws attention to . . .*

- Challenge: Provide a transcript of Martika's audio from Activity 1. Ask learners to find any examples of pathetic fallacy, for example, she talks about playing *in the hot Saxony summer days*, which signifies a happy memory.

> **Assessment ideas:** Ask learners to quickly think of an example of pathetic fallacy they could use in their own writing. They should think of a natural setting or phenomena and the sorts of emotional associations they might have, for example, a still, grey day might signify boredom, or a steep cliff might signify a crisis on confidence. This will help you assess how well learners have understood the success criteria.

3 Writing a sentimental account (50 minutes)

Learning intentions: Consider the effect of non-chronological features. Write a sentimental account.

Resources: Learner's Book, Session 6.6, *Tales from the Riverbank*, Activities 4 and 5

Description: Ask learners to complete Activity 4 as a discussion in pairs. Draw out how the author uses a flashback as a structural device and what it helps convey about his relationship with his father.

Tell learners that they are now going to write their own account of returning home from the point of view of an older person. It will need to be imaginative and sentimental. Introduce Activity 5 and tell learners to choose one of the bullet-point ideas, or think of their own idea.

Allow time for learners to plan their writing. Learners should then complete Activity 5 by writing their accounts.

> **Differentiation ideas:**

- Support: Provide learners with a list of possible structural techniques they could choose from to create a sentimental feeling, for example pathetic fallacy, a flashback or flashforward, a shift in the setting, a shift of focal character, an extended metaphor or a spatial metaphor.

- Challenge: Ask learners to write a greater amount so that it is similar in length to Martika's account (around 400 words).

> **Assessment ideas:** Use AfL techniques to provide purposeful written feedback for Activity 5. Highlight three 'successful' sentences or phrases in the learner's work in one colour where they have created a sentimental feeling using a structural technique – for example, pathetic fallacy or a non-chronological feature. Highlight one sentence or phrase in another colour where a change would improve the learner's writing. Write a short instruction or question to guide the learner in how to make the improvement. Allow time at the beginning of the next session for learners to write their improvements.

Plenary idea

Reflection (5 minutes)

Resources: Completed accounts from Activity 5

Description: Remind learners of the success criteria for Activity 5: to write an imaginative account in a particular voice, creating deliberate emotions and effects. Ask learners to complete the Reflection feature, considering these criteria. Discuss their responses briefly as a class, in particular what they found challenging and how they overcame those challenges.

Homework idea

Learners should complete Workbook Session 6.6.

PROJECT GUIDANCE

A useful sequence for carrying out this project would be as follows.

1   Outline the entire project to the class. Explain what the aim is and what they need to produce and present. For example:

- collaborate in groups to research and present a project on the significance of place in fiction texts

- make a collection of books with distinctive settings

- research meaning and presentation in four books in detail

- discuss your findings and prepare a presentation to share with the class.

2   Organise the class into small groups for the project (a group of four is optimal).

Ask each group to elect a project leader who will coordinate their group's research project. Explain that the project leader's role is to chair discussions and to make sure research and presentations are finished on time. Tell learners that you will be asking each project leader to report to you on their team's progress as they research and prepare their presentations.

3   Allow some class time for each group to decide on their approach to the project, led by the project leader. For example, how will they choose a suitable range of fiction texts? How will they find texts from different genres and cultures? Allow some class time for each group to draw up their longlist of texts. Suggest that they should longlist at least eight books.

4   Next, ask the groups to narrow their lists to four books. Allow time for discussion so that each group can choose the best four texts where the settings seem particularly significant. Learners should then decide how to divide the detailed research into each book equally between them. Set a deadline for the completion of the research.

5   Following their research, allow class time for learners to share their findings. The project leader should lead the discussion. Groups should then discuss how to prepare a presentation on their findings, including its format. Set learners a deadline for completing their presentation materials. Again, you may wish to provide some class time for the preparation of these materials.

6   Ask each group to introduce their research findings to the rest of the class.

7   Meet at least once with the project leaders during the project. Use the meeting to gauge how well their group's research and/or presentation preparation is going. Are they on schedule? Do they need to organise themselves differently? Use dialogue and questioning to guide the project leader in exploring any new options for managing the project. If necessary, meet each group and hold a short discussion about their progress and any obstacles to make sure that their research and presentations are ready on time.

>7 'The Journey Within'

Unit plan

Session	Approximate number of learning hours	Outline of learning content	Resources
7.1 The Tree	2 hours, 30 minutes	Learners identify meanings in a story opening, explore motifs and write an account in the fantasy genre.	Learner's Book Session 7.1 Workbook Session 7.1 ⬇ Language worksheet 7.1
7.2 The farmers	2 hours, 30 minutes	Learners use their voices to convey character, consider formality in dialogue and discuss themes and patterns in a fantasy story.	Learner's Book Session 7.2 Workbook Session 7.2 ⬇ Language worksheet 7.2
7.3 The bronze door	2 hours, 30 minutes	Learners explore time in a text, consider how a theme is presented, explore the effect of setting on character and describe a fantasy setting.	Learner's Book Session 7.3 Workbook Session 7.3
7.4 The crow	2 hours, 45 minutes	Learners consider plot and character development, compare symbols in two texts, explore fantasy stories further and write a monologue.	Learner's Book Session 7.4 Workbook Session 7.4
7.5 Nothing	2 hours, 30 minutes	Learners work out unfamiliar words, consider the effect of anti-climax, explore how beliefs are reflected in a text and analyse the theme of nature.	Learner's Book Session 7.5 Workbook Session 7.5
7.6 Chosen One	2 hours, 30 minutes	Learners react to a story ending, discuss the genre of *Bildungsroman*, listen to the views of others and write their own fantasy story.	Learner's Book Session 7.6 Workbook Session 7.6 ⬇ Differentiated worksheets 7A, 7B and 7C

BACKGROUND KNOWLEDGE

For the teacher

Unit 7 focuses entirely on one story in the fantasy genre, so it may be useful to remind yourself of the conventions of the fantasy genre, and also of *Bildungsroman* books.

The following grammatical and spelling concepts are covered in this unit:

- rules and breaking rules of capitalisation
- formal and informal language and standard English
- vocabulary associated with tactile imagery
- conventions of play scripts
- prefixes, suffixes and root words and their meanings.

It may be useful for you to read up on these concepts before explaining them to learners, if you are not already confident in how they are defined and applied.

Learners are asked to complete several pair discussions in this unit. You may wish to prearrange learners into 'talk partners' to make these discussions as productive as possible. In addition, it is good practice to make sure learners swap talk partners regularly so that individuals have an opportunity to work with a range of their peers and keep their interactions fresh and productive.

For the learner

Learners are likely to be familiar with the fantasy genre from their exposure to popular fantasy novels, movies and video games. In the same way, young adult literature is rich with popular *Bildungsroman* novels, which often deal with the moral development of their protagonists during adolescence. As a result, learners may bring some well-developed genre expectations to this unit. Learners would benefit from making a list of any fantasy books, movies or games they have enjoyed, considering what they like about them. They should do the same for *Bildungsroman* books.

TEACHING SKILLS FOCUS

Metacognition

Metacognition describes the processes involved when learners plan, monitor, evaluate and make changes to their own learning behaviours. These processes enable learners to take control of their learning, helping them to achieve learning goals they have identified for themselves or that have been set for them. Studies show that such processes improve academic achievement across a range of ages, abilities, learning domains and skills such as comprehension, writing, reasoning and problem solving. Learners can also use metacognitive skills to apply what they have learnt in one context or task to another.

As a teacher, you can support learners in developing their metacognitive skills by:

- Stating learning goals explicitly.
- Explaining to learners what success looks like before they start a task.

- Modelling metacognitive strategies using questioning. For example: Have I done something like this before? Which strategies worked or didn't work on a previous task like this? Do I understand clearly what I need to do?
- Helping learners to monitor their own progress towards achieving their goals. For example: encourage learners to self-assess their work and redraft it if necessary or to ask others to help them assess it.
- Allowing learners to feel confident enough to make mistakes and to discuss them and to see them as valuable learning opportunities. Allow time in your planning and lessons for learners to improve their work in response to mistakes.
- Encouraging learners to reflect on and evaluate the metacognitive strategies they have used.
- Discussing how what has been learnt from one task can be applied to another.

7.1 The Tree

LEARNING PLAN

Learning objectives	Learning intentions	Success criteria
9Rv.03, 9Rs.01, 9Ri.01, 9Ri.03, 9Ri.04, 9Ri.06, 9Wv.01, 9Wv.02, 9Wg.04, 9Ws.01, 9Wc.01, 9Wc.02	Learners will: • identify explicit and deeper meanings in a story opening • explore the implications of a motif • write an account using features of the fantasy genre.	Learners can: • understand the implications of explicit information and explore further layers of meaning in a story opening • understand and analyse the purpose and implications of a motif • choose an appropriate structure for a fictional account and write it using features of the fantasy genre.

LANGUAGE SUPPORT

In the story in this unit, there are a number of words that are capitalised in an unconventional way, including the Tree, the Brown Mountain, the Other Worlds, the Chosen One, and a Giant. Remind learners that place names and people's names are proper nouns and need to have capitals. However, the nouns in the examples above are usually common nouns. The writer uses a capital letter for Tree to emphasise that the tree in question is special, and situated in a particular place. In the same way, 'giant' is a common noun that should not have a capital letter, but the author writes a Giant for stylistic emphasis. Note that the writer uses capitals like this only for 'characters', for example, the lake is not capitalised – although it is a significant place in the story, it is not a character in the same way that the Tree is.

Common misconception

Misconception	How to identify	How to overcome
Motifs and symbols are the same thing.	Ask learners to recall a symbol from a previous extract they have studied. (e.g. the, fallen statue of 'Ozymandias' in Session 6.4 is symbolic of the hubris of the arrogant ruler). Ask: *What if a novel featured fallen statues or ruined cities or forgotten places a number of times in the story – what would we call this literary device?* (a motif)	Explain that symbols and motifs can be easily confused because they are both images, ideas, sounds or words that represent something else. The difference is that a symbol may only appear once or twice in a story to help the reader understand a particular idea. A motif appears more often and is used to explain the central idea or theme of the story.

Starter idea

Fantasy predictions (5 minutes)

Resources: Learner's Book, Session 7.1, Getting started activity

Description: Write the title of the story for this unit on the board, 'The Journey Within', and explain that it is a fantasy story. Ask learners to work in pairs to predict what might happen in the story based on the title and the title of the sessions in this unit. Briefly discuss the predictions as a class.

Main teaching ideas

1 Fantasy story opening (45 minutes)

Learning intention: Identify explicit and deeper meanings in a story opening.

Resources: Learner's Book, Session 7.1, 'The Journey Within' Extract 1, Activity 1

Description: Introduce the extract as the opening of the fantasy story 'A Journey Within'. Ask learners to read it twice, then discuss any unfamiliar words and answer any queries about meaning.

To encourage a metacognitive approach in responding to Activity 1, ask learners to think about appropriate reading strategies: *When have you had to choose an appropriate reading strategy before? For what purpose? Have you improved your use of reading strategies over time? If so, how? For this activity, which strategy might you try instead?*

In pairs, learners should compare and discuss their notes before moving on to the second part of the activity, writing their paragraphs.

› Differentiation ideas:

- Support: Learners should be able to find explicit information related to the bullet points, but they may need support when commenting on these. Ask simple questions to encourage learners to focus on how the details make the opening interesting: *What is unusual about the setting? How is the purpose of Aveleen's journey revealed – is it stated anywhere? How does the writer show how Aveleen is feeling? What is surprising about Celegorn's life?*

- Challenge: Remind learners about genre expectations when writing their paragraphs. This is a fantasy story, so how do the details that make the opening interesting match learners' expectations for a story of this genre?

› Assessment ideas:
Ask learners to add a reflection sentence or two about the notes they made for the first part of Activity 1. How useful were their notes when writing their paragraph? What was good or bad about them? What did they like about their partner's notes? What would they do differently when faced with a similar task? An example response might be: 'My notes were hard to follow because I did not organise them under different subheadings. That meant I had to waste time looking things up in the text again to check. Next time, I might use a spider diagram like my partner to organise my notes better.'

2 The motif of the Tree (30 minutes)

Learning intention: Identify explicit and deeper meanings in a story opening. Explore the implications of a motif.

Resources: Learner's Book, Session 7.1, Activities 2 and 3

Description: Ask learners to work in pairs to complete Activity 2. They could draw a grid of magical and real items, actions and concepts and then discuss them as instructed.

Read the Language focus feature as a class, to introduce the concept of a motif. Ask learners to discuss the example of the wedding ring. Ask learners how this differs from a symbol and ensure learners recognise the difference (see Common misconception).

Write *the Tree* on the board. Ask learners why they think 'Tree' has a capital letter (see Language support). Introduce the idea of 'the Tree' as a motif. Learners should then complete Activity 3 as a discussion in pairs.

› Differentiation ideas:

- Support: Provide a grid for learners to complete during Activity 2. Ask questions to focus their responses on the effect of these details on the reader: *What is a waterskin and what does it suggest about Aveleen's world? How is time described? Why are the paths described as devious and false?*

- Challenge: Ask learners to list motifs they know from other books and identify what they mean, for example Harry Potter's scar (a motif for the power of love and for destiny) or singing in *The Lord of the Rings* (a motif for unity and friendship).

different words and to change their tone of voice. Can their partner name the effect they are creating (for example threatening or apologetic)?

Main teaching ideas

1 Performing dialogue (40 minutes)

Learning intention: Use voice to convey character when reading an unseen text aloud.

Resources: Learner's Book, Session 7.2, 'The Journey Within' Extract 2, Activity 1

Description: Introduce the next extract of the story and explain that for Activity 1 learners should read the text aloud in groups. Go through the Speaking tip with the class, then ask learners to organise themselves into groups and assign parts. They should read the extract through for the first time. Once completed, they should swap parts and read it through a second time.

> **Differentiation ideas:**

- Support: You may wish to organise the groups beforehand so that you can support less confident learners using the method outlined in Language support at the start of the session.

- Challenge: Ask learners to discuss the role of the narrator: *How can the narrator help convey character too? What tone should the narrator use?*

> **Assessment ideas:** Monitor learners' performances and give oral feedback about how successfully they are conveying character through their voices. Ask questions to support this: *How do you think the woman farmer is feeling when she says that? What tone would Aveleen use when she says that?*

2 Analysing formality in dialogue (50 minutes)

Learning intention: Consider the effect of formality in dialogue.

Resources: Learner's Book, Session 7.2, Activity 2; Language worksheet 7.2

Description: Before starting Activity 2, use the guidance to introduce Language worksheet 7.2, which contains exercises on formal and informal dialogue. When they have completed the worksheet, spend some time briefly discussing their responses. Address any misconceptions about standard English and formality (see Common misconception).

Explain to learners that so far they have looked at different levels of formality in dialogue. Now they are going to consider its effect, too. Ask learners to read the Language focus feature in the Learner's Book. As a class, briefly discuss the effects of the two examples and address any queries and misconceptions.

Read Activity 2 together, and point out that learners are being asked to focus on the *effect* created by the dialogues in the extract and the levels of formality in each. Learners should complete the activity, including examples from the text to support their analysis.

> **Differentiation ideas:**

- Support: Some learners may need help identifying and commenting on the formality of the dialogues. Consider pairing learners, allowing them to discuss their ideas before they write their analyses. In particular, ask questions to help learners interpret the effect the dialogues create:

  - *How can you tell what the relationship is between the two farmers from how they speak to one another?*

  - *Can you give an example from the text?*

- Challenge: Ask learners to summarise Celegorn's character in the extracts they have read so far, using three adjectives that are not based on his appearance (for example wise, commanding, mysterious) and to give examples from the text, especially the dialogue. Extend this by asking learners to do the same for Aveleen.

> **Assessment ideas:** Ask learners to share what they have written to assess how well they have met the success criteria. Have learners understood how formality can be used to convey character? Have they commented on the effect of both formal and informal dialogue?

3 Exploring the fantasy genre (45 minutes)

Learning intention: Discuss themes and patterns in a fantasy story.

Resources: Learner's Book, Session 7.2, Activities 3 and 4

Description: Read the information in Activity 3 to the class, and make sure that learners understand that a quest is a common structural device in the fantasy genre. In pairs, learners should discuss

Aveleen's encounter with the farmers in this context. Learners should then complete Activity 3, using the bullet points and their discussion to structure their responses.

Explain to learners that they will be working in pairs to discuss the story so far, looking at its themes and patterns. Introduce Activity 4 and ask learners to discuss each bullet point in turn, taking time to explore their ideas in depth and where they agree and disagree.

When they have finished, learners should complete the Reflection feature.

> **Differentiation ideas:**

- Support: For Activity 3, provide learners with a sheet containing sentence starters to help them organise their writing: *The problem is . . . , One farmer thinks . . . , The other thinks . . . , The solution Aveleen suggests is . . . , This shows that Aveleen is . . .*

- Challenge: Ask learners to write a short summary of their predictions using their knowledge of the patterns and themes so far, as well as their genre expectations. They should put these aside for now; they will revisit them at the end of the unit.

> **Assessment ideas:** A metacognitive approach encourages reflection and evaluation. Ask learners to evaluate the depth and quality of their discussions:

- What was successful or unsuccessful about them?

- How did their comments contribute to the discussion?

- Did their disagreements affect the discussion in a positive or negative way?

- What would they change about how they tackled the task?

Give learners a minute to think of a way they could apply what they have learnt from this discussion task to another in the future, for example they may ask their partner more open questions or use a timer so that they have equal time to speak and explain without interruption. Ask learners to share their thoughts on this. You could record these so you can remind learners to apply them in a future task.

Plenary idea

Session reflection (10 minutes)

Description: Ask learners to read the Summary checklist. They should give themselves a score out of 10 for each point to indicate how well they think they have achieved the success criteria. Learners could share their scores with a partner and identify where the difference in their scores for one criteria was the greatest. The learner with the higher score should then ask the learner with the lower score what they found difficult and, if possible, explain or address any misconceptions. The pair should find a further criteria to discuss where they swap roles.

Homework idea

Learners should complete Workbook Session 7.2.

7.3 The bronze door

LEARNING PLAN

Learning objectives	Learning intentions	Success criteria
9Rv.02, 9Rs.01, 9Ri.01, 9Ri.03, 9Ri.04, 9Ri.07, 9Ri.08, 9Ww.01, 9Ww.03, 9Wv.01, 9Wv.02, 9Wc.04, 9Wp.04	Learners will: • explore the way time is used to structure a narrative text • consider how a theme is presented and how it relates to other texts • explore the effect of setting on character • describe an imaginative fantasy setting.	Learners can: • analyse the way time is used as a structural device in a narrative text • explain how a theme is presented and explore it in relation to other texts • comment on how setting can impact character • write a description of a fantasy setting to create specific effects.

LANGUAGE SUPPORT

Some activities in this session focus on how the imagery used to describe a setting can affect character. The Writing tip asks learners to remember to use tactile imagery for this purpose, so it may be useful to recap this type of sensory imagery.

Ask learners what *tactile* means (related to the sense of touch). Encourage learners to think of this in a wider sense: tactile imagery conveys things that can be felt as well as touched. Provide a list of words to support this:

• texture (smooth, abrasive, coarse, dented, etched, gritty, mushy, etc.)
• temperature (cool, mild, sizzling, crisp, boiling, bracing, cosy, etc.)
• touch (flexible, damp, sticky, limp, flimsy, greasy, stiff, etc.)
• movement (drag, clap, stir, fall, sway, lift, shove, etc.)

Starter idea

A memorable place (5 minutes)

Resources: Learner's Book, Session 7.3, Getting started activity

Description: Ask learners to close their eyes and imagine they are in a place they have been that had a real impact on them. How did this place make them feel? What sights, sounds and smells are there? In pairs, learners should describe their place to each other. Encourage learners to use visual, aural and tactile imagery to convey the scene and why it had such an impact.

Main teaching ideas

1 The theme of time (50 minutes)

Learning intention: Explore the way time is used to structure a narrative text. Consider how a theme is presented and how it relates to other texts.

Resources: Learner's Book, Session 7.3, 'The Journey Within' Extract 3, Activities 1 and 2

Description: Ask learners to read Extract 3 of the story. Allow time for them to discuss in pairs what they have read, focusing on how time is presented in the extract. Introduce Activity 1 and read the information together on how the writer uses time as a structural device. Ask learners to continue their discussions based on the bullet points.

Move on to Activity 2 and remind learners of some of the ideas about time they explored in Unit 4. Ask them to discuss how these ideas are presented in 'The Journey Within'.

To support a metacognitive approach, write the success criteria about time as a structural and thematic device on the board. Make sure learners understand these criteria by asking them to identify the key words to help them structure their writing precisely:

- *I can <u>analyse</u> the way <u>time</u> is used as a <u>structural device</u> in a narrative text.*
- *I can <u>explain</u> how a <u>theme</u> is <u>presented</u>.*

Learners should complete Activity 2, writing an analysis of what the story so far shows about time. They should comment on time as both a structural device and as a theme. Remind learners that they should use carefully selected references from the text to support their points. When everyone has completed their paragraph, come together as a class and share some of the paragraphs.

> **Differentiation ideas:**

- Support: Provide a writing frame that focuses learners' responses on the success criteria. You could also provide a list of words they should aim to include in their responses (for example *structural device*, *narrative time frame*, *shift of tense*, *flashback*, *theme*, *past*, *present*, *future*).
- Challenge: Extend Activity 2 by asking learners to refer to other texts in their analysis. They should look back at Unit 4 and compare how time is presented in 'The Journey Within' with a text of their choice from Unit 4, commenting on any similarities or differences and their effect.

> **Assessment ideas:** After Activity 2, ask learners to assess their paragraphs against the success criteria, especially the key words they identified. How well does their paragraph address the success criteria? What could they do to improve it? Allow some time here for learners to redraft their work.

2 Inside the mountain (25 minutes)

Learning intention: Explore the effect of setting on character.

Resources: Learner's Book, Session 7.3, Activity 3

Description: Learners should start by reading Extract 3 again. Ask them for a few suggestions

about how Aveleen feels about her experiences inside the mountain, then read Activity 3 to the class. Tell learners to take notes as they discuss the bullet points. Allow time for learners to have a full discussion of all the points and to write an answer to the following question: *What effect does the setting have on Aveleen?*

After completing Activity 3, ask each pair of learners to share an example of the language the writer uses (words, phrases, imagery, figurative language) to reveal Aveleen's emotions. Record these on the board if you think it will be useful. Then discuss the answer to the question above about the effect the setting has on Aveleen.

> **Differentiation ideas:**

- Support: Remind learners of the difference between types of imagery (visual, aural and tactile) and the different types of figurative language (similes, metaphors, hyperbole, etc.).
- Challenge: Widen the discussion to what the inside of the mountain represents in terms of Aveleen's journey. For example, it can be read as a spatial metaphor for the temptation to give up and settle for an easy life, free of responsibility. What other ideas do learners have?

> **Assessment ideas:** Monitor learners' paired discussions during Activity 3 to assess how well they are commenting on Aveleen's feelings and the effect of the setting on her decisions and character.

3 A fantastical setting (55 minutes)

Learning intention: Describe an imaginative fantasy setting.

Resources: Learner's Book, Session 7.3, Activity 4; dictionaries

Description: Ask learners to briefly recall Aveleen's emotions inside the mountain and to write these down as a list of abstract nouns (awe, wonder, comfort, contentment, admiration, completion, thrill, enchantment, reassurance, familiarity). Tell learners that they are now going to write a scene that conveys the same emotions using their own imagination.

Read the instructions for Activity 4 and ensure learners understand the purpose and audience for the writing. Before they start, ask a volunteer to read the Writing tip, then briefly explore the emphasis on tactile imagery (see Language support at the start of the session). Do not allow access to dictionaries at this point. Learners should then complete Activity 4.

> **Differentiation ideas:**

- Support: Create a planning sheet so that learners can organise their ideas before writing. This could include prompts such as: *a visual image, a tactile image, a simile using an aural image* or *synonyms for happiness.*

- Challenge: Ask learners to include a moment in their description where there is a turning point in the mood of the character in response to the setting (in the same way that Aveleen remembers her mission). Learners should use the same language choices and techniques to convey this change.

> **Assessment ideas:** Learners should complete the Peer-assessment activity in the Learner's Book. One way to support metacognitive development is to give learners time to think about and learn from their mistakes, so ensure that learners discuss the accuracy of each other's spelling in a sensitive way and allow time for them to use dictionaries and correct any mistakes. They could discuss strategies for remembering how to spell such words correctly in the future.

Plenary idea

Sharing fantastical settings (15 minutes)

Resources: Completed descriptions from Activity 4

Description: Ask learners to share their writing with the rest of the class. Write the success criteria on the board: *Write a description of a fantasy setting to create specific effects.* Ask learners to comment on something that had a specific effect on them as they were listening, such as a tactile image or a phrase of emotive language.

CROSS-CURRICULAR LINK

Art (creating an imaginative scene): 'The Journey Within' can be interpreted as a journey Aveleen goes on 'within' herself (inside her own mind) rather than in reality. Learners could represent this in a piece of art. For example, they could draw the fantastical scene inside the mountain as if it was inside Aveleen's head.

Homework idea

Learners should complete Workbook Session 7.3.

7.4 The crow

LEARNING PLAN

Learning objectives	Learning intentions	Success criteria
9Rv.03, 9Ri.01, 9Ri.03, 9Ri.04, 9Ri.08, 9Ra.02, 9Ra.04, 9Wv.01, 9Wc.01, 9Wc.03, 9Wc.04, 9Wc.05, 9Wc.07, 9SLm.03, 9SLs.01, 9SL.02, 9SLr.01	Learners will: • consider the significance of plot and character development • compare the use of symbols in two texts • explore the content of fantasy stories and readers' reactions to them • write a monologue in the voice of a particular character.	Learners can: • comment on how plot and characters are developed in a story and what this means • identify the meaning of symbols and compare how they are used in different texts • respond to readers' reactions about the content of fantasy stories, and express their own response • write a monologue in the voice of a character to entertain the reader.

LANGUAGE SUPPORT

In this session, learners are asked to give their opinion on different views of the story so far. In activities like these, it is common for learners to limit their language to phrases such as 'I think . . .'. Support learners by preparing them with functional phrases and structures that will allow them to be more nuanced and precise. Present learners with a selection of phrases they can use for offering and explaining opinions. This selection should range from simple expressions, such as *In my opinion . . .*, *I feel that . . .* and *I prefer . . .*, to more advanced constructions, such as *My initial reaction is . . .*, *There is part of me that thinks . . .* and *I've always thought . . .*

Starter idea

Talking animals (5 minutes)

Resources: Learner's Book, Session 7.4, Getting started activity

Description: Ask learners to discuss any books or films they know that feature talking animals. In what genres of books or films do such animals appear? Do they like such books and films? Why, or why not? What do talking animals add to the narrative?

Main teaching ideas

1 Plot, character and symbols (30 minutes)

Learning intentions: Consider the significance of plot and character development. Compare the use of symbols in two texts.

Resources: Learner's Book, Session 7.4, 'The Journey Within' Extract 4, Activities 1–3

Description: Introduce Activity 1, then ask learners to read the next extract and make notes as instructed to understand what is happening at this point in the story. Learners should then move straight on to Activity 2 using their notes from the first activity to help them. This should be carried out as a pair discussion to begin with, then together as a class to discuss ideas.

Write *symbol*, *motif* and *theme* on the board. Ask learners to think about this unit so far and to discuss the difference between the meanings of the three words (a symbol is something concrete that represents something abstract like an idea; a motif is a recurring idea, image or symbol; a theme is the core meaning of a story, which is reinforced by motifs and symbols). Ask learners about the talking crow. Do they think it is real or symbolic? If symbolic, what does it represent?

Read the Reading tip to the class and remind learners that not everything in a story should be interpreted figuratively. Then introduce Activity 3 and ask learners what they remember about 'Chasm' from Unit 6. They should then complete the activity as a discussion in pairs before again reporting back to the class. Do learners agree on the significance and symbolism of the crater? Can the crater be classed as a spatial metaphor as Milford Sound was is 'Chasm'?

> **Differentiation ideas:**

* Support: Join in with pairs as they discuss the similes in Activities 2 and 3. Ask questions to focus their discussions on character development and symbolism:
  * *What does Aveleen put up with to reach the crater?*
  * *What does this tell you about her?*
  * *Does it fit with what came earlier in the story?*
  * *What does Aveleen's angry reactions say about her?*
  * *Why do you think she dislikes the crow as soon as she sees it?*

* Challenge: Extend Activity 3 by asking learners to explain which of the two symbols (the crater here and Milford Sound in 'Chasm') they prefer and why.

> **Assessment ideas:** Monitor learners' discussions to gauge the depth of their responses to the learning intentions. Listen in particular for the features learners are picking out as evidence of the character development and symbolism.

2 Reactions to fantasy stories (45 minutes)

Learning intention: Explore the content of fantasy stories and readers' reactions to them.

Resources: Learner's Book, Session 7.4, Activities 4 and 5

Description: Ask learners to recall the characters Aveleen encounters on her journey to the lake. Read the introduction to Activity 4 and remind learners that Aveleen notices something familiar about all the characters she meets. Learners should complete the activity as a discussion in pairs, but come together as a class to discuss the final bullet point. Why have these characters been included? What do they represent?

Ask for a show of hands from learners to indicate whether they enjoy fantasy stories in general or not. Then ask how much they are enjoying this story and to give reasons why or why not. Explain that they are now going to explore different reactions to the story – their own and other people's.

Read the Speaking tip to the class, then ask for two volunteers to read Marcus and Sofia's responses in the Learner's Book. Introduce Activity 5 and ask learners to complete parts **a** and **b** as a paired discussion. Advise them that they will be summarising this discussion so they may want to take brief notes in a suitable format as they talk. Allow plenty of time for learners to discuss their opinions and explanations and their preferences and contexts. Remind them to refer to the text to support their views.

Finally, learners should independently write a short (100–150 words) summary of the ideas covered in their discussion for part **c**.

> **Differentiation ideas:**

- Support: Learners may need support giving and explaining their opinions so provide them with a list of functional language they can use (see Language support).

- Challenge: Ask learners to think how they could persuade someone who dislikes the fantasy genre to change their mind. They should write down three persuasive reasons, for example 'Although they are not based in the real world, fantasy stories deal with what it means to be human in an imaginative way.'

> **Assessment ideas:** Before learners write their summaries, they should work in their pairs to complete the Peer-assessment feature, feeding back to each other using the prompts in the bullet points.

3 Writing a monologue (60 minutes)

Learning intention: Write a monologue in the voice of a particular character.

Resources: Learner's Book, Session 7.4, Activity 6

Description: Tell learners they are now going to imagine they are Aveleen, at the point in the story when she reaches the crater and the chasm opens, and explore how she feels at that moment. To do this, set up a 'thought tunnel' (see Main teaching idea 3 in Session 5.3 for full instructions on setting up this activity). One learner will walk through the 'tunnel' as Aveleen. The learners on one side should speak the negative thoughts Aveleen might be having (for example *Celegorn didn't tell me about the chasm*). Learners on the opposite side should imagine her positive thoughts (*There must be a way across* or *I will not give up now after everything I've been through!*).

Learners should listen carefully to each other so that they do not repeat the same words and expressions: encourage learners to react quickly if someone else says what they were about to say and express a similar sentiment in a different way or think of something else.

After the 'thought tunnel' experiment, read the instructions for Activity 6 as a class. Emphasise that learners should focus on writing their monologue in Aveleen's voice, using ideas from the 'thought tunnel'. They should write their monologue in the form of a play script.

> **Differentiation ideas:**

- Support: Remind learners of some of the conventions for writing and setting out a playscript: stage directions should appear between a pair of brackets; stage directions for character movements should be in the present tense, for example *(stands up)*; stage directions for character reactions, behaviour or tone of voice should use adjectives, adverbs or the past participle, for example *(angry)* or *(seriously)* or *(shocked)*. Remind learners of things to avoid as well, for example no speech marks are required unless a character is quoting something or someone else.

- Challenge: Extend this activity by asking learners to include the appearance of the crow in their monologues. The extended scene should end just as the crow is about to speak.

> **Assessment ideas:** Use AfL techniques to provide purposeful written feedback for Activity 6. This should only relate to the relevant success criteria and activity instructions; it should not focus on grammar, spelling, syntax, etc. Highlight three 'successful' sentences or phrases in their work in

one colour and one sentence or phrase in another colour where a change would improve the learner's response. Write a short instruction or question to guide the learner in how to make the improvement. The next activity provides time for learners to write their improvements.

Plenary idea

Aveleen's monologue (15 minutes)

Resources: Completed monologues from Activity 6

Description: Ask learners to share their monologues with the help of a partner: one person should perform Aveleen's words and the other should read the stage directions and make any sound effects. Give informal feedback on how well they have captured Aveleen's voice and her conflicting feelings, as well as on the use of stage directions and sound effects.

Homework idea

Learners should complete Workbook Session 7.4.

7.5 Nothing

LEARNING PLAN

Learning objectives	Learning intentions	Success criteria
9Rv.01, 9Rs.01, 9Ri.01, 9Ri.08, 9Ra.05, 9Wg.04, 9Wg.05, 9SLm.02, 9SLm.03	Learners will: • work out the meanings of unfamiliar words • consider the structural effect of anti-climax • explore how beliefs about life are reflected in a text • discuss and analyse the theme of nature.	Learners can: • choose appropriate strategies to work out the meanings of unfamiliar words • explain the effect of an anti-climax on a text • comment on how beliefs about life, including fate and fortune, are reflected in a text • discuss the theme of nature in a text and then write a formal analysis.

LANGUAGE SUPPORT

Some of the unfamiliar words in this session's extract have prefixes and suffixes attached to a root word. Use this session to reinforce the spelling and meaning of common prefixes, such as *in-*, *un-* and *dis-*, and common suffixes, such as *-ous*, *-able* and *-ly*.

Help learners to understand that common prefixes change the meaning to the opposite or negative of the root word, and that suffixes show the word type. For example, the suffixes *-able* and *-ous* indicate that the word is an adjective (unthink*able*, incredul*ous*). The suffix *-ly* often indicates that the word is an adverb (distracted*ly*). Recognising these prefixes and suffixes will help learners to determine the type of word they are hearing or reading, offering another possible route into working out the meaning of unfamiliar words.

Starter idea

Fortune and fate (10 minutes)

Resources: Learner's Book, Session 7.5, Getting started activity

Description: Ask learners to read the four statements about fate and fortune. In small groups, they should discuss what the words mean in the different contexts. Are learners familiar with the different meanings? Challenge each group to come up with a sentence of their own for each word, or to give examples of a further meaning, for example *The old woman looked at my hands and told my fortune.*

Main teaching ideas

1 Exploring anti-climax (50 minutes)

Learning intentions: Work out the meanings of unfamiliar words. Consider the structural effect of anti-climax.

Resources: Learner's Book, Session 7.5, 'The Journey Within' Extract 5, Activities 1 and 2; dictionaries

Description: Explain to learners that they are reaching the end of the story. Ask them to recall what they know about story structure. What would they expect to happen at this point (the *climax* of the story, involving a dramatic moment)?

Introduce Activity 1. Ask learners to recall strategies for working out the meaning of unfamiliar words (contextual, morphological and etymological clues). Learners should read Extract 5 straight through once. They should then read it again and discuss the meaning of the underlined words with a partner. Ask them to write definitions of what they think the words mean, then check them in a dictionary.

Ask learners what they think about this, the climax of the story. Was it what they were expecting? Draw out the idea that in fact this extract is an *anti-climax* and briefly explain what this means using the Key word definitions. Explain that it is structural choice made by the writer, using the introduction to Activity 2. Ask learners why the author might have chosen to use an anti-climax at this point of the story. Learners should then complete Activity 2 on their own, analysing the effect of the anti-climax.

> **Differentiation ideas:**

- Support: Learners may need help remembering strategies for working out word meanings or using a dictionary efficiently. Ask questions

to remind them: *Can you use the surrounding words to work out the meaning? What organisational clues can you use to find a word quickly in a dictionary* (guide words at the top of each page)?

- Challenge: Ask learners to explain how they worked out a word meaning and to grade how close their meanings were to the dictionary definitions.

> **Assessment ideas:** Learners could peer assess each other's expectations for the end of the story. Tell each pair to feed back something they really liked about the other's prediction and why, and something they did not agree with and why.

2 Fantasy and 'real life' (25 minutes)

Learning intention: Explore how beliefs about life are reflected in a text.

Resources: Learner's Book, Session 7.5, Activity 3

Description: Ask learners to name some of the fantastical or magical things in the story so far (a talking crow, a world inside a mountain, etc.). Next, ask them to name some things that would be recognisable in 'real life' (the bundle of wheat, Aveleen's boots, etc.). Then ask the same questions about the rules of Aveleen's world. You may wish to explore this in scientific terms (see Cross-curricular links).

Write *Fortune* and *Fate* on the board and introduce Activity 3. Discuss the meanings of fortune and fate in the activity description. Learners should complete the activity as a discussion in pairs. Use the Speaking tip to remind learners to listen to and question each other in a respectful way when discussing belief systems.

After the discussion, learners should complete the Reflection feature on their own.

> **Differentiation ideas:**

- Support: It may help learners to provide them with a list of functional language they can use to help them discuss and disagree about complex topics in a respectful way. Such language helps learners acknowledge the existence of a different point of view before stating their own. For example: *Some people may disagree, but . . . , I could be wrong, but . . . , It's a difficult issue, but . . . , To the best or my knowledge . . . , I think it is reasonable to say . . .* and *Although I can see both points of view . . .*

- Challenge: Ask learners to give examples of different meanings of fortune and fate. For example: a fortune can be a large amount of money, goods or property; someone's fate is something that happens to someone, often final or negative, such as death or defeat.

> **Assessment ideas:** Monitor learners' discussions to gauge how well they are commenting on how beliefs about life are reflected in a text. Use open questions to encourage learners to explain their thinking: *To what extent do you think good or bad luck plays a role in Aveleen's journey? How much does fate play a part in the story? How do you feel about such beliefs?*

3 The theme of nature (45 minutes)

Learning intention: Discuss and analyse the theme of nature.

Resources: Learner's Book, Session 7.5, Activities 4 and 5

Description: Ask learners to recall one of the themes of the story so far (time). Introduce Activity 4 and explain that nature is another key theme. Have a brief class discussion about elements of nature that have appeared in the story so far, then go through the bullet points learners should include in their discussion. Draw out any prior knowledge about how writers show the relationship between humans and nature, for example pathetic fallacy in Session 6.5.

Learners should complete Activity 4 as a discussion in pairs before briefly coming back together as a class to discuss ideas. Ask learners what role nature plays in the story. Do the natural objects, animals and environments have a deeper, symbolic meaning? Does the writer use the pathetic fallacy?

Introduce the writing task in Activity 5. Learners should then write their analyses in line with the bullet points in the description.

> **Differentiation ideas:**

- Support: Allow extra time for learners to complete Activity 5. Offer your own questions to help them find evidence from the texts and structure their response:
  - *How will you organise your writing?*
  - *What words could you quote from the text to show that?*
- Challenge: Remind learners that a theme is the core meaning of a story. In addition to the bullet points, ask them to comment on

what they think the story has to say about the relationship between humans and the natural world.

> **Assessment ideas:** Provide written feedback for Activity 5, highlighting a number of successes. Make sure your feedback is task-focused and set a target in the form of a question about how learners could improve their learning. For example: *Your analysis includes lots of good points mixed up in one paragraph. Can you think how you could organise and structure these points in a more effective way?*

Plenary idea

Dictionary definitions challenge (15 minutes)

Resources: Dictionaries

Description: Organise learners into small teams and give each team a dictionary. Challenge learners to find the dictionary definitions of the following words from the extracts so far. Each team member should take a turn and find the dictionary definition as quickly as possible. You may wish to discuss how to use a dictionary efficiently before you start. Use the following words:

weary (adj.)	recoil (verb)
precipice (noun)	resistance (noun)
incapable (adj.)	reassuring (adj.)
banish (verb)	harmony (noun)

You could extend this activity by asking learners to find synonyms for these words in a thesaurus.

CROSS-CURRICULAR LINK

Science (real science vs. science fiction): Fantasy stories often contain many elements that do not exist in real life, such as giants or cities inside mountains. The reader is asked to 'suspend disbelief' and accept these fantastical elements. However, fantasy stories also have to be rooted in reality for them to make any sense. Ask learners to identify all the elements and features in the story that are consistent with 'real world' science (how gravity and light work). Which features are not consistent in this way (the strange misleading paths)? What effect do both of these have?

Homework idea

Learners should complete Workbook Session 7.5.

7.6 Chosen One

LEARNING PLAN

Learning objectives	Learning intentions	Success criteria
9Ri.01, 9Ri.03, 9Ri.04, 9Ri.08, 9Ra.01, 9Ra.05, 9Ra.02, 9Ww.01, 9Wv.01, 9Wv.02, 9Ws.01, 9Wc.01, 9Wc.03, 9Wc.04, 9Wp.04, 9SLs.01, 9SLg.01, 9SLg.02, 9SLg.04	Learners will: • express their reactions to the ending of the story • discuss whether the story fits the genre of *Bildungsroman* • listen to the views of others about the full story • write their own fantasy story.	Learners can: • comment in detail on the ending of a story • identify the features of *Bildungsroman* in a story • understand and respond to the views expressed by others about a text • write a fantasy story using appropriate literary, language and structural techniques.

LANGUAGE SUPPORT

In Activity 3, help learners improve their listening skills by asking them to predict what they might hear from each of the students in the audio. Before listening, ask questions that will prepare learners for the content of the audio. Here, learners are asked to make notes on Jack's views on minor characters, so you could ask:

• Who are the minor characters?
• What are they like?
• Do you think they are real or imagined?

You could also prepare a list of specific words or phrases that you would like learners to listen out for; in Lara's audio, you could ask them to listen out for the word 'mentor'. After listening, ask learners:

• What words came before and after 'mentor'? ('a' and 'figure')
• How did Lara define what type of person a mentor is?
• According to Lara, what is a mentor's job?

Starter idea

Predicting the ending (5 minutes)

Resources: Learner's Book, Session 7.6, Getting started activity

Description: Remind learners about how they wrote about and discussed their expectations for the final part of the story in Session 7.5. Ask learners to think about Aveleen's story so far and to consider how it might end. Working on their own, learners should note down their predictions. Who do they think the Chosen One might be and why? Learners should then discuss their ideas in pairs.

Main teaching ideas

1 Reactions to the ending (20 minutes)

Learning intentions: Express their reactions to the ending of the story. Discuss whether the story fits the genre of *Bildungsroman*.

Resources: Learner's Book, Session 7.6, 'The Journey Within' Extract 6, Activities 1 and 2

Description: Tell learners to read Extract 6 – the final part of the story – and then complete Activity 1, discussing their reactions to the ending of the story. Open up the discussion to the whole class.

Write *Bildungsroman* on the board and ask learners if they have come across the word before. Explain its German etymology: *Bildung* (education or formation) + *roman* (novel). Introduce Activity 2 and ask learners to discuss in pairs whether the story fits the genre of the *Bildungsroman*.

> Differentiation ideas:

- Support: Ask learners some open questions to stimulate their discussions. For example: *What does Aveleen learn about herself during the story? How does her quest shape or change her? What do you think her journey represents?*

- Challenge: Ask learners if they have read or know of any other famous *Bildungsroman* books, for example *The Catcher in the Rye* (J. D. Salinger), *The Hunger Games* (Suzanne Collins), *Great Expectations* (Charles Dickens), *Aristotle and Dante Discover the Secrets of the Universe* (Benjamin Alire Sáenz). They could identify the genre features in these or any others they know of.

> Assessment ideas: Monitor learners' paired discussions during Activity 1 to assess how well they are expressing their ideas about the story ending.

56 🎧 2 Listening to other reactions (40 minutes)

Learning intention: Listen to the views of others about the full story.

Resources: Learner's Book, Session 7.6, Activities 3 and 4

> ⬇ **Download the audioscript for Activity 3 from Cambridge GO (Track 56).**

Description: Explain to learners that they will now be considering the meaning of the whole story. Introduce Activity 3 and explain that learners will have to take notes on the views of four different people that they hear speaking. You may wish to prepare learners for this listening exercise using the advice in Language support at the start of the session.

Share the Listening tip, then play the audio for the first time and ask learners to listen only. Afterwards, ask open questions to gauge how well they have picked up the overall meaning. If necessary, play the audio again before repeating it for a third time while learners make their notes.

Ask learners to organise themselves into groups of three or four, then read through Activity 4. Before learners start their discussion, to encourage a metacognitive approach, ask learners to think about a time when they have held a group discussion in the past. Ask: *What do you remember about your discussion? Was it effective in allowing everyone to contribute? How could you organise yourselves to have a more effective discussion than last time? Will you assign roles or make some ground rules?*

Learners should then complete Activity 4, using their notes to discuss the views they have heard in the audio.

> Differentiation ideas:

- Support: Prearrange the groups for this activity so that members will provide suitable levels of support for each other. Encourage learners to assign a chairperson to ensure that all group members are given a chance to contribute. If necessary, provide a transcript of the audio for learners to follow.

- Challenge: After their discussions, ask learners to write their own interpretations of what the story means.

> Assessment ideas: Ask learners to think about their group discussions. How successful were they? Did each member have enough time to speak? Did people listen carefully? Did people have a chance to ask questions or challenge opinions? Was their discussion controlled or chaotic and what effect did that have? How might they organise themselves differently next time?

3 Planning a short fantasy story (25 minutes)

Learning intention: Write a fantasy story.

Resources: Learner's Book, Session 7.6, Activity 5; Differentiated worksheets 7A, 7B and 7C

Description: Tell learners that the last task of this unit is to write their own short fantasy story, but first they need to plan their writing. Introduce Activity 5, the task, the word count and the audience. Ask learners to look back through their Learner's Book to remind themselves of the skills and genre knowledge they have developed. Remind them that they will need to plan their stories carefully.

Before learners begin their writing, hand out Differentiated worksheets 7A, 7B or 7C and explain that these can be used to help with their planning.

> Differentiation ideas:

- Support: In addition to the differentiated planning worksheets, remind learners to revisit their fantasy names work from Language worksheet 7.1.

- Challenge: Ask learners to choose a non-chronological structure for their story, for example a flashforward or flashback.

> Assessment ideas: Providing some informal written feedback on learners' plans will help you assess how well they have developed their genre knowledge. Comment on any aspects of the plan that might need to be clarified when they write their stories.

4 Writing a short fantasy story (50 minutes)

Learning intention: Write a fantasy story.

Resources: Learner's Book, Session 7.6, Activity 5; completed Differentiated worksheets

Description: Learners should write their stories using their completed plans. Afterwards, they should complete the Peer-assessment feature and then edit or redraft their work.

> Differentiation ideas:

- Support: Allow extra time for learners to write and edit their stories.
- Challenge: Consider setting a strict word limit of 500 words and no more. Encourage learners to edit their stories to make every word count!

> Assessment ideas: Provide effective written feedback for Activity 3. Effective feedback should always be linked to the task and any success criteria. It should be written clearly, be detailed and constructive and should identify strengths and weaknesses. It should begin by saying what a learner has done well and should provide guidance on how a learner can improve. Such feedback should also be prompt so that the task is fresh in learners' minds.

Plenary idea

Quick-fire blurb challenge (10 minutes)

Description: Remind learners what a blurb is (a brief summary of the story designed to make people want to buy the book), then explain that they are going to write an engaging blurb for their story as quickly as possible. They should include elements of plot, character and setting, but no spoilers. Tell them to write in the present tense. For example: *The Tree has spoken but who is the Chosen One? Tenacious Aveleen travels high into the mountains in search of a new leader.* Give learners just five minutes to write the blurbs underneath their completed stories.

Homework idea

Learners should complete Workbook Session 7.6.

PROJECT GUIDANCE

A useful sequence for carrying out this project would be as follows.

1. Outline the entire project to the class. Explain what the aim is and what they need to produce and present. For example:
   - collaborate in groups to come up with an idea for a new fantasy television series
   - hold creative workshops to discuss the 'world' their series will be set in, its central characters, conflicts and rules, and an overall plot across ten episodes
   - present their ideas to the class in an imaginative way.

2. Organise the class into small 'creative teams' for the project (a group of four is optimal). Ask each group to elect a 'show runner' who will coordinate their group's project. Explain that the show runner's role is to lead discussions and to make sure presentations are finished on time. Tell learners that you will be asking each show runner to report to you on their creative team's progress as they discuss ideas and prepare their presentations.

3. Allow some class time for the first creative workshop to discuss initial ideas, led by the show runner. They should start with a 'world-building' session as described in the Learner's Book.

4. Next, allow time for a second workshop so that teams can come up with a plot to take place in their fantasy worlds, guided by the bullet-point prompts in their books.

5. Following their creative workshops, the teams should decide on how they are going to present their ideas and how they will divide the work needed to prepare and present them. Set teams a deadline for completing their

CONTINUED

presentation materials. Again, you may wish to provide some class time for the preparation of these materials.

6   Meet at least once with the show runners during the project. Use the meeting to gauge how well their creative team's presentation preparation is going. Are they on schedule? Do they need to organise themselves differently?

Use dialogue and questioning to guide the show runners in exploring any new options for managing the project. If necessary, meet each team and hold a short discussion about their progress and any obstacles to make sure that their presentations are ready on time.

7   Ask each team to present their ideas.

> 8 Different lives

Unit plan

Session	Approximate number of learning hours	Outline of learning content	Resources
8.1 The aeroplane	2 hours, 30 minutes	Learners explore drama, movement, set design, characters and themes. They also consider how conflict can be shown through language choices.	Learner's Book Session 8.1 Workbook Session 8.1
8.2 Mrs Manzi	2 hours, 30 minutes	Learners compare how characters are presented within a play and write a scene with contrasting characters.	Learner's Book Session 8.2 Workbook Session 8.2
8.3 A different voice	2 hours, 30 minutes	Learners explore the content, structure and point of view of an informative article, and write their own feature article.	Learner's Book Session 8.3 Workbook Session 8.3 ⬇ Language worksheet 8.1 ⬇ Differentiated worksheets 8A, 8B and 8C
8.4 He for she	2 hours, 30 minutes	Learners explore the content and techniques of a persuasive speech and consider the effects of different pronoun choices. Learners also write and deliver a persuasive speech.	Learner's Book Session 8.4 Workbook Session 8.4 ⬇ Language worksheet 8.2
8.5 The transporter	2 hours, 30 minutes	Learners compare the presentation of characters in two texts, consider genre conventions and respond to views about story openings.	Learner's Book Session 8.5 Workbook Session 8.5
8.6 A strange ship	2 hours, 30 minutes	Learners explore the conventions of science fiction and the functions of dialogue and narrative. They also write part of a science-fiction story.	Learner's Book Session 8.6 Workbook Session 8.6

BACKGROUND KNOWLEDGE

For the teacher

This unit uses extracts from a play, feature articles, a persuasive speech and a science-fiction novel. As these are distinct forms, with a range of differing language features, it will be useful to ensure you are familiar with their linguistic conventions. In addition, the following language topics are supported, so you could prepare by reading these sections during your planning:

- vocatives and forms of address
- present and past tense verbs
- pronouns
- British and American spelling
- semantic fields.

CONTINUED

For the learner

The following would be useful background reading for learners:

- Drama: Some plays can be watched or read online free.
- Speeches: Many of these are available to read on history websites, and there are also plenty of audio and video recordings of more recent speeches available online.
- Articles: These could be from newspapers and magazines, either in print or online; blog articles would also be useful.
- Novels and short stories in the genres of fantasy and science fiction.

TEACHING SKILLS FOCUS

Cross-curricular learning

The basic concept of cross-curricular learning is simple: connecting information between different subjects, such as links between English and science or English and maths. A useful way of finding links between English and other subjects is to read the texts that will be studied in class and then brainstorm for possible links based on the content. While planning your teaching, create a simple table that notes the links between texts and other subjects and topics. Here is an example based on the cross-curricular links in this unit:

Session	Subjects and topics	Textual connections	Cross-curricular links
8.1	Science and geography: climate change; the changing Earth; climate	The play *I Want to Fly* is set in Zimbabwe.	Zimbabwe experiences rainy seasons, droughts and deforestation. Learners could research these topics.
8.4	Science: genes and reproduction – sex determination	Emma Watson's UN speech for the HeForShe campaign encourages gender equality.	Learners could research how biological science determines sex through a physical description of anatomy and understanding chromosomes. Then, learners could consider whether 'sex' is a scientific label and 'gender' is a social or cultural label.
8.6	Maths: speed, distance and time Science: light and sound; observing the universe; a star is born	The novel *Binti* involves space travel between planets.	Learners could research distances in space, then calculate the time it would take for a spacecraft to reach those planets or stars at a given speed.

8.1 The aeroplane

LEARNING PLAN

Learning objectives	Learning intentions	Success criteria
9Rv.03, 9Ri.01, 9Ri.03, 9Ri.04, 9Ra.05, 9SLp.01, 9SLp.03	Learners will: • use voice and movement to convey dramatic ideas • explore how physical action, set design and symbol show character and theme • consider the way conflict is shown through language choices.	Learners can: • read and perform a play extract, using voice and movement to convey dramatic ideas • understand how physical action, set design and symbol convey theme • analyse the way conflict is shown in language choices.

LANGUAGE SUPPORT

The play *I Want to Fly* expresses conflict both between characters and in language choices. One of the writer's language choices is to use contrasting language in dialogue and in stage directions when describing characters' actions. For example, Yinka and Mankwinji contrast as characters because Yinka wants to fly to a new life, but Mankwinji believes her daughter is trapped within the life of the village.

This central conflict between the desires of the characters is reflected in the language of the play. Words and phrases such as *flying*, *want to fly*, *fly high*, *visit* and *dream* communicate Yinka's desire for a new life. In contrast, words and phrases such as *limping*, *laid a trap*, *won't be able to fly* and *destined to remain* express Mankwinji's feeling that it will not be possible to escape and emphasise how dialogue and action adds to characterisation and expresses the themes of the play.

Starter idea

The impact of film and theatre sets (20 minutes)

Resources: Learner's Book, Session 8.1, Getting started activity

Description: Explain that sets and locations are an important part of storytelling in film and theatre, for example, using Oxford University for *Hogwarts* in the Harry Potter films. Organise learners into groups of six to eight and give them ten minutes to create two or three of the sets listed below using only the tables, chairs, or any other items in the classroom, as well as their own bodies. Emphasise that they should try to suggest a place using the furniture as a symbol, for example, desks can be placed together to create a long conference table,

chairs can be arranged in fours to symbolise front and back car seats, etc. The sets to create are:

- a family dinner at a dining table
- a business meeting at a conference table
- a couple at a restaurant
- someone having a coffee alone at a street-side table outside a café
- three people in a car
- five or seven people on a bus.

After 10 minutes, ask learners to discuss the Getting started activity. Remind them to consider how sets connect with the characters and conflicts in a film. Also, ask learners to discuss what they had to think about when creating their sets in the classroom and how they were able to suggest a place by using tables, chairs, etc. as symbols.

Main teaching ideas

1 Performing a scene (60 minutes)

Learning intentions: Use voice and movement to convey dramatic ideas. Explore how physical action, set design and symbol show character and theme.

Resources: Learner's Book, Session 8.1, *I Want to Fly* Extract 1, Activities 1 and 2

Description: Read the introduction to the extract to the class, then either read the extract yourself or ask for three volunteers to read the stage directions and the parts of Yinka and Mankwinji.

Use the information in Language support at the start of the session to explain the contrast between Yinka and Mankwinji and how the writer shows this through scripted language choices and actions. Give the verb choices listed above as examples, as well as Yinka *miming flying like a bird* and *flying a paper aeroplane* contrasted with Mankwinji *limping slowly* as examples of contrasting actions.

Ask learners to emphasise these and other scripted language choices and actions when reading, discussing and performing this scene in pairs. Point out that these are important aspects of performing dramatic scenes. Read the Speaking tip as a class, reminding learners to use these ideas during Activity 2. Then, organise learners into pairs and ask them to complete Activities 1 and 2 together.

> **Differentiation ideas:**

- Support: Pick a confident learner to play the part of Yinka while you play the part of Mankwinji. Act out the scene together in front of the class, showing learners how you can express character through speech, gesture and movement. Then ask learners to repeat the techniques you demonstrated, adding new ones of their own, as they perform the scene in their pairs.

- Challenge: Ask learners to write a paragraph reflecting on their choices of speech, gesture and movement in the scene they performed. They should comment on whether their choices helped the performance and if they would make different choices if they had to perform the scene again.

> **Assessment ideas:** As learners perform the scene, watch and listen for how they express the characters' feelings and desires. Specifically, look for examples

of learners performing Yinka's mime of flying and Mankwinji's slow limp; stressing key words such as *fly*, *flying dream* or *broken*, *trap*, *remain* as they read and perform the characters' dialogue.

2 Analysing language in *I Want to Fly* (55 minutes)

Learning intention: Consider the way conflict is shown through language choices.

Resources: Learner's Book, Session 8.1, Activities 3 and 4

Description: Read the Language focus feature to learners. Remind them how they used miming flying, limping and other actions to express Yinka's and Mankwinji's characters, as well as how the verb choices express the difference between the characters.

Point out that the writer's stage directions indicate that the two sets of *I Want to Fly* are intended to contrast with each other and show two different worlds or ways of life. Emphasise that when learners come to write their notes and analysis for these two activities, they should consider *how* the sets contrast and *why* the writer chose these sets. Learners should then complete Activities 3 and 4 on their own.

> **Differentiation ideas:**

- Support: Write a list on the board of different categories of language learners can analyse, for example, verb choices (see Language support above), adjectives and nouns such as Yinka's *rich, strong voice, flamboyant wings* and Mankwinji mentioning *hunters* and *a trap*, as well as Mankwinji's questions and what they imply about Yinka's life and Mankwinji's expectations of her daughter. Learners can refer to these examples in their analyses.

- Challenge: After Activity 4, ask learners to write an additional paragraph explaining other language choices that could have symbolised Yinka's dreams of a different life. Give the example of the song 'Over the Rainbow', which symbolises this kind of dream through imagery ('over the rainbow skies are blue' and 'over the rainbow . . . all your dreams come true'). Ask learners to think of other symbols that express a similar idea.

> **Assessment ideas:** Read learners' analyses. Assess whether they investigated the language of the play in detail, in particular how the writer contrasts

Yinka's and Mankwinji's language (that is, how the nouns, verbs and adjectives of each contrast in meaning), the specifics of the set design (that is, the poor and simple surroundings contrasted with expensive-looking furniture and paintings) and how Yinka's desires are symbolised through props such as paper aeroplanes and magazines about aeroplanes.

Plenary idea

Dramatising conflict (15 minutes)

Description: Ask each learner to think of scenes in novels, plays or films that show dramatic conflict. In small groups, learners should discuss and reflect on the techniques that writers and directors use to dramatise conflict between characters and central ideas such as good versus evil or dreams versus reality. Ask learners to consider some or all of the following:

- language choices, both description and character dialogue

- location, sets, setting, lighting (for example forest in *A Midsummer Night's Dream*; light, darkness and night in *Romeo and Juliet*; a character's home shown as shadowy, such as a detective's dark office, an ancient castle, etc.)

- characters' movements and appearance – hairstyles, clothing or costumes (for example contrasts of black and white clothing, the use of hats or cloaks)

- symbols and objects that characters fear or value (the ring in *Lord of the Rings*, lightsabres in *Star Wars*).

CROSS-CURRICULAR LINKS

Science and geography (climate/the changing Earth): *I Want to Fly* is set in Zimbabwe, which has a tropical climate and weather that varies widely within its various regions, experiencing both rainy seasons and droughts. Learners could be asked to research Zimbabwe's weather patterns and compare them with the weather patterns of their own area. Also, Zimbabwe faces some environmental issues due to deforestation. Learners could research the impact that deforestation has in different parts of the world and the impact it has on the global climate.

Homework idea

Learners should complete Workbook Session 8.1.

8.2 Mrs Manzi

LEARNING PLAN

Learning objectives	Learning intentions	Success criteria
9Rg.04, 9Ri.01, 9Ri.07, 9Wv.01, 9Ws.01, 9Ws.02, 9Wc.01, 9Wc.07, 9SLm.02, 9Lg.02, 9SLg.03, 9SLg.04, 9SLp.01, 9SLp.02, 9SLp.03	Learners will: • read a scene from a play aloud in pairs • explore the way relationships between characters are presented • compare how contrasting characters are presented • write a drama scene featuring contrasting characters.	Learners can: • read an unseen script aloud with confidence and expression • analyse the way that relationships between characters are presented in drama • comment on the representation of two contrasting characters • write a drama scene featuring contrasting characters.

LANGUAGE SUPPORT

In this session, learners explore a play extract in which forms of address, such as *my dear* and *Ma'am* have a key role in establishing character relationships. It may help to explain forms of address and related concepts, particularly vocatives.

A 'form of address' is what we call someone in writing or while speaking. Forms of address may be formal (*Her Royal Highness*, *Mr President*) or informal (*dear*, *darling*, *you*).

Vocatives refer to the person or group being spoken to ('*Mina*, dinner's ready', '*Patrick*, there's

someone at the door for you'). Vocatives can also be used to indicate intimacy or the relative status between people ('*Sir*, may I leave the classroom?', 'It's time to go, *dear*').

In writing, vocatives are normally followed by a comma. This is important to distinguish when a vocative is used to directly address rather than referring to someone in the third person:

* *Ruby, will you walk with me?*
* *Will you walk with me, Ruby?*
* *Ruby walked with me.*

Starter idea

Who inspires you? (15 minutes)

Resources: Learner's Book, Session 8.2, Getting started activity

Description: Give learners a definition of the word 'inspire' (to fill someone with the desire or ability to do something creative or challenging). Point out that we can be inspired in many different activities, for example in learning, sports, exploration, music, art, writing or how to lead a good life. Organise learners into pairs and ask them to discuss the Getting started activity.

Main teaching ideas

1 Exploring character relationships (20 minutes)

Learning intention: Read a scene from a play aloud in pairs.

Resources: Learner's Book, Session 8.2, *I Want to Fly* Extract 1, Activity 1

Description: Organise learners into pairs and allow 10–15 minutes for them to read Extract 2 together for Activity 1. They should read the extract two or three times silently to themselves as preparation for reading aloud in their pairs. Emphasise that when they read aloud they should read with expression and emotion in order to bring the character to life.

Afterwards, remind learners of the Starter idea and ask them to consider which adults could be an inspiration for Yinka.

> **Differentiation ideas:**

* Support: Pick two confident readers to perform Extract 2 at the front of the class. Ask learners to identify where their peers were particularly expressive or confident when reading the extract. Encourage them to imitate the same confident and expressive techniques as they read Extract 2 themselves for Activity 1.

* Challenge: Ask learners to read Extract 2 twice or more in their pairs, but taking turns in reading the two roles.

> **Assessment ideas:** Ask learners to use the Reflection questions in the Learner's Book to self-assess their level of confidence and expression when reading aloud.

2 Comparing characters (40 minutes)

Learning intentions: Explore the way relationships between characters are presented. Compare how contrasting characters are presented.

Resources: Learner's Book, Session 8.2, Activities 2 and 3

Description: Using the information in the Language support above, briefly discuss forms of address and vocatives. Point out that forms of address can indicate different levels of formality between people, or between characters in fictional dialogue. Then give learners 10–15 minutes to write their responses to Activity 2 on their own. Remind them to use specific examples from the extract.

Explain that in Extract 2, we can guess that Mrs Manzi is likely to be a more inspirational person for Yinka than her mother, based on what we have seen so far. Give the example of Yinka being interested in Mrs Manzi's possible transfer and move to town, which could indicate that Yinka admires Mrs Manzi for moving away from the village to start a new life. Then put learners into small groups and ask them to discuss Activity 3 together. Remind learners to explore everyone's point of view, and try to understand where and why they agree or disagree on their responses.

> **Differentiation ideas:**

- Support: Prompt learners' thinking in part **a** of Activity 3 by explaining how the desires and values of Yinka, Mankwinji and Mrs Manzi contrast with each other – for example, Yinka dreams of a better life, whereas Mankwinji worries Yinka will always be trapped in poverty, while Mrs Manzi believes Yinka can fulfil her dreams.

- Challenge: Add a fourth question for learners to discuss as part of Activity 3: *Is it possible to see Yinka's mother as trying to protect her daughter? If yes, how? If no, why not?*

> **Assessment ideas:** Listen to the group discussions and assess how well learners: take turns to speak; focus on the specific points raised by the questions; explore and discuss where they agree and disagree; and guide the direction of the discussion in how they contribute (for example focusing on the questions, asking peers to clarify their points).

3   Considering characters for a dramatic scene (65 minutes)

Learning intention: Write a drama scene featuring contrasting characters.

Resources: Learner's Book, Session 8.2, Activities 4 and 5

Description: As a class, read the introductory text to Extract 1 from Session 8.1, as well as the text before Activity 4 in 8.2 to remind learners of the set design for *I Want to Fly*. Remind them how this contrasts Yinka's poor life circumstances with a wealthier lifestyle.

Read the character descriptions of Shumba and Aunt Sihle in the Learner's Book and point out that these characters inhabit the wealthier setting. Ask: *What do these descriptions tell us about Shumba and Aunt Sihle?* Write key words from learners' answers on the board, for example *Shumba is <u>wealthy</u>, Shumba is a <u>hypocrite</u>* and *Aunt Sihle is <u>kind</u>.*

Organise learners into pairs to discuss Activity 4. Explain that they should make notes on Shumba's and Aunt Sihle's characters and possible storylines, to use in the next activity.

After the discussions, read Activity 5 and the Writing tip to learners, then ask them to complete the activity on their own. Emphasise that they should be aiming to create conflict between characters in their scene. Remind them to use the layout of play scripts, using the format of the extracts to guide their structure and layout.

> **Differentiation ideas:**

- Support: Give learners some further suggestions of what they could include in their scene if they are struggling with their own ideas. For example: *Shumba is proudly showing Aunt Sihle some very expensive clothes he has bought. Aunt Sihle gets angry, saying he is wasting money that they could have used to help Yinka's family.*

- Challenge: Ask learners to create a third character, a daughter to Shumba and Aunt Sihle, and make her contrast with Yinka – perhaps she is spoilt, or has no dreams of her own. Tell learners their scene should show conflict between all three characters.

> **Assessment ideas:** Learners should complete the Peer-assessment feature.

Plenary idea

Reflecting on contrasting characters (10 minutes)

Description: Ask learners to think of a favourite novel, play or film and then list the major characters. In pairs, they should discuss how these major characters contrast with one another and what conflicts and themes this brings out in the story. Use a sketch like the example below to get learners thinking, or ask learners to help you create an example from another book they know.

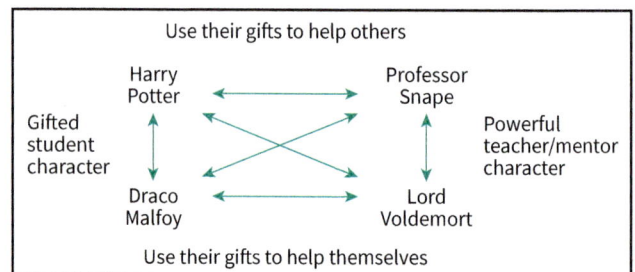

Homework ideas

Learners should complete Workbook Session 8.2.

8.3 A different voice

LEARNING PLAN

Learning objectives	Learning intentions	Success criteria
9Rs.01, 9Ri.02, 9Ri.03, 9Ri.04, 9Ra.02, 9Ra.05, 9Wv.01, 9Wg.02, 9Wg.05, 9Wc.04, 9Wp.03, 9SLm.03, 9SLs.01	Learners will: • listen to and answer questions about people's experiences of disability • explore the content, structure, viewpoint and effects of an informative article • consider how narrative viewpoint affects a text • write a feature article on the subject of disabilities.	Learners can: • listen to, make notes on and explain people's experiences of disability from an audio • explain the effects of content, structure and viewpoint in an informative article • understand how different narrative viewpoints affect a text • write an engaging feature article, making appropriate structure and language choices.

LANGUAGE SUPPORT

In this session, learners examine an extract from an autobiography, a form of personal writing. Different forms of personal writing, such as letters, diaries and autobiographies, share some common linguistic features. Often in these kinds of texts, the majority of verbs will be in the past tense, because the text records actions, events, feelings and attitudes after they have happened.

However, an interesting aspect of these kinds of texts is that the present tense can also be used for effect. For example, in the extract in this session the writer uses the present tense not to describe events that are happening at that moment, but to communicate particularly strong emotional memories as they are brought to mind: *I recall this beautiful little face with big blue eyes looking at me.*

Language worksheet 8.1 gives learners further practise with different uses of the present tense.

Starter idea

Active listening through paraphrasing (15 minutes)

Resources: Learner's Book, Session 8.3, Getting started activity

Description: Either set learners the discussion in the Getting started activity, or use the following alternative to prepare them for the listening exercise in Activity 1.

Define 'paraphrasing' to learners as *restating the meaning of what you have read or listened to using other words.*

Emphasise that paraphrasing explains or clarifies what you read or listened to and that it is an important skill for active listening, helping them concentrate, understand, respond to and remember what they hear.

In groups of four, learners should take turns telling a one-minute story about something that happened to them (it can be anything). After each learner has told their story, the others should paraphrase it for the rest of the group. When all four learners have told their stories, ask the groups to discuss whether paraphrasing helped them to concentrate, understand and remember more than they would normally.

Main teaching ideas

1 Practising paraphrasing (35 minutes)

Learning intention: Listen to and answer questions about people's experiences of disability.

Resources: Learner's Book, Session 8.3, Activity 1; Language worksheet 8.1

> ⬇ **Download the audioscript for Activity 1 from Cambridge GO (Track 59).**

Description: Go through the information in the Language support feature at the start of the session. Then, give learners Language worksheet 8.1 to complete on their own.

Next, tell learners that you are going to play an audio recording, and that they should listen and make notes. Explain that the three speakers on the audio will be talking about their personal experiences of disability. Emphasise the point from the Language support – that speakers and writers use the present tense for a variety of reasons, not just when referring to events that are happening now.

Read the Listening tip to learners and point out that paraphrasing and active listening can help them concentrate, understand and remember more of what they read and listen to. Remind them to take notes and emphasise they will use these notes to answer questions afterwards, paraphrasing what they hear. Play the audio recording twice while learners make notes. Afterwards, ask learners to write their answers to Activity 1 on their own.

> **Differentiation ideas:**

- Support: Pause the audio recording after each speaker to give learners more time to make their notes for each part of Activity 1.

- Challenge: After the activity, ask learners to write a paragraph summarising all the difficulties mentioned by Alisha, Larry and Hamid.

> **Assessment ideas:** Read learners' answers to Activity 1. Assess whether they have used their own words in restating and paraphrasing what Alisha, Larry and Hamid said rather than quoting them exactly.

2 Exploring biographical texts (50 minutes)

Learning intentions: Explore the content, structure, viewpoint and effects of an informative article. Consider how narrative viewpoint affects a text.

Resources: Learner's Book, Session 8.3, 'Just crash through it', Activities 2–4; Differentiated worksheets 8A, 8B and 8C

Description: Read the introduction to the text to the class and Activity 2. Then ask learners to read the extract again, making notes in response to the bullet points.

Read Activity 3 as a class, and explain any key concepts in questions **a–d** that learners may need help with. For example, in writing 'voice' can have both a specific and a more general meaning. To explain the specific voice, use examples of a narrative voice that is clearly not the writer's own, such as Harper Lee using the voice of Scout Finch to narrate *To Kill a Mockingbird* or Suzanne Collins using the teenage voice of Katniss Everdeen to narrate *The Hunger Games* (you could ask learners for other examples). Clarify the general meaning of voice in writing by comparing it to speech. Point out that people have an individual way of speaking: they may have an accent or use a dialect; they may speak very formally or use a lot of slang; they might sound older or younger in their speech or writing.

Using the guidance, hand out Differentiated worksheets 8A, 8B or 8C to learners and allow 15 minutes for them to complete the activities for more practice on the use and effect of first- and third-person voice. Then, organise learners into pairs and give them 15–20 minutes to discuss Activity 3 together. Before they start, read the Speaking tip and emphasise the importance of being kind and respectful during discussions of sensitive topics like this.

Next, ask for a volunteer to read Activity 4 to the class. Explain the different effects of a writer's perspective with a quick example, such as a written account of a traffic accident. Point out that we can read written accounts from the following perspective:

- someone who witnessed the accident through the window of their home

- someone who witnessed the accident as they were crossing the road

- someone who was a passenger in one of the cars involved in the accident
- someone driving one of the cars in the accident
- a police officer who attended after the accident
- a paramedic who treated people involved in the accident.

How might these different perspectives have different effects on the reader? After briefly considering this as a class, organise learners into pairs and ask them to discuss Activity 4 together.

> **Differentiation ideas:**

- Support: Before learners complete the worksheets and discuss Activity 3, remind them about first-, second- and third-person pronouns and who they refer to: first person refers to the speaker or writer (I, me, we, us); second person refers to the audience (you, your); third person refers to third parties (she, her, him, his, it, they, theirs).

  Point out that writing in the third person also includes referring to people by their name, for example, *Mina walked over*, *Mr Smith entered the classroom*.

- Challenge: Add an extra question to Activity 3 for learners to discuss: *Personal writing such as letters, diaries and autobiographies usually uses the first person, whereas fiction writers tend to use either the first or third person, and writing in the second person is rare. Why is this?*

> **Assessment ideas:** Ask learners to use the questions in the Reflection feature to self-assess the effectiveness and sensitivity of their discussions.

3 Write a feature article (40 minutes)

Learning intention: Write a feature article on the subject of disabilities.

Resources: Learner's Book, Session 8.3, Activity 5

Description: Read the Writing tip, then remind learners of the key points they should keep in mind when writing their feature article: audience (use language that will appeal to teenagers and young adults), and purpose and approach (to inform readers what it is like to live with disabilities, but the article should be interesting and entertaining).

Remind them also of the key structural features of a newspaper or online feature article:

- Headline/title: Grab the reader's attention.
- Subheading: One or two short sentences that give readers the main idea of the article.
- Introductory paragraph: Tell the reader what is interesting and important about the topic.
- Body paragraphs (using subheadings if useful): Paint a picture and bring the article to life by including details from sources (mention Alisha, Larry, Hamid and Rosaleen by name and use quotations from them).
- Concluding paragraph: Leave a memorable impression.

Learners should aim to write about 400 words.

> **Differentiation ideas:**

- Support: Give learners explicit direction on how to frame their article. Tell them to imagine they are a journalist who has interviewed Alisha, Larry, Hamid and Rosaleen and will now write an article about what they learnt. They should frame the article as a 'day-in-the-life' of a disabled person, so readers can imagine what it is like. They should aim to help the reader understand how the interviewees live their lives, and include details the reader will find interesting.
- Challenge: Ask learners to write the article in the first person, as if they are Alisha, Larry, Hamid or Rosaleen informing and entertaining readers about their life and experiences.

> **Assessment ideas:** Assess whether learners have used language appropriate to a teenage or young adult audience, for example, not overly formal but rather with a conversational tone, and perhaps with references to things (such as school, sports or peer groups) of interest to this age group. Have they used an appropriate structure, that is, a headline, subheading, intro, body and concluding paragraphs?

Plenary idea

Different narrative viewpoints (10 minutes)

Description: Ask learners to reread the four text examples on the Differentiated worksheet 8C. Point out that A and B are fiction and that C and D are non-fiction. Then ask learners to discuss these questions in pairs:

- *How would you describe the different effects of the first- or third-person versions of the fiction text?*

- *How would you describe the different effects of the first- or third-person versions of the non-fiction text?*

- *Are the differences between first and third person the same across fiction and non-fiction texts? Give your partner reasons for your answer.*

Homework idea

Learners should complete Workbook Session 8.3.

8.4 He for she

LEARNING PLAN

Learning objectives	Learning intentions	Success criteria
9Rv.02, 9Rv.03, 9Rg.03, 9Ri.02, 9Ri.03, 9Ri.09, 9Ra.02, 9Ra.05, 9Wv.01, 9Wg.03, 9Wg.04, 9Wc.05, 9Wp.04, 9SLm.01, 9SLm.04, 9SLm.05, 9SLp.04, 9SLp.05, 9SLr.02	Learners will: • explore the content and techniques used in persuasive speeches • consider the effects of different pronoun choices • write and deliver a persuasive speech.	Learners can: • identify and comment on the techniques used in a persuasive speech • analyse the effects that different pronoun choices have on a reader or audience • write and deliver a persuasive speech for a specific audience, using appropriate techniques.

LANGUAGE SUPPORT

In this session, learners examine how personal pronouns are used persuasively in a speech. The use of the first-person singular pronouns, such as *I*, *me* and *my*, can make a speaker or writer sound direct and sincere. On the other hand, using first-person plural pronouns, such as *we*, includes the audience, and can make it seem as if the speaker and audience are on the same side. Additionally, use of second-person pronouns, such as *you* can

make listeners in the audience feel as if they are being directly addressed.

It may also be useful to remind learners that pronouns have a wide range of grammatical functions, and to review the categories of pronouns from Session 2.6.

Language worksheet 8.2 gives learners additional practise with pronouns in a persuasive context.

Common misconception

Misconception	How to identify	How to overcome
Pronouns are words that replace or stand in for nouns.	Write these three examples on the board. Then ask learners to identify the pronouns and the words that they replace. a *I have lots of pets, but it is difficult because my family does not like looking after them.* b *I asked my teacher if she liked cinema.* c *'Are you from around here?' 'Why did you ask that?'*	Point out the following: a *them* replaces or stands in for the single word *pets* b *she* stands in for the whole noun phrase *my teacher* c *that* replaces or stands in for a whole clause, that is, 'Why did you ask "Are you from around here?"' Point out that the traditional definition of a pronoun is a word that replaces *a* noun. This is true, but pronouns can also replace *larger* units, such as noun phrases or whole clauses.

Starter idea

Gender identity and growing up (10 minutes)

Resources: Learner's Book, Session 8.4, Getting started activity

Description: Point out that male and female is a binary categorisation, consisting of two options. However, some people view gender as non-binary – that is, they recognise more than two gender identities. Read the Getting started activity to learners and ask them to think about the challenges young people like themselves face, then discuss their thoughts in pairs.

Main teaching ideas

1 Exploring features of a persuasive speech (35 minutes)

Learning intention: Explore the content and techniques used in persuasive speeches.

Resources: Learner's Book, Session 8.4, 'Gender equality is your issue too', Activities 1 and 2

Description: Ask for a volunteer to read aloud the speech in the Learner's Book. After they have read it, ask learners: *Who is the 'your' in the title of the speech?* Use wait time (count at least three seconds in your head) to encourage learners' thinking. If necessary, ask the follow up question: *Does 'your'* refer to *men/boys* or *women/girls?* Finally, prompt learners' thinking on the overall meaning of the speech by asking: *How does the title of the speech and the campaign name, HeForShe, summarise the main ideas of the speech?* Get several responses.

Point out that although the speech is about improving gender equality for all, it takes a particular approach to the issue by focusing on how men and boys are affected by gender inequality, not just women. It asks for men and boys to help, rather than just suggesting what women and girls can do.

Read the instructions for Activities 1 and 2 and take questions to ensure learners understand what the focus of their discussions should be. Then, organise learners into pairs and ask them to complete both activities. After 15 minutes, suggest that learners move on to Activity 2 if they have not already.

> **Differentiation ideas:**

- Support: Sit with pairs and help them identify examples of the language features listed in Activity 2 by making suggestions and asking questions to guide their thinking. For example give an example and then ask: *Could this be an example of . . .?* After learners answer, ask them to explain how the example you gave them does or does not match the particular bullet point in Activity 2.

- Challenge: For Activity 2, ask learners to work together to write one or two paragraphs that discuss the effectiveness of the persuasive techniques used in the speech.

> **Assessment ideas:** Ask learners to note down one or more examples of each language feature listed in Activity 2 to assess how well they have identified them from the speech.

2 Persuasive pronouns (45 minutes)

Learning intention: Consider the effects of different pronoun choices.

Resources: Learner's Book, Session 8.4, Activity 3; Language worksheet 8.2

Description: Start by reading through the Language focus feature and explaining any key points using the Language support feature at the start of the session.

Hand out Language worksheet 8.2 and ask learners to complete the activities. Then ask learners to read though Emma Watson's speech and on a copy of it, highlight every occurrence of the pronouns *I*, *you*, *your*, *we*, *yourself* and *me*. (There are other pronouns in the speech, but learners should focus on these six to begin with.)

When they have identified the pronouns, ask learners to go through the speech again and make notes on the following questions: *What pattern do you notice in the speaker's use of pronouns? What is the effect of the speaker using pronouns in this pattern?*

Come together to review responses briefly as a class before learners write their analyses for Activity 3.

> **Differentiation ideas:**

- Support: Write these sentences from the opening and closing parts of the speech on the board, highlighting the pronouns as marked.

  - *I am reaching out to **you** because **I** need **your** help. **We** want to end gender inequality – and to do that **we** need everyone to be involved.*

  - *I am inviting **you** to step forward, to be seen to speak up, to be the 'he' for 'she'. And to ask **yourself** if not **me**, who? If not now, when?*

- Suggest that the pattern of pronoun use and the main effects can be seen in these sentences and ask learners to focus on these sentences, as well

as any other examples they identify from the speech, in their analysis.

- Challenge: The majority of pronouns are first person (*I*, *we*, *me*) and second person (*you*, *your*, *yourself*), but there are some interesting uses of the third person *them* and *they* when the speaker is describing the effects of gender discrimination towards men. Ask learners to include comments on this use of the third person in their analysis.

> **Assessment ideas:** Assess if learners identify the following patterns and effects in pronoun use: use of *I* to express the speaker's honesty and caring for the issue; use of *you* to directly address the audience in general and also men and boys specifically; use of *we* to create a sense of a team jointly facing a challenge (that is, the speaker, the United Nations, the audience and men and boys all working together on the issue); use of *you*, *your*, *yourself* and *me* (along with rhetorical questions) to suggest to the audience they can and should support the HeForShe campaign.

3 Writing and delivering a speech (50 minutes)

Learning intention: Write and deliver a persuasive speech.

Resources: Learner's Book, Session 8.4, Activities 4 and 5

Description: Explain that learners are going to plan, write, edit and then deliver their own persuasive speech like the one in this session. Explain that they should choose a topic they care about, as this will make their speech more persuasive and engaging. They could use one of the suggestions on Language worksheet 8.2, or think of their own idea. Remind them that their purpose is to convince their audience to agree with their ideas. You could suggest the following structure:

- Greet the audience, then introduce your topic with a 'problem-solution hook' (for example *Do you fear the effects of climate change? Then you probably already know that burning coal, gas and oil for electricity and heat is the largest single source of global greenhouse gas emissions. We can reduce this and diminish the effects of climate change by . . .*).

- Present three points that show three separate parts of the problem and three solutions for them.
- Conclude with a memorable sentence that sums up your message.

Remind learners that they should use the techniques from Activity 2 and choose pronouns carefully.

Read the Writing tip to learners and then ask them to draft their speeches for Activity 4. After they have finished their first drafts, ask learners to spend 10–15 minutes editing and improving their speeches.

Finally, learners should deliver their speeches to the class for Activity 5. Remind them to vary the pace and volume of their voice and to use gestures to emphasise their key points.

> **Differentiation ideas:**

- Support: Give learners more detail on how to present the three points identifying parts of the problem:
  - Present a part of the problem as a statement: *Burning coal, gas or oil to fuel our home adds to climate change.*
  - Then present statistics, evidence or facts as a solution: *We can use renewable energy such as wind or solar energy instead of fossil fuels to generate electricity.*
  - End with a positive statement: *Renewable energy can renew our world.*

  Explain to learners they can use this approach to each of the three points they make in their speech.

- Challenge: Ask learners to try to memorise their speech and deliver it without notes. Alternatively, learners could reduce the speech to key words and phrases during Activity 4 and use those as a guide rather than reading the speech from the full draft.

> **Assessment ideas:** When learners have delivered their speeches, ask the class to feed back on them using the Peer-assessment feature.

Plenary idea

Persuasive and unpersuasive language (10 minutes)

Description: Read the following two examples to learners (or write on the board). Point out that the first version is from the original HeForShe speech; the second version has been altered to demonstrate less persuasive language.

> I am reaching out to you because I need your help. We want to end gender inequality – and to do that we need everyone to be involved. I am inviting you to step forward, to be seen to speak up, to be the 'he' for 'she'. And to ask yourself if not me, who? If not now, when?

> You need to help us. Gender inequality must end – and it's your job to make that happen otherwise it will continue. You should step forward, you should speak up and be 'he' for 'she'. Can there possibly be any good reason why you are not already doing this now?

Organise learners into pairs and ask them to identify the differences in language use between these two versions. Ask learners to discuss why the language used in the first is persuasive and why the language used in the second is unpersuasive.

CROSS-CURRICULAR LINK

Science (genes and reproduction/sex determination): In this session learners have considered gender and gender stereotypes. Point out that the terms 'sex' and 'gender' can have overlapping or distinct meanings, that is, 'sex' and 'gender' can be seen a synonyms for *biological differences* or this biological meaning can be reserved for 'sex' with 'gender' referring to social differences. Learners could research how science determines sex, for example, in terms of anatomy or chromosomes. They could also discuss whether 'sex' and 'gender' have roughly the same meaning or instead, if and how the meanings differ in important ways.

Homework idea

Learners should complete Workbook Session 8.4.

8.5 The transporter

LEARNING PLAN

Learning objectives	Learning intentions	Success criteria
9Ri.01, 9Ri.07, 9Ri.08, 9Ri.10, 9Ra.01, 9Ra.02, 9Ra.04, 9Wc.06, 9Wp.02, 9SLm.03	Learners will: • explore the features and effect of a futuristic story • compare the presentation of young characters in two texts • respond to different views about a story opening.	Learners can: • identify the features of a futuristic story and analyse their effects • compare the presentation of characters in two texts on similar themes • give a thoughtful response to different views about a story opening.

LANGUAGE SUPPORT

The extract used in this session is from *Binti*, by Nnedi Okorafor, a Nigerian-American writer. Some words in the extract, such as *realized* and *scandalized*, use American spellings. This would be a good area to review with learners, as there are variations within English globally and learners will come across differences in spelling in texts they read.

The main differences in British and American spelling:

• **ise** or **ize** – realise/realize, scandalise/scandalize

• **our** or **or** – colour/color, labour/labor
• **yse** or **yze** – analyse/analyze, paralyse/paralyze
• **ll** or **l** – travelled/traveled, traveller/traveler
• **ence** or **ense** – defence/defense, pretence/pretense
• **ogue** or **og** – dialogue/dialog, analogue/analog

Although both British and American spellings are valid, learners should be consistent and not switch between British and American spellings within the same piece of writing.

Starter idea

Imagining future settings (15 minutes)

Description: Explain that writers have often tried to imagine the future in stories. Mention some famous stories, such as Plato's *Republic* (375 BCE), Thomas More's *Utopia* (1516), Aldous Huxley's *Brave New World* (1932) and George Orwell's *Nineteen Eighty-Four* (1949). Point out that when writers imagine a positive future setting it is called a utopia (or utopian); a negative future setting is called a dystopia (or dystopian).

Put learners into small groups and give them ten minutes to discuss one or two stories (books or films) that are set in the future, and to decide if the setting is utopian or dystopian. Then come together as a class for each group to share the utopian or dystopian stories they discussed.

Main teaching ideas

1 Comparing characters in two texts (45 minutes)

Learning intention: Explore the features and effect of a futuristic story. Compare the presentation of young characters in two texts.

Resources: Learner's Book, Session 8.5. Activities 1 and 2

Description: Ask for a volunteer to read Extract 1 to the class. Before they begin, tell learners to listen for parts of the story that seem unusual and parts that seem normal (Activity 1a). After the reading, organise learners into pairs and ask them to reread the extract together and this time to make notes on the unusual and normal parts that they have just been listening out for. Point out that learners can use any note-taking method, as explained in the Writing tip, but that columns or a two-column table could suit this task.

When they have completed Activity 1a, allow ten minutes for the discussion in part b. Learners should then complete the Peer-assessment feature.

They should stay in their pairs to complete Activity 2. Remind them to start by rereading Extract 1 of *I Want to Fly* in Session 8.1.

> **Differentiation ideas:**

- Support: Suggest the following steps to help learners compare the extracts from this session and Session 8.1: identify key descriptive words in both extracts, analyse how language is used for effect in the two extracts and explain the similarities and differences in how language is used between the two extracts.

- Challenge: Ask learners to identify and compare specific language features in both extracts: metaphors, similes, personification, words with positive or negative connotations, dynamic verbs, sensory imagery, symbolism, etc.

> **Assessment ideas:** For Activity 2, read learners' notes. Several direct references, examples or quotations from both extracts are necessary for the comparison task of Activity 2, so assess how successfully learners have done this.

2 Comparing two texts (30 minutes)

Learning intention: Compare the presentation of young characters in two texts.

Resources: Learner's Book, Session 8.5, Activity 3

Description: Outline on the board the following essay plan for learners to use for the comparison in Activity 3:

- Introduction: Write one or two sentences introducing how the experiences of young people are presented in both extracts (20–30 words).

- Paragraph 1: Set out examples/quotations from both extracts of key descriptive words and phrases that present experiences of young people (50–60 words).

- Paragraph 2: Analyse the language techniques used in the examples from both extracts, for example figurative language, symbolism, etc. (50–60 words).

- Paragraph 3: Explain the effects on the reader of the two presentations of young people's experiences (50–60 words).

- Conclusion: Write one or two sentences summarising your main points (20–30 words).

Learners should then use the notes they made in Activities 1 and 2, and this plan, to respond to Activity 3 independently.

> **Differentiation ideas:**

- Support: Ask learners to comment on the following points in their essays: the different effects of a drama text compared to a prose text; the similarities and differences in symbolism (flight, birds and aeroplanes in 8.1 and *a transporter* like *a prayer stone* in this session); the similarities and differences between Yinka's *passion* and Binti's *silent prayer*.

- Challenge: Give learners a higher word count (for example 350 words) and ask them to expand their conclusion to include their personal response to how young people's experiences are presented in both extracts.

> **Assessment ideas:** Read learners' comparisons. Assess whether they have: written approximately 250 words; used a range of examples/quotations from both extracts; named and analysed the language techniques used; explained effects on readers; used connectives to contrast; and used accurate spelling, punctuation and grammar.

3 Reader reactions (50 minutes)

Learning intention: Explore and respond to different views about a story opening.

Resources: Learner's Book, Session 8.5, Activities 4 and 5

Description: Write the opening sentence from Extract 1 on the board: *I powered up the transporter and said a silent prayer.* Point out that the phrase *the transporter* identifies the science-fiction setting. In other genres, the opening sentences could be used to place a character in the same scenario, that is, a journey towards a better life. Give the following examples:

- I mounted my horse, asked the Lord for help, then galloped towards the frontier. (western)

- The ship's sails flapped as I stood on deck and prayed for a successful voyage. (historical)

- I made a wish, then floored the accelerator pedal, speeding away. (contemporary)

Note that the type of transport is different in each case, helping the reader identify genre and setting.

Introduce Activity 4 and read the speech bubble as a class. Tell learners that they should make notes during their discussion, which they will use in the next activity, then give learners 15–20 minutes to discuss the activity.

After the discussion, learners should write their summaries for Activity 5 on their own.

> **Differentiation ideas:**

- Support: Offer learners some key steps for success in these tasks:

    1 Understand the instructions (summarise the different views discussed).

    2 Make clear notes during the discussion (use bullet points, focus on the main ideas, combine repeated points, etc.).

3 Write the summary in a concise, formal style, using linking phrases (first, second, finally, etc.).

4 Check the final version for spelling, punctuation, grammar and word count.

- Challenge: Instead of writing a summary, ask learners to write a short essay in which they argue for the two best opinions about story openings they heard. They should summarise all the views from the discussion and then explain which views they think are best (including their own) and why.

> **Assessment ideas:** Ask learners to use the Reflection feature in the Learner's Book to self-assess their confidence and ability in expressing their views in the discussion.

Plenary idea

Comparing ideas in similar genres (10 minutes)

Description: Ask learners to recall the opening of *Binti* and how the writer establishes character, setting, genre and themes in the story's opening. Next, write these two story premises on the board:

- *In 1849, a young woman sets out on horseback to seek a new life in California during the Gold Rush.*

- *In 2549, a young woman takes a space flight to start a new life in the human colony on Mars.*

Organise learners into pairs and ask them to discuss what might be similar and what might be different in the presentation of the character, setting and theme in these two stories.

Homework idea

Learners should complete Workbook Session 8.5.

8.6 A strange ship

Learning objectives	Learning intentions	Success criteria
9Rv.02, 9Rs.01, 9Ri.01, 9Ri.04, 9Ri.07, 9Wv.01, 9Ws.01, 9Wc.01, 9Wc.03, 9Wc.07, 9SLm.03	Learners will: • explore how conflict, mystery and tension are created in fiction • learn about the conventions of science fiction • consider the functions of dialogue and narrator's voice • write part of a futuristic story.	Learners can: • analyse how a writer has created conflict, mystery and tension in a science-fiction extract • understand the conventions of science-fiction writing • explain how dialogue and narrator's voice can be used to structure a story • continue a futuristic story, using appropriate voice, language and structural features.

LANGUAGE SUPPORT

In the extract in this session, the writer uses a semantic field linked to science and technology. Learners may find it useful to recap the use and effect of semantic fields, which could be linked back to the work on extended metaphors in Session 1.5.

Remind learners that a semantic field is a collection of words and phrases linked to the same topic or idea. For example, *lesson*, *students*, *teacher*, *classroom*, *desks*, *board*, etc. all belong to a semantic field linked to school/education.

Writers may choose words from a particular semantic field to describe seemingly unrelated things to create an overall metaphorical meaning. For example, sporting competitions are often described using words from the semantic field of battle or conflict (*the other team attacked, our team's defence was bad, they invaded our territory on the pitch*). The semantic field in this extract includes words such as *body scan*, *astrolabe*, *ship*, *space*, *creatures*, *technology*, *breathing chamber* and *oxygen*. These help establish the futuristic setting and atmosphere of the story.

Starter idea

The language of science fiction and fantasy (15 minutes)

Resources: Learner's Book, Session 8.6, Getting started activity

Description: Write these two story extracts on the board

A *It was quite by accident I discovered this incredible invasion of Earth by lifeforms from another planet. As yet, I haven't done anything about it; I can't think of anything to do.* (from *The Eyes Have it,* by Philip K. Dick)

B *And many kinds of serpents they saw in the water, and wonderful dragons searching the sea, and on the cliff-slopes, monsters of the ocean were lying at full length.* (from *The Story of Beowulf*)

Ask learners to discuss the following questions in small groups:

- *One of these extracts is from a fantasy story and the other is from a science-fiction story. Which is which?*

- *What language in each extract helps you identify their story as fantasy fiction and science-fiction?*

- *What do you think are the differences and similarities between fantasy and science-fiction stories?*

Briefly share ideas as a class before moving on to the main activities.

Main teaching ideas

1 Science-fiction storytelling (30 minutes)

Learning intentions: Explore how conflict, mystery and tension is created in fiction. Learn about the conventions of science fiction.

Resources: Learner's Book, Session 8.6, *Binti* Extract 2, Activities 1 and 2

Description: Ask for a volunteer to read the extract to the class. Then remind learners about the concepts of genre, fantasy and science fiction as follows:

- Genre: A category of art, music or literature; works in the same genre will share similar form, content, technique and style.

- Fantasy: A literary genre that uses elements from myth or fairy stories, such as strange creatures, and actions or events that do not follow natural laws of reality.

- Science fiction: A literary genre that includes futuristic ideas such as advanced technology, for example exploration of other planets, time travel and parallel universes.

Learners should then complete Activities 1 and 2 in pairs.

> **Differentiation ideas:**

- Support: Support learners' exploration of key features of the extract in Activity 1 by suggesting that they focus on the part of the extract involving the guard, looking at the direct speech and checking the Glossary for a definition of *scowl*.

- Challenge: Ask pairs to work together to write a paragraph that argues *Binti* is *either* fantasy fiction *or* science fiction. They must give reasons for their answer and use direct references and short quotations from both extracts to support their views.

> **Assessment ideas:** Learners should complete the Reflection feature to self-assess their learning from these activities.

2 Analysing dialogue and narration (35 minutes)

Learning intention: Consider the functions of dialogue and narrator's voice.

Resources: Learner's Book, Session 8.6, Activity 3

Description: Read Activity 3 to learners. Explain that dialogue in fiction has many purposes and effects, including moving the story forward, revealing characters' personalities, dramatising conflict between characters and allowing readers to imagine characters talking, arguing, etc. Point out that dialogue, especially in the form of direct speech, contrasts with narrative text, which instead is used to describe a setting, character, an action or event.

Emphasise that when learners write their answers for Activity 3 they should use direct references to and short quotations from Extract 2 to support their analysis. They should then complete the activity on their own.

> **Differentiation ideas:**

- Support: Tell learners to focus their analysis for this activity on just part of the extract, from *'Step forward,' the guard said* to *But even I didn't know exactly what it could and couldn't do.*

- Challenge: Ask learners to write three paragraphs as follows: Paragraph 1: What the interaction between Binti and the guard reveals; Paragraph 2: How the presentation of the guard increases sympathy for Binti; Paragraph 3: The most important effects of dialogue in this scene.

> **Assessment ideas:** Ensure that learners have supported their analysis of Binti and the guard with direct references and short quotations from Extract 2.

3 Writing futuristic fiction (60 minutes)

Learning intention: Write part of a futuristic story.

Resources: Learner's Book, Session 8.6, Activity 4

Description: Remind learners what they learnt about plot structure in Unit 1: a plot has a beginning, a middle and an end, but writers may reorder events to create different effects. Give an example suitable for science fiction, such as: *Professor Alpha wants to take over the world* (beginning). *So he invents an indestructible robot and attacks a city. The military fights back but is defeated because the robot is too powerful* (middle). *Then, the robot turns against Professor Alpha and rules over him as well as everyone else* (end).

Recap what has happened in *Binti* so far by reading through the bullet points in Activity 4, then read the Writing tip. Emphasise that the section learners will write will be part of the middle of the plot, so they should introduce complications and conflicts – this can be new characters who oppose Binti, or events that create a setback or an obstacle to success, for example, the spaceship develops a problem or crashes. Remind learners they should invent futuristic devices and names to create the style and content of a science-fiction story.

> **Differentiation ideas:**

- Support: Suggest the following for the next part of the plot: *Binti goes through a door at the end of the blue corridor. Inside this new room is an extraordinary-looking screen with strange buttons and dials that lets her see what is happening on different planets . . . she sees exotic landscapes and strange creatures. Then, she sees someone using an edan like hers. It does something amazing.*

- Challenge: Get learners to create a new character for their section and tell them to include direct speech that shows conflict between Binti and this new character.

> **Assessment ideas:** Learners should complete the Self-assessment feature to evaluate their storytelling.

Plenary idea

Discussing sci-fi (10 minutes)

Description: Tell learners that Nnedi Okorafor, the author of *Binti*, has described her writing as Africanfuturism. She defines this as *a sub-category of science fiction* with a concern for *visions of the future* but *rooted first and foremost in Africa.*

Organise learners into small groups and ask them to discuss:

- how *Binti* conforms to the conventions of science fiction

- how *Binti* does not conform to the conventions of science fiction – do learners agree or disagree with Okorafor that it is in a sub-category?

CROSS-CURRICULAR LINK

Maths (speed, distance and time); science (light and sound, observing the universe): The text in this session includes space travel so learners could research on space-related topics. They could link maths and science by first researching distances in space (the distance between Earth and other planets or between the Sun and the next nearest star). Then they could calculate the time it would take for a spacecraft to reach those planets (or star) at a given speed. Alternatively, they could research space probes such as *Voyager 1* and *2*, as these probes reached several outer planets in the solar system and give an idea of the speeds and distances involved.

Homework idea

Learners should complete Workbook Session 8.6.

PROJECT GUIDANCE

Prepare learners for this project by reading out and explaining aspects of the task as described in the Learner's Book. Then organise learners into groups and explain they will compile their anthology by breaking down the project into smaller tasks that will be allocated to specific group members. You could encourage camaraderie by suggesting that learners give their teams a name.

Give learners a sample project plan and encourage them to use it in organising themselves as a team:

1   Initial planning meeting in teams.

2   Use the internet and library to research writing in different voices, for example writers from around the world, stories involving unusual people or 'outsiders' to society in different times and places.

3   Meet as a group to share research and agree what research will be included in anthology.

4   Meet as a group to divide the project into smaller tasks and allocate the smaller tasks to individual group members. Some of the smaller tasks could be:

- designing the anthology front cover and title

- designing individual pages

- putting the anthology together – writing, drawing or printing.

5   Share the anthology with the rest of the class.

Give learners a schedule for the anthology project which works backwards from a completing deadline, for example:

- a date for sharing the completed anthology with the class

- a date for putting the anthology together

- a date by which they should have allocated all the smaller tasks

- a date by which their initial research should have finished.

> 9 Strange and unusual

Unit plan

Session	Approximate number of learning hours	Outline of learning content	Resources
9.1 Stranger in a strange land	2 hours, 30 minutes	Learners explore meaning and language choices in a poem and discuss structural effects.	Learner's Book Session 9.1 Workbook Session 9.1
9.2 A strange meeting	2 hours, 30 minutes	Learners explore language, plot and characterisation in *Macbeth*, understand the conventions of tragedy and compare two texts.	Learner's Book Session 9.2 Workbook Session 9.2 ⬇ Differentiated worksheets 9A, 9B and 9C
9.3 Fun with *Macbeth*	2 hours, 30 minutes	Learners explore modern versions of *Macbeth* and write their own version.	Learner's Book Session 9.3 Workbook Session 9.3
9.4 An unusual job	2 hours, 30 minutes	Learners discuss features of an article, consider representation and write a feature article.	Learner's Book Session 9.4 Workbook Session 9.4 ⬇ Language worksheet 9.1
9.5 Unusual endings	2 hours, 30 minutes	Learners explore conventional and unconventional endings and write their own unconventional ending.	Learner's Book Session 9.5 Workbook Session 9.5
9.6 A twist in the tail	2 hours, 30 minutes	Learners explore how a writer blends elements from science fiction, comedy and thrillers, and consider ambiguity in language such as puns and double meanings.	Learner's Book Session 9.6 Workbook Session 9.6 ⬇ Language worksheet 9.2

BACKGROUND KNOWLEDGE

For the teacher

The following are useful areas of background knowledge for texts and topics you could consult as preparation for teaching this unit:

- Shakespeare's language and blank verse
- the text of *Macbeth* and different versions of the play in film and prose forms
- analysis of metaphorical language, that is, source and target distinction (source = the thing being used to describe; target = the thing described)
- the format, layout and language of feature articles (print and online)
- plot structure and shape in stories; genres and types of endings
- lexical (word) and grammatical (structural/ syntactic) ambiguity in language.

CONTINUED

For the learner

The following would be useful preparation for learners as they approach this unit:

- reading Shakespeare's *Macbeth* (versions of the play are available online)
- reading modern versions of *Macbeth*, for example *Call Me Mac* (available online)
- watching TV or film versions of *Macbeth*, including modern versions such as BBC's *Shakespeare Retold*
- reading newspaper and magazines articles (print or online)

- reading short stories; many are available online, but the following are recommended to help learners prepare for activities in later sessions of the unit:
  - 'The Gift of the Magi' by O. Henry
  - 'The Long Rain' by Ray Bradbury
  - 'The Veldt' by Ray Bradbury
  - 'Taste' by Roald Dahl
  - 'The Hitch-Hiker' by Roald Dahl
  - 'The Plantation' by Ovo Adagha
  - 'Mrs. Sen's' by Jhumpa Lahiri.

TEACHING SKILLS FOCUS

Differentiation

Differentiation previously referred to ranking learners according to ability; however, today this more often refers to good practice in terms of adapting teaching to differences across the spectrum of learners.

There are a number of ways to include differentiation within your teaching:

- Planning: Defining clear learning intentions and preparing a wide range of activities.
- Teaching: Using a variety of activities, teaching approaches and questioning techniques.

- Learners' needs: Repeat teaching of topics and reviewing learners' progress.
- Resources: Collect useful resources that are appropriate for learners, and use classroom displays, posters and other exhibits and memory aids.

This approach to differentiation can be seen as a cyclical process:

planning → teaching → learners' needs → resources and then back to further planning → adjustments to teaching, etc.

9.1 Stranger in a strange land

LEARNING PLAN

Learning objectives	Learning intentions	Success criteria
9Rv.01, 9Rv.02, 9Rv.03, 9Rs.01, 9Ri.01, 9Ri.04, 9Ri.07	Learners will: • explore meaning in a poem • consider the effect of language choices on meaning • discuss the effect of structural choices in a poem	Learners can: • explore meaning and make inferences about a poem • analyse how language choices are used to influence meaning in a poem • discuss the effect of structural choices in a poem, including an ambiguous ending

LANGUAGE SUPPORT

This session is a good opportunity to emphasise that writers shape and control the language of literary texts such as novels, short stories and poems, to achieve specific effects. Although all writers do this, literary texts usually contain more experimentation with imagery, word choice and sentence structure than 'non-literary' texts such as leaflets, instruction manuals, textbooks and encyclopedias.

One particular language technique used by the writer of the poem in this session is moving the position of clause elements to emphasise a particular meaning. You can illustrate this to learners using the beginning of 'This Landscape, These People'. The line is:

> *My eighth spring in England I walk among*
> *The silver birches of Putney Heath*

This can be read as: adverbial / subject / verb / adverbial:

> [During] *my eighth spring in England / I / walk / among the silver birches of Putney Heath.*

More typical non-literary structures would be subject / verb / adverbial / adverbial:

> *I / walk / among the silver birches of Putney Heath / [during] my eighth spring in England*

> *I / walk / [during] my eighth spring in England / among the silver birches of Putney Heath*

The writer orders the clauses in this way to emphasise that he has been in England for eight years – the fact that he is walking is less significant. Learners will see that this meaning takes on greater impact as the poem progresses.

Starter idea

A new country (15 minutes)

Resources: Learner's Book, Session 9.1, Getting started activity

Description: Briefly discuss with learners some things that people might find different if they move to a new country, such as the language, climate/weather, food, economies with more or fewer opportunities, currency/ money, and people's customs and behaviour. Learners should then discuss the Getting started activity in pairs.

Main teaching ideas

1   Analysing poetry (60 minutes)

Learning intentions: Explore meaning in a poem. Consider the effect of language choices on meaning.

Resources: Learner's Book, Session 9.1, 'This Landscape, These People' Extract 1, Activities 1 and 2

Description: Read the introduction to the poem in the Learner's Book. Then read Extract 1 to the class, once at a normal pace, then a second time more slowly.

Ask for three volunteers to read the instructions for Activities 1 and 2 and the Reading tip. Prompt learners to start thinking about the meaning of the poem by asking the following questions:

- *The second stanza describes a scene in which a child feels that they are prevented from experiencing things that are interesting and valuable. How does the poet use imagery to convey those feelings?*

- *What sensory imagery is used in the third and fourth stanzas (Part II), for example, imagery that appeals to the senses of touch, sight and taste, as well as movement?*

When a learner responds to one of these questions, ask the class to comment and briefly discuss the responses. Then organise learners into pairs and give them 20 minutes to make notes on Activity 1.

They should then work independently to write the analysis for Activity 2, using their notes from Activity 1.

> **Differentiation ideas:**

- Support: Offer specific questions to guide learners' analyses for Activity 2: *In the second stanza, what are being described as 'an exhibit in a glass case' and 'an antique chair' What are the* frontiers *that the poet refers to? How does it feel to be at the frontier, or boundary, of something you want to touch? What food is mentioned in the fourth stanza? What connotations does the food have in relation to the country being described?*

- Challenge: Ask learners to write an analysis of the description and imagery in all four stanzas (not just second and fourth) for Activity 2.

> **Assessment ideas:** Assess how well learners have analysed the things *used to* describe and the things *being described* (second stanza) – for example: an exhibit in a glass case used to describe England from the poet's point of view; an antique chair blocked by a rope also used to describe England from the poet's point of view. Also assess how many examples of sensory imagery they have identified (fourth stanza).

2 Exploring poetry (60 minutes)

Learning intention: Explore meaning in a poem. Consider the effect of language choices on meaning. Discuss the effect of structural choices in a poem.

Resources: Learner's Book, Session 9.1, 'This Landscape, These People' Extract 2, Activities 3 and 4

Description: Read Extract 2 to learners – again do so once at a normal pace, then a second time more slowly. Afterwards, read through Activity 3 and recap pastoral imagery if necessary (this is imagery that shows an idealised, romanticised or perfect image of life in the country). Then give learners 20–25 minutes to write their analysis for Activity 3.

Ask for a volunteer to read the Language focus information to the class. Emphasise that by writing an ambiguous ending a poet (or author) is inviting different interpretations of the overall meaning of the text from different readers.

Organise learners into small groups. Ask each group to nominate one learner to chair the discussion. The chairperson should keep track of time and make sure all the bullet points in Activity 4 are discussed (approximately five minutes on each bullet point). Come together as a class to briefly share ideas at the end.

> **Differentiation ideas:**

- Support: For Activity 3, give learners these specific questions as hints of what to analyse in Extract 2: *What imagery from nature (plants, water, etc.) does the poet use? How does this help to create a sense of an idealised, romanticised or perfect country scene?*

- Challenge: Give learners 20 minutes for Activity 4 and ask them to make notes on key points of their discussions. After 20 minutes, ask groups to report back on these points to the rest of the class.

> **Assessment ideas:** Ask learners to use the questions in the Reflection feature to self-assess their analysis of and confidence in discussing poetic structure.

Plenary idea

Last lines (15 minutes)

Description: Point out that the last line of any poem – whether it is ambiguous or very clear – can have a huge impact. Both types of ending can have *resonance* for the reader: echoes and interpretations of the line will stay with the reader afterwards.

Write these last lines from different poems on the board:

- *The lone and level sands stretch far away.*

- *Good fences make good neighbours.*

- *Beauty is truth, truth beauty – that is all / Ye know on earth, and all ye need to know.*

- *So long lives this, and this gives life to thee.*

- *To this country I have come. / Stranger or an inhabitant, this is my home.*

Organise learners into pairs and ask them to discuss which lines they find most interesting and why. They should consider how the poet has used language to prompt and provoke particular thoughts and feelings.

Homework ideas

Learners should complete Workbook Session 9.1.

9.2 A strange meeting

LEARNING PLAN

Learning objectives	Learning intentions	Success criteria
9Rv.01, 9Rv.02, 9Rv.03, 9Ri.01, 9Ri.04, 9Ri.08, 9Ri.10, 9Ra.01, 9Wp.02, 9SLs.01	Learners will: • explore language, plot and characterisation in an older play • consider metaphorical meaning • learn about the conventions of tragedy • compare the plot and moral messages of two texts.	Learners can: • understand features of an older play, including language, plot and characterisation • explain how a playwright has used metaphor to reflect meaning • understand the conventions of tragedy • compare the plot of two texts, including their moral messages.

LANGUAGE SUPPORT

Much of the writing in Shakespeare's plays takes the form of blank verse, so it may be useful for learners to understand this structure while they explore the language of *Macbeth*.

Blank verse is a verse line of ten syllables with five stresses and no rhyme. (The lack of rhyme is why the verse is called blank.) A typical line is ten syllables in a pattern called iambic pentameter, which has alternating unstressed (/) and stressed (U) syllables:

˅ / ˅ / ˅ / ˅ / ˅ /
And all our yesterdays have lighted fools

The number of syllables and pattern of stresses sometimes varies, but blank verse is the basic rhythmic pattern in *Macbeth*. Shakespeare also sometimes uses rhyme as a way of emphasising something important about an event, scene or character.

Starter idea

Ideas about *Macbeth* (5 minutes)

Resources: Learner's Book, Session 9.2, Getting started activity

Description: Ask learners to pair up and discuss the Getting started activity together. They should make a list of things they already know about *Macbeth*, study the image in the Learner's Book for ideas about the story, then discuss how they would feel if someone predicted they would be rich, famous and head of their country in the future (prime minister, president, monarch). Point out that at the beginning of the story, Macbeth is a general in the army but then he hears a prediction that he will one day be King of Scotland.

Main teaching ideas

1 Language and character in *Macbeth* (35 minutes)

Learning intention: Explore language, plot and characterisation in an older play.

Resources: Learner's Book, Session 9.2, Activities 1 and 2

Description: At the start of the session, allow two minutes for learners to study the image for Activity 1, considering whether they would trust or mistrust the weird sisters and why. Organise learners into groups of four and allow 15–20 minutes for them to complete Activity 1. Remind them to refer to the Glossary to help with unfamiliar words.

As a class, read the Reading tip and briefly recap what a soliloquy is if necessary. Learners should complete Activity 2 independently, then pair up and compare their answers, discussing any differences.

> **Differentiation ideas:**

- Support: Before they start Activity 2, explain to learners that they can reflect on both the literal and metaphorical meanings of Shakespeare's lines. Give this example from earlier in *Macbeth*:

Original	Modern translation
MALCOLM Hail, brave friend! Say to the King the knowledge of the broil, As thou didst leave it.	**MALCOLM** Hello, brave friend! Tell the King about the battle and how it was when you left it.
CAPTAIN Doubtful it stood, As two spent swimmers, that do cling together And choke their art.	**CAPTAIN** It was uncertain who would win. The two armies were like tired swimmers clinging together, making it impossible for them to stay afloat.

- Challenge: After learners have completed the matching activity, ask them to write five new modern translations for **A** to **E**. For example, **A** could also be translated as: *If I can move on when this is done, then it would be best to get it over and done with quickly.*

> **Assessment ideas:** Read learners' translations for Activity 1c. Assess whether they have understood the meaning of Shakespeare's lines by checking their translation of the line *Macbeth! That shalt be king hereafter* to an appropriate modern version, such as: *Macbeth! That shall be king in the future. / Macbeth! Who will be king in the future. / Macbeth! Who is going to be king after this time* etc.

2 Analysing metaphorical meaning (70 minutes)

Learning intention: Consider metaphorical meaning.

Resources: Learner's Book, Session 9.2, Activities 3 and 4; Differentiated worksheets 9A, 9B and 9C

Description: Recap with learners the key stages in writing a summary in relation to the activities in this session:

1 Understand the text (that is, understand the quotations from Activities 1 and 2).

2   Understand the instructions (that is, the instructions for Activity 3).

3   Make notes using bullet points, focus on main ideas and combine repeated points.

4   Write the summary in a clear, formal tone; be concise; use linking expressions.

5   Edit the final version (check spelling, punctuation and grammar).

When learners are clear on what they need to do, ask them to write their summaries for Activity 3.

Hand out Differentiated worksheets 9A, 9B or 9C and allow learners approximately 20 minutes to complete them.

For Activity 4, first read Macbeth's soliloquy (*And all our yesterdays . . .*) aloud, then go through the instructions for Activity 4. Point out that learners can use the same process as on the worksheets – that is, the candle, actor and tale are the *things being used to describe* and so learners should analyse and write about *the things described* for each of them for Activity 4.

> **Differentiation ideas:**

* Support: For Activity 4, ask learners to draw a table to plan out what to say for the thing being described and the thing being used to describe. In the second column write *candle*, *actor* and *tale*. Then, ask learners to make notes for their analysis on the thing being described for the candle, actor and tale. Suggest they write one or two sentences for each of the three metaphors. They can use these notes when writing up their analyses.

* Challenge: As well as analysing the three metaphors of the candle, actor and tale, ask learners to include an analysis of the metaphorical meaning of *All our yesterdays* and *Told by an idiot, full of sound and fury / Signifying nothing* for Activity 4.

> **Assessment ideas:** Learners should use the Reflection feature to self-assess their analysis of Shakespeare's language.

3 Exploring tragedy (35 minutes)

Learning intentions: Learn about the conventions of tragedy. Compare the plot and moral messages of two texts.

Resources: Learner's Book, Session 9.2, Activities 5 and 6

> ⬇ **Download the audioscript for Activity 5 from Cambridge GO (Track 68).**

Description: Read Activity 5 to the class and explain that you are going to play an audio recording about the conventions of tragedy. Explain that they should make notes as they listen. Remind them that they can use any note-taking method they like (tables, bullet points or spider diagrams) as long as their notes are clear and cover the main points.

Before playing the recording, read the Key word definition of 'tragedy' and explain the idea of *the conventions of tragedy* as a description of the literary tradition and genre of tragedy. Remind them to listen out for the typical features of tragedy, such as typical plots, narrative structures, characters and themes. Then play the recording while learners make notes.

Read Activity 6 as a class, then write the summary of 'The Red-Headed League' below on the board:

* *Jabez Wilson meets with Sherlock Holmes about the suspicious Red-Headed League and Vincent Spalding.*

* *Holmes discovers a link between the Red-Headed League and a planned bank robbery.*

* *Holmes and Watson wait to catch the bank robbers in the dark bank cellar.*

* *Spalding (who is in fact John Clay) and another man break into the bank.*

* *Holmes and Watson capture Spalding/John Clay. The other man escapes.*

* *Holmes explains to Watson how he solved the mystery of the Red-Headed League.*

Point out that Spalding/John Clay is motivated by greed. Then put learners into pairs and ask them to discuss Activity 6 together. Remind them to focus on identifying the similarities and differences in the narrative structures, themes and moral messages of the two texts.

> **Differentiation ideas:**

* Support: For Activity 6, point out that there are similarities in the plots of both texts: a character has dark motivations for greed or

power but in the end suffers for their actions. Ask learners: *The plots of* Macbeth *and 'The Red-Headed League' have similarities, but are the moral messages of both texts also similar? What differences in moral messages do you think the texts have?* They should consider these questions during their discussion.

- Challenge: In addition to discussing the narrative structure and moral messages of the two texts, ask learners to discuss these questions: *Who is the protagonist in each story? What is the outcome for the protagonist in the end?*

> **Assessment ideas:** Evaluate learners' comments on the similarities and differences in both texts, namely both Macbeth and Spalding plan bad actions but both are defeated in the end; the protagonist of 'The Red-Headed League' is Sherlock Holmes but the protagonist of *Macbeth* is Macbeth himself – an anti-hero. This differences makes *Macbeth* more clearly a tragedy because the protagonist experiences the reversal and fall whereas in 'The

Red-Headed League' the ending is a success for Holmes.

Plenary idea

Tragedy: reversals and falls (5 minutes)

Description: Remind learners that a key part of tragedy is the downfall of the protagonist. Point out that this is usually a character who is good in many ways but who suffers a reversal of fortune – often through their own bad choices – that sets them on a path to their downfall. For example, Macbeth starts as a heroic general but after killing King Duncan, he ends up on a path of self-destruction.

Organise learners into pairs and ask them to discuss any stories they have read or films they have seen that use the conventions of tragedy and show a reversal and fall for the main character.

Homework idea

Learners should complete Workbook Session 9.2.

9.3 Fun with *Macbeth*

LEARNING PLAN

Learning objectives	Learning intentions	Success criteria
9Rv.01, 9Rv.03, 9Rg.04, 9Ri.01, 9Ri.04, 9Ri.10, 9Ra.01, 9Ra.02, 9Ww.01, 9Wc.01, 9Wc.07, 9Wp.04	Learners will: • explore content and meaning in updated versions of *Macbeth* • compare two different versions of the same story • plan and write their own version of the play.	Learners can: • analyse language and meaning in different versions of *Macbeth* • make thoughtful comparisons of different versions of *Macbeth* • devise new ideas for the play and write an original version.

LANGUAGE SUPPORT

In this session, learners examine a text in which adjectives play a particularly important role: to give an atmospheric description of the characters and setting of the Indian film *Paddayi*, a modern retelling of *Macbeth*. Point out to learners how important lively, vivid and interesting adjectives are in building description and atmosphere, and in communicating significant features.

In the article in this session, adjectives convey the conflict between a simple, traditional world and a more complicated, aggressive new world.

You could discuss what the adjectives add to the description in these phrases:

- a <u>beautiful</u> <u>coastal</u> village
- <u>traditional</u> fishing using <u>wooden</u> boats
- <u>aggressive</u> methods
- <u>able</u> fishermen
- <u>inaccessible</u> <u>new</u> world
- <u>poetic</u> reflections
- Madhava's <u>tragic</u> situation.

Starter idea

Adapting *Macbeth* (15 minutes)

Resources: Learner's Book, Session 9.3, Getting started activity

Description: Write five literary and film genres on the board, for example *science fiction*, *detective fiction*, *fantasy*, *western* or *superhero*. Organise learners into groups of three or four and ask them to pick one of the genres, then complete the Getting started activity by discussing their ideas for turning *Macbeth* into a story for their chosen genre. Come back together as a class to share ideas. Make a note on the board of how many times each genre was picked and discuss why some genres were popular and some unpopular with learners.

Main teaching ideas

1 Understanding adaptations of *Macbeth* (40 minutes)

Learning intention: Explore content and meaning in updated versions of *Macbeth*.

Resources: Learner's Book, Session 9.3, 'Macbeth in a new India', 'Call Me Mac', Activities 1 and 2

Description: Ask learners to turn to Activity 6 in Session 9.2 in the Learner's Book and ask a volunteer to read the bullet-point summary of the plot of *Macbeth*. (You could also write this on the board before the lesson starts.) Explain that in this session, learners will be exploring the concepts behind two modern adaptations of *Macbeth*; they should keep in mind the basic plot and themes from this bullet-point list as they do so.

Ask learners to read the first extract ('A poetic retelling of Macbeth in a new India'). For Activity 1, they should use their preferred note-taking method (table, spider diagram, etc.) to make notes on the first article.

Read Activity 2 and the Reading tip as a class. Recap *narrative voice* and *tone* as follows:

- Narrative voice is the sense of the narrator's personality in a piece of writing, created through the style of writing and the relationship established with the reader (a formal/informal voice, use of slang (or not), someone's age, whether the text feels humorous or serious).

- Tone is the attitude of the writer towards the subject of the text; readers can often identify a writer's tone through their word choices.

Emphasise that for Activity 2, learners should look at the writer's word choices to consider how these develop ideas about voice and tone. Then ask learners to read the text 'Call Me Mac' before pairing up and responding to Activity 2.

> **Differentiation ideas:**

- Support: Read 'Call Me Mac' to learners first, emphasising the comic and sarcastic tone. Then ask learners to practise reading the text to each other in a similar way before completing Activity 2.

- Challenge: Ask learners to write a paragraph that describes the voice and tone of 'Call Me Mac', referring to specific word choices and using short quotations to support their points.

> **Assessment ideas:** Learner pairs could swap their notes for Activity 1 and give each other feedback on what they find useful about their partner's note-taking method and on improvements they could make to this method.

2 Comparing two texts (25 minutes)

Learning intention: Compare two different versions of the same story.

Resources: Learner's Book, Session 9.3, Activity 3

Description: Outline (verbally or on the board) the following plan for learners to use when writing their comparison for Activity 3:

- Introductory paragraph: Write one or two sentences introducing the comparison – that is, how the two texts retell *Macbeth* in different ways (25–35 words).

- Paragraph 1: Using examples/quotations from both texts, explain the attitudes and values expressed in each text (50–60 words).

- Paragraph 2: Analyse and name the language techniques used in both texts, for example tone and voice, figurative language, symbolism (50–60 words).

- Paragraph 3: Explain the effects on the reader of the two texts and say which one you prefer and why (50–60 words).

- Concluding paragraph: Write one or two sentences summarising the main points (25–35 words).

Learners should then complete Activity 3 independently.

> **Differentiation ideas:**

- Support: Ask learners to specifically consider the following issues in their comparison: whether making the Madhava character a poor fisherman creates more sympathy for him than the original Macbeth character; whether making Mac sarcastic in 'Call Me Mac' makes him more likeable than the original Macbeth character; why or why not Madhava is more sympathetic; why or why not Mac is more likeable.

- Challenge: Ask learners to include a third text in their written comparison – the idea they discussed in the Starter idea. They should write about which text they preferred and why

(if the third was developed into a complete novel, graphic novel, play or film).

> **Assessment ideas:** Assess whether learners have: written approximately 250 words; explained the attitudes and values expressed in both texts; analysed the language techniques used, particularly use of tone and voice; said which text they prefer and why; used connectives to contrast, for example *on the other hand, in contrast, however*; used accurate spelling, punctuation and grammar.

3 Write a prose version of *Macbeth* (60 minutes)

Learning intention: Plan and write their own version of the play.

Resources: Learner's Book, Session 9.3, Activity 4

Description: Read Activity 4 to learners. Point out that when adapting the text, the writers matched the original character roles to equivalent roles; Macbeth is a Scottish general in the original but becomes a head chef or rich chief executive in the adaptations – both of them also roles that have power and status. Point out that settings also have some links to the original background of Scottish courts and castles – a successful restaurant and a powerful oil company are also places where people compete for powerful positions. Suggest to learners that when they write their prose versions of *Macbeth* they should think of a role and setting that will bring out the theme of seeking power within a large organisation.

Refer learners to the summary of what happens in *Macbeth* in Activity 6 in Session 9.2. For this activity, they must tell the story of Macbeth's meeting with the weird sisters, his feelings about Duncan and his later suffering, so they should focus their 500 words on this part of the story.

Allow 30–40 minutes for learners to write a first draft. They should then edit and redraft their work to improve the story, checking the accuracy of the spelling, grammar and punctuation too.

Finally, ask learners to complete the Peer-assessment exercise and in the time remaining (or for homework) to write a final draft of their version of *Macbeth*, making improvements based on feedback and their own assessment.

> Differentiation ideas:

- Support: Encourage learners to start by imagining Macbeth's role and the setting. Macbeth's role could be something straightforward like a politician or a powerful business person (male or female) or something less predictable like a computer gamer, a comedian, an animal or even an alien. The setting could be a nation or country, a powerful company or something unusual like a virtual game world, a TV show, a forest, a jungle or another planet.

- Challenge: Give learners 20 minutes to write a first draft then immediately begin writing a second draft (over another 20 minutes) to improve on the story. Afterwards, they should edit and check their work for accuracy, and do the Peer-assessment feature as described above.

> Assessment ideas: The Peer-assessment feature should be used for assessment in this activity.

Plenary idea

Choosing versions of Macbeth (10 minutes)

Description: Give learners four brief outlines of the versions of Macbeth they have considered in this session:

- Macbeth is a poor fisherman in modern-day India.
- Macbeth is a detective in modern-day Scotland.
- Macbeth is head chef of a successful modern-day restaurant.
- Macbeth is an ambitious deputy in a modern-day powerful oil company.

In pairs, ask learners to identify and discuss the similarities and differences between these four outlines. Which version would they most like to see as a play or a film and why?

Homework ideas

Learners should complete Workbook Session 9.3. As an alternative homework activity, learners could complete a third draft of their prose version of Macbeth (Activity 5).

9.4 An unusual job

LEARNING PLAN

Learning objectives	Learning intentions	Success criteria
9Rs.01, 9Rs.02, 9Ri.02, 9Ri.03, 9Ri.06, 9Wv.02, 9Wv.03, 9Ws.02, 9Wc.04, 9Wc.05, 9Wp.02, 9SLm.02, 9SLm.03, 9SLs.01, 9SLg.04	Learners will: • practise note-taking and summarising skills based on an interview text • discuss the effect of structural features in an article • consider how representation is linked to readership and structural choices • write a feature article for an adult audience.	Learners can: • take accurate notes and summarise information for a specific purpose • participate in a group discussion to explore the structural features of a text • understand how representation is linked to readership and structural choices • use appropriate language and organisational features to write a feature article for an adult audience.

LANGUAGE SUPPORT

The article in this session uses a question-and-answer format so this may be a good opportunity to review question types with learners. Remind them that in interviews, open questions are likely to get better responses than closed questions. Note also that calling a sentence *a question* might refer to its form (it ends with a question mark), its usage (what the purpose of the sentence is) or both. Sometimes a sentence is written in the form of a question but is not really seeking an answer or information in response. For example, questions can be seen as more closed or more open. More closed questions include **exclamatory questions** and **declarative questions** (*Haven't you got tall?*), **rhetorical questions** (*How should I know?*) and **yes-no questions** (*Is Ruby at home?*). More open questions include **alternative questions** (*Would you like water or milk?*) and **wh-questions** or **information questions** (*What have been the greatest challenges in your life so far?*).

Language worksheet 9.1 offers learners additional practise with different types of questions.

Starter idea

Becoming an astronaut (10 minutes)

Resources: Learner's Book, Session 9.4, Getting started activity

Description: Briefly outline some of the things that people need to have in order to be an astronaut (a master's degree in maths, science, etc.; two years or 1000 hours of experience as a pilot on jet aircraft; excellent leadership, teamwork and communications skills, etc). Then organise learners into pairs to discuss the Getting started activity. Ask learners to also discuss how their real life as an astronaut (if they would accept the challenge) would differ from what they typically see as 'life in space' in science-fiction films or read about in science-fiction stories.

Main teaching ideas

1 Write a biographical summary (65 minutes)

Learning intention: Practise note-taking and summarising skills based on an interview text.

Resources: Learner's Book, Session 9.4, 'Interview with astronaut Christina Koch', Activities 1 and 2; Workbook Session 9.4

Description: To prepare for the focus of this session, ask learners to complete the Focus and Practice sections of Workbook Session 9.4. Afterwards, ask them to explain how they summarised the information about Anna Jeffs: *What information did you cut? What information did you keep? How did you know what was important to keep and what you could cut?* Get several responses from different learners. If possible, prompt them to expand on *how* they summarised, for example, did they decide what to cut beforehand or just start writing and kept going until they finished? The idea here is to get learners to share their thinking and writing methods with the rest of the class.

Next, ask for several volunteers to read their analysis and comparison in answer to the Practice activity. Briefly discuss similarities and differences between their written answers. Write any key points common to their analyses and comparisons on the board.

Read Activities 1 and 2 in the Learner's Book as a class so learners understand what is expected from their first reading of the text. Point out that they will be writing a biographical summary of Christina Koch so they should keep this in mind when reading the interview.

Read the Writing tip, then remind learners of the sequence for writing a summary: understand the text; understand the instructions; make notes; write the summary; edit the summary. Suggest that as this is biographical, they could follow a chronological structure in their summary – start with points earlier in Koch's life or astronaut training, then move to later events. Learners should then read the article and complete the two activities on their own.

When learners have finished Activity 2, they should return to the Workbook and complete the Challenge activity on their own. Afterwards, learners should swap their two articles with a partner and discuss and compare how they used language differently in the two versions.

> **Differentiation ideas:**

- Support: Remind learners about the techniques of scanning and skimming and how both can be used to make notes for Activity 1. For example, learners are asked to make notes on Koch's experiences, views and feelings so they could scan the text to find relevant information. For an overview of information about Koch they can skim headings, subheadings and the first sentence of each paragraph.

- Challenge: Ask learners to write their initial summary for Activity 2 in 100 words as stated. Then ask them to cut this summary to just 50 words.

> **Assessment ideas:** Assess if learners' summaries are within the 100-word limit, have accurately communicated details from the text about Koch's life or astronaut training, and show accurate spelling, punctuation and grammar.

2 Exploring the features of articles (65 minutes)

Learning intentions: Discuss the effect of structural features in an article. Consider how representation is linked to readership and structural choices.

Resources: Learner's Book, Session 9.4, Activities 3 and 4; Language worksheet 9.1

Description: Briefly run through the information about question types in the Language support feature at the start of the session. Then hand out Language worksheet 9.1 and allow 10–15 minutes for learners to complete the worksheets.

Read the Key word definition of *paraphrasing*, then organise learners into pairs and ask them to discuss Activity 3 together, making notes on their answers to the two bullet points.

Write this explanation of *representation* on the board: *Representation is how texts present identities such as someone's gender, age, ethnicity or nationality. Representation is also how social and political issues and events are presented in film, TV programmes and written texts.*

Answer any questions learners have about this explanation, then join up pairs into groups of four for the structured discussion in Activity 4. They should spend 4–5 minutes on each of the bullet-point questions. Suggest that one learner act as a timekeeper for the group and another learner take notes during the discussion. Each group should combine their two sets of notes from Activity 3 into

a single set. Remind learners to read the Reading tip and consider its points during their discussion.

After the discussion, groups should report back the key points to the class.

> **Differentiation ideas:**

- Support: For Activity 3, give learners these three possible explanations why the writer might have organised the text in a question-and-answer format and used Christina's own words:

  1 Questions make good headings and subheadings and answers give about a paragraph of text in reply.

  2 Questions can be phrased to prompt interesting answers and using Christina's own words communicates her personal qualities.

  3 Using Christina's own words and questions shows that the writer met her in person and asked her interesting things.

  Ask learners to decide which is the best explanation and why.

- Challenge: For Activity 4, ask learners to write three additional questions the interviewer could ask Christina then share them with the class at the end of the session. They should explain why and how their new questions would continue the positive representation in the article.

> **Assessment ideas:** Listen out for relevant points as learners report back on their discussions. In particular, listen for ideas about why the question-and-answer format is effective, why paraphrasing Koch's words might not be appropriate and how the article's representation of Koch is appropriate for the target audience.

Plenary idea

Representation in language and media texts (10 minutes)

Description: Remind learners of the explanation of *representation* covered in this session. Emphasise that representation is relevant to film, theatre, television and literary texts. Put learners into pairs and ask them to discuss two examples of films, TV programmes, comics or novels they know that have:

- a negative representation of someone's gender, age, ethnicity or nationality

- a positive representation of someone's gender, age, ethnicity or nationality.

Ask learners to discuss *how* negative or positive connotations about gender, age, ethnicity or nationality are communicated through media images or language in their two examples.

> **CROSS-CURRICULAR LINK**
>
> **Science (light and sound/the Moon):** Learners could be asked to find out what conditions are like in space or on the Moon (light and dark, gravity, temperature, lack of atmosphere) and therefore what equipment human beings need as astronauts to help them survive there.

Homework ideas

Learners should complete Activity 5 for homework. As part of this, encourage learners to read several feature articles to familiarise themselves with the style and format. Give them the following tips for their writing:

- Audience: Use language that will appeal to adults.
- Purpose and approach: Explain why Christina Koch is a positive role model for young women and also explain Christina's background and achievements.
- Format: Feature article for a newspaper or magazine (printed or online).
- Structure:
  - Headline/title – grab the reader's attention.
  - Subheading – one or two short sentences that give readers the main idea of the article.
  - Introductory paragraph – explain what is positive and interesting about Christina Koch.
  - Body paragraphs (can use subheadings for paragraphs) – paint a picture of Christina Koch's personality, life and achievements.
  - Concluding paragraph – leave a memorable impression.

At the start of the next session, learners could use the Self-assessment feature in the Learner's Book to evaluate their writing.

9.5 Unusual endings

LEARNING PLAN		
Learning objectives	**Learning intentions**	**Success criteria**
9Rs.01, 9Ri.03, 9Ri.04, 9Ra.01, 9Ra.02, 9Wv.01, 9Wc.01, 9Wp.04, 9SLg.03	Learners will: • explore the effects of unconventional endings • write an unconventional ending to a story • read and discuss the implications of a conventional ending.	Learners can: • analyse the effects of unconventional endings • write an unconventional ending to a story to create an effect • read and discuss the implications of a conventional ending.

LANGUAGE SUPPORT

The extract in this session offers an opportunity to recap ways of punctuating parenthetical information in sentences. Use the following sentence from the extract as an example:

Outside was dark and I looked into the sky, at the stars, knowing the pink one was home.

Encourage learners to identify other ways in which this sentence could have been punctuated:

- With dashes: *Outside was dark and I looked into the sky – at the stars – knowing the pink one was home.*

- With brackets: *Outside was dark and I looked into the sky (at the stars) knowing the pink one was home.*

Remind learners that brackets, dashes and double commas allow writers to insert words, phrases or clauses into a sentence. These are usually explanations, afterthoughts or asides added to, but kept partly separated from, the main meaning of the sentence. In the example from *Binti*, the phrase *at the stars* explains that the character is looking at something specific rather than just staring at the night sky – she is recognising her home even though she is millions, perhaps billions, of miles away.

Starter idea

Story endings (10 minutes)

Resources: Learner's Book, Session 9.5, Getting started activity

Description: Remind learners of the different types of story endings (happy/comic, sad/tragic, tragi-comic, cliffhanger and twists). Explain that another way of looking at story endings is to consider whether the plot events are resolved or left unresolved. Give these examples:

- a story about a detective trying to solve a crime – at the end either the villain is caught and punished (resolved) or the writer does not reveal who committed the crime (unresolved)

- a love story – at the end either the couple get married (resolved) or the writer leaves the ending uncertain.

Ask learners to discuss the Getting started activity in pairs.

Main teaching ideas

1 Conventional and unconventional endings (40 minutes)

Learning intention: Explore the effects of unconventional endings.

Resources: Learner's Book, Session 9.5, Activity 1

Description: Explain that we can group together resolved and conventional endings, and unresolved and unconventional endings. A resolved and/or conventional ending is usually as the reader would expect: the villain gets caught, the couple lives happily ever after, etc. Unconventional endings often leave things unresolved.

Organise learners into pairs and ask them to read the three story endings in the Learner's Book. Allow approximately 20 minutes for them to complete Activity 1 together, then share ideas for conventional and unconventional endings as a class.

Follow this up with a class discussion about the overall effects of conventional and unconventional endings. Ask: *What effects are there when the reader's expectations are fulfilled with conventional endings? What effects are there when the reader's expectations are overturned with unconventional endings?*

> **Differentiation ideas:**

- Support: Before learners discuss the three story endings, read *Abiola* aloud to the class. Point out that readers might expect Chidi to come back and take revenge on Abiola, which could be a conventional ending. To create an unconventional ending, learners should think of unexpected developments that could work in the story, for example, Abiola becomes emperor but then Ethiopia is attacked by another country, or he becomes emperor but then develops a severe illness and his advisers decide he cannot rule properly. Learners should continue with Activity 1 using these ideas.

- Challenge: Ask learner pairs to write a paragraph summarising and explaining the different effects on readers of conventional and unconventional story endings.

> **Assessment ideas:** Ask learners to self-assess their speaking and listening skills during the class discussion using the following questions:

- What did I learn from listening to my peer's contributions to the group discussion?

- How did I feel about contributing to the large group discussion?

- What could I do to improve how I listen and contribute to large group discussions?

2 Responding to and writing endings (60 minutes)

Learning intention: Write an unconventional ending to a story.

Resources: Learner's Book, Session 9.5, Activities 2 and 3

Description: Read the introductory information 'Back to *Binti*' and Activity 2 to learners. Ask for three volunteers to read one summary each. Prompt learners' thinking about the summaries by asking them: *What are some of the differences between A, B and C?* Write key words from learners' answers on the board.

Organise learners into groups of three and give them 15–20 minutes to discuss Activity 2 together, spending 4–5 minutes on each bullet point. They should elect a member of the group to be a timekeeper but every member of the group should write their own notes during the discussion, as these will be useful for the writing exercise in Activity 3.

After the discussion, tell learners to assign each member of their group one of the summaries (A, B or C) so they can write it up as a complete ending to the story. Before they start writing, verbally summarise each one to focus learners on the key plot elements they should include in their ending:

A Haro finds Binti and uses the *edan* to defeat the gang.

B Binti has become a powerful and feared leader who will do anything to retain power.

C Binti's daughter, Amiri, is offered a place at Ooma University.

Suggest that learners use imagery, description, direct speech and varied sentence structures to make the writing engaging for their reader. Learners then complete Activity 3 on their own.

> **Differentiation ideas:**

- Support: Offer learners some first lines for their endings, so they can continue from there. For example:

  - *The* edan *is too powerful for any one person to control, so I speak with Haro about how we will share its power in the battle with the Shari.*

  - *At first, I worried about going to war with Alcentor, but after I saw how they treated the captured Oomarian soldiers I no longer had any doubts.*

  - *I see Amiri in her room packing for university. I go to speak with her about the adventure I never had that she now can.*

- Challenge: Ask each learner to write two or three different endings for Activity 3. They could then write a paragraph explaining which of their endings they think is best and why.

> **Assessment ideas:** Learners should complete the Peer-assessment feature in the Learner's Book to evaluate each other's writing for Activity 3.

3 Discussing endings (30 minutes)

Learning intention: Read and discuss the implications of a conventional ending.

Resources: Learner's Book, Session 9.5, Activity 4

Description: Ask for a volunteer to read the text that introduces the last paragraph of *Binti*, then ask for another to read the last paragraph of the novel. Prompt learners' thinking about the ending of *Binti* by asking: *What contrasts are described in this final paragraph?* Get several responses from different learners and briefly discuss then. Then, organise learners into pairs and ask them to discuss Activity 4 together.

> **Differentiation ideas:**

- Support: To get the discussion started, point out the revealing contrasts in the last paragraph that seem to relate to the type of ending: physical distance in space contrasted with emotional closeness to family; a dark sky contrasted with Binti's pink home planet.

- Challenge: Ask learners to write one or two paragraphs explaining their ideas in response to each of the bullet points in Activity 4.

> **Assessment ideas:** Listen to learners' paired discussions. Assess if they identify a positive development for Binti by the end of the novel (she reconnects with her family). Assess also if they give a personal response – whether they enjoyed the idea – and support it with details from the extracts, or with other reasons (for example they like happy endings).

Plenary idea

Responding to story endings (10 minutes)

Description: Ask learners to think of two stories they know well (they can be films, short stories or novels), one with an ending they really like and one with an ending they really dislike. Working in pairs, learners should explain to each other what they like and dislike about the ending of their two example stories. Is it because they are conventional, unconventional or something else?

Homework idea

Learners should complete Workbook Session 9.5.

9.6 A twist in the tail

LEARNING PLAN

Learning objectives	Learning intentions	Success criteria
9Rv.02, 9Rv.03, 9Rs.01, 9Ri.01, 9Ri.03, 9Ri.04, 9Ri.07, 9Ra.01, 9Ra.02, 9Wv.01, 9Wg.02, 9Ws.01, 9Wc.03, 9Wc.04, 9SLm.03	Learners will: • explore how a writer blends elements of different genres • discuss meanings and predict an ending • consider the effects of puns and double meanings • write their own story with a surprise ending.	Learners can: • analyse a story that blends different genre elements • understand the structure of a story with a surprise ending • comment on the effects of puns and double meanings • write a story with a surprise ending.

LANGUAGE SUPPORT

It may be useful for learners to understand that they can create jokes and humorous effects by deliberately using words that sound the same (or similar), or crafting sentences using grammar that offers more than one possible meaning. Below are some examples and explanations.

Using words that sound the same (or similar): *What do you call an alligator in a vest? An investigator!* Here the speaker is deliberately using the word *investigator* because it sounds similar to *in*, *vest* and *gator* (abbreviation of *alligator*).

Using words with multiple meanings: *Why did the tree go away? Because it was time to leave!* Here the speaker is deliberately using the word *leave* because it means both 'to depart' and 'when a tree grows new leaves'.

Using sentences with ambiguous grammar: *Praveen cooked dinner with lots of colourful vegetables and his mother's apron.* Here the writer is deliberately using grammar that could mean either *Praveen cooked dinner with lots of colourful vegetables while wearing his mother's apron* or *Praveen cooked dinner putting lots of colourful vegetables and his mother's apron in.*

Starter idea

A twist in the tail (15 minutes)

Resources: Learner's Book, Session 9.6, Getting started activity

Description: Read the following summary of O. Henry's *The Gift of the Magi* to learners:

> Jim and Della are married and have no money. They have only two possessions that they love: Jim's gold pocket watch and Della's beautiful long hair. It's Christmas Eve, and Della is desperate to get Jim the perfect gift. She wants to buy him a chain for his pocket watch but she cannot afford it. Suddenly she realises she can sell her hair to a wig maker. Della sells her hair and gets enough money to buy a chain for Jim's watch. When Jim comes home from work he pulls a package out of his coat pocket and hands it to Della. Inside, there are expensive hair combs that Della had been wanting for a long time, but which are now completely useless. Hiding her tears, she gives her gift of the watch chain to Jim. Jim collapses onto their old sofa and tells Della that he sold his watch to buy her combs.

Then organise learners into pairs and ask them to reflect on 'the twist' in this story as they discuss the Getting started activity.

Main teaching ideas

1 Exploring short story elements (45 minutes)

Learning intentions: Explore how a writer blends elements of different genres. Discuss meanings and predict an ending.

Resources: Learner's Book, Session 9.6, 'To Serve Man' Extracts 1 and 2, Activities 1 and 2

Note: Please note that there are no audio recordings for the text extracts in this session.

Description: Read the introduction to Extract 1 to learners, then ask a volunteer to read the extract itself. Afterwards ask learners what elements of the three genres mentioned in the introduction – science fiction, humour/comedy and thriller/suspense – they can see in the extract. Encourage them to offer specific details and give examples from Extract 1 in their answers. Write key words from learners' answers on the board.

When you have gathered one or two responses for each genre from different learners, give them 15–20 minutes to write a paragraph in response to Activity 1.

When all learners have finished, as a class, read the paragraph about surprise endings that comes before Extract 2, then ask for another volunteer to read the extract. Organise learners into pairs and ask them to discuss Activity 2 together.

> **Differentiation ideas:**

- Support: After learners have read Extract 1, outline some common elements of science fiction, comedy and thrillers to learners on the board: science fiction (aliens, space travel, time travel, advanced technology, future societies); comedy (humorous, strange or silly situations, people or creatures with a funny appearance, mocking of important people); thrillers (a situation not being what it seems, a threat or danger to someone (or a group) from strange visitors showing up).

- Challenge: Ask learners to work together to write a paragraph that explains their thoughts on the two bullet points in Activity 2.

> **Assessment ideas:** Read learners' paragraphs for Activity 1. Assess whether they have given specific examples of each of the three genres and whether they have given specific examples from the text, such as: the Kanamits being aliens from another planet (science fiction); the Kanamits having an amusing, unattractive appearance (comedy); and the threat implied by the Kanamits' superior technology and intelligence (thriller).

2 Analysing ambiguity (75 minutes)

Learning intention: Consider the effects of puns and double meanings.

Resources: Learner's Book, Session 9.6, Activity 3; Workbook Session 9.6; Language worksheet 9.2

Description: Write the example of a pun from Workbook Session 9.6 on the board: *He was trying to remember what caused lightning when it struck him.* Underline or draw a circle around *struck*, then read the explanation.

Next, give a definition of a pun: *a joke that uses the different possible meanings of a word or that there are words which sound alike but have different meanings.* Emphasise that words with different possible meanings or which sound alike but have different meanings can create ambiguity, which sometimes has humorous effects. Learners should then complete Workbook Session 9.6 on their own.

Outline the information in the Language support feature at the start of the session. Then organise learners into pairs, hand out Language worksheet 9.2, and give learner pairs 20–30 minutes to discuss the examples and write their answers on the worksheets. Go through the answers as a class before moving on.

Recap the Language focus information about puns. Point out that a pun often relies on the ambiguity or double meaning of a word as they saw in the Workbook session. Ask a volunteer to read Extract 3 to the class, then learners should work on their own to complete the analysis.

> **Differentiation ideas:**

* Support: Explain the idea of words with multiple meanings on the board with an annotated diagram and example. For example:

  draw → to create a picture

  → to finish a game with an equal score

  → to pull or drag something

* Explain that writers and speakers can deliberately use words like these to create ambiguity, for example: *The sketch artists had a competition. It was a draw.* Learners should then complete the Language worksheets as described above.

* Challenge: When they have completed their analyses, ask learners to write an alternative title for the story 'To Serve Man'. Their title must also include a pun, be ambiguous in some way or involve a play on words or grammar.

> **Assessment ideas:** Ask learners to self-assess their understanding of ambiguity by asking themselves the following questions:

* Do I find it easier to notice ambiguity when it is due to single words or when it is due to grammar?

* If I find one easier that the other, why is this?

* What can I do to improve my understanding of ambiguity at the word and grammar level?

Plenary idea

Spoiler alert! (15 minutes)

Description: Ask learners: *What is a spoiler and why do some people not want to hear spoilers* (when someone gives away an important plot point or the ending of a story)? Discuss responses. Emphasise that spoilers are connected to key information in a story, such as the direction it takes, what happens to the characters, the development of events, reversals and twists, and the ending.

Organise learners into pairs and ask them to discuss:

* a film or story they know where it would be important not to give any spoilers

* what is it about the information given in the spoiler that makes it 'key' and potentially able to ruin the surprise or suspense in the story.

Finish by suggesting that learners use what they have learnt in this plenary in planning and writing their story for homework for Activity 4 (see below).

Homework ideas

Learners should write their short stories for Activity 4 as homework. Explain that they should read the Writing tip in the Learner's Books and use it as guidance in writing their story. You could also suggest the following:

* *Avoid predictable and unsatisfying surprise endings such as revealing the story's events as 'all being a dream'.*

* *Do not use endings or twists that people will too easily recognise from other stories they know.*

* *Give the reader clues during the beginning and middle of your story that they will not pay too much attention to, and then use those clues in your surprise ending.*

Remind learners to use imagery, description and varied sentence structure and to redraft, edit and correct any errors as needed. After learners have written their stories, ask them to swap them with a partner and use the Peer-assessment exercise in the Learner's Book to give each other feedback. You could also ask learners to read their finished stories to the rest of the class.

PROJECT GUIDANCE

Prepare learners for this project by reading out and explaining aspects of the task as described in the Learner's Book. Emphasise that learners first need to choose a theme for the session that will appeal to their readers. Then, organise learners into teams and explain they will design, create and produce the session by breaking the project down into smaller tasks that will be allocated to specific group members as they have done for previous projects.

You can suggest the outline below for the session; however, explain that learners should alter the sequence, number and type of texts/extracts and activities as appropriate for their topic. They may only want or need one text extract, for example.

1   State what will be learnt in the session as a list of three or four bullet points.

2   Describe a 'Getting started' activity or question for discussion that gets people thinking about the topic or practising skills.

3   Create a short paragraph to introduce the first text or extract.

4   First text.

5   Activity 1: Design an activity that will help people examine the format, content or language of the first text or extract (perhaps note-taking or a question to discuss).

6   Activity 2: An activity that will help people examine the format, content or language of the text (perhaps further questions to discuss or an instruction to examine specific aspects of the text or extract).

7   A short paragraph to introduce the second text or extract.

8   Second text.

9   Activity 3: An activity that will help people examine the format, content or language of the second text (perhaps analysing something in more detail, such as a writer's use of figurative language, grammar or some other language feature).

10 Activity 4: An activity that practises writing in a similar style and format to the texts studied and using similar language skills.

11 Add a self- or peer-assessment activity to check what they have learnt and to decide what they can do to improve their understanding of the topic or language studied in the session.

12 Summary checklist: Statements that link back to the learning intentions at the start of the session.

Give learners a schedule for the learning session project that works backwards from a deadline for completion.

> Acknowledgements

Text reproduced from *Developing the Cambridge learner attributes* with permission from Cambridge Assessment International Education

Excerpts from the Approaches to learning and teaching series, courtesy of Cambridge University Press and Cambridge Assessment International Education: cambridge.org/approachestolearning

Cover image created by Justin Rowe

Acknowledgements for the digital resources can be located in the Digital Teacher's Resource